Modernization, Exploitation and Dependency in Latin America

Modernization, Exploitation and Dependency in Latin America

Germani
González Casanova
and Cardoso

Joseph A. Kahl

Transaction Books
New Brunswick, New Jersey

Library of Congress Catalog Number: 75-43190.
ISBN: 0-87855-584-6.

Printed in the United States of America.

HM
22
L3K33

Library of Congress Cataloging in Publication Data
Kahl, Joseph Alan, 1923-
   Modernization, exploitation, and dependency in Latin America.

   Includes bibliographies and index.
   1. Sociology—History—Latin America. 2. Germani, Gino. 3. González Casanova, Pablo, 1922- 4. Cardoso, Fernando Henrique.
I. Title.
HM22.L3K33   301'.098   75-43190
ISBN 0-87855-584-6

To the memory of
LEONARD REISSMAN

The intellectuals in Latin America are important because they are the voices of those who cannot speak for themselves.

—Fernando Henrique Cardoso

Preface

This book presents to readers of English the contributions of three contemporary Latin American sociologists: Gino Germani, Pablo González Casanova and Fernando Henrique Cardoso. It offers a digest of their most important writings and interprets those writings in the context of the events in their lives which shaped their work. The biographical material comes from interviews with the authors themselves. The book is addressed to three audiences: (1) students of Latin American socioeconomic development who wish to share the insights of outstanding local scholars about the process of social change; (2) social scientists in the United States who are seeking to reorient their disciplines away from abstract model-building and toward analysis of crucial public issues, and wish to see how that is being done in other countries; (3) sociologists and political scientists who are interested in the emergence of their disciplines under varying circumstances that illustrate the interplay between life and thought, between biographical and national events and the theories of social science.

Since the book takes a personal perspective for each of its subjects, it is appropriate for me to set down the events in my life which led me to write it. I first went to Mexico in 1955 and at that time became acquainted with González Casanova, a sociologist of my own generation. I have returned to Mexico every year since then and our professional association has grown into a personal friendship that I greatly value. Through stimulating conversations with him over the years, I have learned a lot about Latin American society and also about the men who study it, and these new ideas have in turn affected my own views of the aims and methods of our discipline. In addition, I lived for a year in Brazil in 1960 and had the chance to travel not only in that country but also to Argentina and Chile; while in Buenos Aires I met Germani, and on a return trip to that city to attend a conference at his invitation in 1964, I met Cardoso. I have since had several occasions to renew acquaintance with both of them.

These personal relationships made it easy and pleasant to arrange a series of tape-recorded interviews for the exploration of the social stimuli which influence individual scholarship. The formal interview with González Casanova was the shortest of the three, since it occurred in 1970 when he was pressed with his new duties as rector of the National Autonomous University of Mexico; however, I have relied upon memory to add material from other conversations with him over the years. Cardoso came to Ithaca in the spring of 1971 for our talks, and Germani visited me in Cuernavaca in December of that year. González Casanova spoke in Spanish, Cardoso alternated between Spanish and English and Germani used English. I have taken great liberties in treating their spoken words as well as in making translations from their published works, always striving for graceful written English; this often required condensations as well as juxtapositions of sentences from different sequences. I am grateful to my three colleagues for providing the material and for permitting my liberties. Each one has read the chapter on his own work, has corrected errors of detail, and has at times challenged my interpretations. I believe the presentation of their own ideas as it now stands is faithful to their intent, but of course the interpretations and emphases reflect my own biases and limitations.

A preliminary version of the manuscript (or parts of it) was read by a number of friends who have offered useful suggestions: Peter Berger, Harley L. Browning, Stanley M. Davis, Tom E. Davis, Dennis Gilbert, Irving Louis Horowitz, Eldon Kenworthy, Michael Maccoby, Leonard Reissman, Rodolfo Stavenhagen, Marjorie Urquidi and Victor L. Urquidi.

I have enjoyed secretarial assistance from Robyn Jacobs and Sharon Haskins, and institutional support from the Latin American Studies Program and the Department of Sociology of Cornell University, as well as helpful copy editing by Susan C. Ferris.

This book was written in Cuernavaca, Morelos, Mexico and Ithaca, New York, U.S.A., and was finished in June 1973, therefore it does not cover publications that appeared after that date.

CONTENTS

Preface

1. The New Sociology in Latin America   1

2. Gino Germani   23

3. Pablo González Casanova   74

4. Fernando Henrique Cardoso   129

5. Conclusion   195

Indexes   211

Modernization, Exploitation and Dependency in Latin America

1
The New Sociology in Latin America

In the years immediately following World War II, the social sciences came to maturity in Latin America. I define maturity in intellectual movements as the ability to absorb the best ideas and techniques available in worldwide sources and add to them in creative ways that nourish the sources themselves. In most instances, such maturity is a collective rather than an individual accomplishment, for it requires enough institutional support to encourage the joint participation of a large group of men and women with a common focus. Without the institutions, the individuals could not devote full attention to intellectual work and gain their livelihood from it, and without the stimulus of colleagues they would be unlikely to find the response and criticism that sustain motivation and correct errors.

Before the war, there were some Latin Americans who wrote about social trends, but they had no permanent institutional backing in their own countries and found little resonance abroad. They were mostly amateur essayists or *pensadores* who were trained and supported as lawyers and bureaucrats. The best among them tended to illuminate the peculiarities of their own national scene rather than the regularities of social structure and change throughout the continent. The postwar years required a new type of social science that was fully professional and that explained national trends in comparative, international terms. This book tells the story of three men who were leaders in transforming sociology in that direction: Gino Germani of Argentina, Pablo González Casanova of Mexico and Fernando Henrique Cardoso of Brazil. Although the book focuses on sociology and political science (there is little distinction between them in Latin America) the story must begin with economics, since much of sociology has developed as a

1

response to the relative neglect by economics of certain essential themes concerning the process of development.

What changed the situation after the war? Perhaps the central influence was the fact that the governments of the larger countries tried for the first time to produce rapid economic development through a deliberate policy of industrialization and turned to the social sciences, particularly economics, for guidelines. The new programs superseded earlier policies of laissez faire growth and were responses to the shocks of the Great Depression and the war. The depression had cut off the external markets for agricultural and mineral products that were the traditional bases of the Latin American economies. As foreign earnings evaporated, local manufacturing plants stepped in to supply simple consumer goods that were previously imported but could no longer be afforded. When the war came the export of agricultural and mineral products resumed, and indeed some reached boom proportions; however, the supply of manufactured goods in world markets disappeared because the advanced countries had all converted to war production. That situation led to a further growth of local manufacturing capacity, and it also led to an accumulation of foreign-exchange reserves.

The crisis point came at the end of the war. As the Latin American countries began to import manufactured goods once more, they saw their foreign-exchange reserves dissipated in a wave of purchases, many of which were luxury goods that had been so long denied to the local elites who had money to spare. New Cadillacs became common on the streets of Buenos Aires, Rio de Janeiro and Mexico City. It soon became clear that a buying spree of such dimensions would be short-lived and that foreign-exchange reserves had to be conserved for more essential purposes. Furthermore, local manufacturers begged for protection against renewed foreign imports, and local industrial workers demanded that their jobs be guaranteed. The slow and rather spontaneous process of industrialization that began two decades earlier had now reached the point where further growth depended on deliberate government action.

There seemed at the time to be a natural alliance of political forces with enough creativity and strength to design and implement a new policy. Intellectuals and politicians formulated the words, and they in turn mobilized support from industrialists and factory workers, as well as from government bureaucrats who sought expansion of their own activities. The central theme of the proposed policy was nationalism, expressed in a language of populism that seemed to offer something to each of the emerging or "progressive" sectors in society (ignoring the peasants, who were a majority of the population but had no voice). The program called for aiding the local industrialists or "national bourgeoisie" through higher tariffs, cheap government credit and foreign-exchange subsidies on the import of necessary machinery and raw materials. It promised the creation of many new factory jobs for the masses that were shifting rapidly from rural to urban locations, and it offered them government support for higher wages and more fringe benefits in the form of social-security systems. It called for a rapid expansion by the government of the infrastructure needed for industrialization, including roads, electricity and modern schools and universities, all of which gave work and power to the intellectuals and the bureaucrats. The entire package was tied in an enticing ribbon of modernization and national independence: Latin America would be transformed from a backward and subordinate agricultural and mineral zone that supplied bananas and tin to the advanced countries (depending upon those sales for prosperity) into a respected participant in the world scene. Diversified economies would grow as a result of steady expansion of internal production and consumption and they would provide their own stimulus to prosperity, becoming more "autonomous" as they became less "dependent" on exports of primary products. It was universally believed that only complex industrial societies could utilize the benefits of modern technology and thereby reach high standards of living, and it was an article of faith that only advanced countries could enjoy the glories of stable democracy, true independence and national pride. All of this was about to come to pass in Latin America.

Within the social sciences, the most sophisticated and by far the most influential version of this optimistic spirit was generated in the offices of the United Nations Economic Commission for Latin America (the organization referred to by its initials as ECLA in English or CEPAL in Spanish) located in Santiago, Chile. Its leader was the Argentine economist and banker Raúl Prebisch. ECLA offered full-time research jobs to professional economists, gave advanced training to younger men from all over the continent in short courses and seminars and gathered official statistics and published them in standard form that allowed comparisons of one country with another, leading toward generalizations about the process of development. But most important of all, it shaped and publicized the ideology of *desarrollismo* or "developmentalism." The ECLA approach matured in the decade of the 1950s before the birth of the Alliance for Progress, and it was in contradiction to the laissez faire philosophy that dominated the Eisenhower administration. Paradoxically, the heartland of this new ideology of deliberately fostered national development (which implied a series of measures against the interests of the advanced countries that benefited from the status quo, especially the United States) was an international agency whose funds were mainly supplied by the advanced countries. Fortunately, it was an agency of the worldwide United Nations rather than the regional Organization of

American States; the latter was dominated if not suffocated by the United States, but the former had greater freedom to develop an independent line of thought.

The prime importance of the new ideology was in defining the central issues: It focused on a few key points and ignored all others. Although technical economic analysis and careful empirical research advanced the argument, the proposed solution was already contained as seed within the formulation of the problem. As is always the case, the theoretical perspective dominated the discussion by shaping its boundaries.

The perspective that was formulated in ECLA kept evolving and went through three main stages: deterioration in the terms of trade, emphasis on central planning and promotion of a regional common market. The first of these emphasized that Latin America, as a region that lived by the export of primary products, agricultural and mineral, was suffering from a steady deterioration in the international terms of trade that was "unfair." Both theoretical arguments and statistical data were mustered to support this position. It was asserted that world prices of primary products were steadily falling relative to those of manufactured goods, so Latin America received less and paid more in its trade with the advanced countries. The theory stated that demand (and thus prices) for primary products in world markets did not increase at the same rate as general consumption, since technological advances made it possible to use raw materials more effectively and to substitute one for another. Furthermore, as people got richer they spent a declining proportion of their incomes on food. By contrast, the cost of manufactured goods kept rising as products became more sophisticated and as labor costs increased in the advanced countries; the situation was made worse by monopolistic elements that artificially boosted prices. Some long-term statistical series seemed to support this argument, and certainly the short-term trends in the mid-fifties gave it credence, as declining demand for primary products after the end of the Korean War caused Latin American exports to suffer. Economists are still engaged in controversy over the validity of the theory of deteriorating terms of trade, but it has become part of the basic set of assumptions that are used by most Latin American writers in assessing their situation; thus, it guides thought and policy regardless of its degree of truth.

The new perspective weakened the base of the older free-trade arguments that called for policies of laissez faire and extolled the benefits of "comparative natural advantage." By contrast, the revised view suggested that wise policy would call for an attempt by the exporting countries to form combines and try to force prices up on world markets (which met with some limited success in the later agreements on sugar and coffee), but even more it indicated that the only long-term solution was to produce more manufactured goods at home. Otherwise, the nations of miners and peasants would slip further behind rather than begin to catch up with the advanced countries.

The men of ECLA urged their countries to promote rapid industrialization by means of deliberate national plans (written by economists, of course). Each country should take stock of its situation and then produce a coherent set of guidelines that would indicate the proper policies on tariffs, import quotas and exchange rates, suggest government investments' in both infrastructure and basic industries and provide standards for foreign private investment. In essence, this was a policy that called for diversion of the profits from export sales of primary products from the pockets of the owners of mines and plantations to the more "progressive" hands of government and private investors in modern manufacturing facilities, even at the cost of inflation and higher prices to consumers. And it called for an entirely new style of government, away from mere peace-keeping and the building of public monuments toward technical guidance of the entire economic process.

The economists who were rethinking the theory of development in the decade of the fifties were able to offer valuable suggestions for the improvement of national financial accounts and for the formulation of various sets of "target" plans for both private and public investment. And when outside agencies, such as the World Bank and later the Inter-American Development Bank and the Alliance for Progress, began to make large loans for development projects, the written plans became important as bargaining tools in requests for money. Despite all the zigzags in execution that were forced by the short-term compromises that accompanied political instability, the plans did assist in the mobilization of support from local industrialists, workers and bureaucrats for various schemes of industrialization based on "import-substitution." Usually the effective argument was a simple one: Foreign exchange was a key bottleneck, so the obvious remedy was to produce manufactured goods at home that were previously being imported. It called for a variety of governmental measures that would give both import protection and credit encouragement to the industries that had gotten started during the years of the depression and the war, plus help in the starting of new ones. And it usually emphasized those goods that were already in demand and were being imported on a large scale, which meant goods that the middle and upper classes could affort to buy—the most flamboyant example being automobiles.

In the late forties and early fifties, the policy seemed to meet with considerable success. There were, for example, industrial booms in Argentina, Brazil and Mexico. But toward the end of the fifties some problems came to the forefront of attention. The rate of industrial expansion tended to slow down in many countries once the demands of the limited fraction of the population with money to spend were met; the masses remained marginal to these new consumption markets. Foreign exchange remained a bottleneck, since demand for imports merely shifted from consumer goods to the capital goods and raw materials needed for industrial production. And to make matters worse, the concentration on industry to the detriment of agriculture and mining often had the effect of slowing export expansion. Furthermore, as local producers began to move in the direction of intermediate and capital goods, they found themselves increasingly dependent on sophisticated technology that had to be bought from the advanced countries, either by royalty contract or by inviting the foreigners to become partners in local enterprises. The very tariff walls set up to protect local manufacturers also had the unanticipated consequence of encouraging outsiders to move in and open their own factories, and with their great advantages in technical, managerial and financial resources, they often drove the local firms out of business.

Even governments felt the pinch, and to pay for their investments in infrastructure they expanded the local money supply, producing rapid inflation, and borrowed more from abroad. Soon repayments on these external debts, combined with the outflow of profits and royalties in the private sector, added up to annual sums that were greater than the inflow of new loans and investments: the poor countries began sending capital to the rich ones. To meet their old debts, the governments called for even larger programs of new aid to the developing nations, and President Juscelino Kubitschek of Brazil publicized a grand scheme called Operation Panamericana, which was the forerunner of U.S. President John F. Kennedy's Alliance for Progress.

Social tensions often seemed to increase along with the pace of industrialization. Improvements in public health measures lowered death rates dramatically, but birth rates stayed high and a population expansion of unprecedented vigor resulted. The growing masses of citizens moved toward the cities looking for work, since the agricultural zones did not develop at a rate that could absorb them. But the new industries were based on labor-saving technology, imported from the advanced countries where labor was scarce and expensive, and therefore jobs in factories did not increase at the same rate as did physical production; indeed, the proportion of the population in industrial jobs in much of Latin America remained stable throughout the period, at a level about half of what it had been in the advanced countries when they went through a comparable stage of industrialization.

The benefits of economic growth were being distributed in ways that increased the gap between rich and poor. The new industrialists were becoming very rich indeed, and those workers who managed to get the limited number of good jobs in modern industry were improving their levels of living, but the peasants remained as poor as ever, and unemployment was on the rise in both rural and urban zones. These disparities came to public notice at the same time that the local role of foreign manufacturing firms— the "multinational corporations"—was growing, and populist politicians suggested a causal connection. It appeared that modern industrialization benefited the local rich, segments of the middle class and urban proletariat and foreigners, at the expense of the vast mass of the people. The national-populist sentiments that had glued together the earlier political alliance in favor of industrialization were outraged by expanding foreign influence and by increasing signs of exploitation of the poor, and the alliance began to disintegrate.

The economists at ECLA eventually recognized these problems, but faced two constraints in suggesting solutions: their technical expertise was not supposed to extend to social and political matters, and their institution depended upon the support of conservative Latin American governments that would not welcome attacks upon their key constituency in industry. Thus ECLA could recommend a Latin American common market that would allow expansion of local industries to a large enough scale to meet the requirements of modern production, and could on occasion suggest mild efforts at redistribution of income to increase internal demand for industrial products, or even softly murmur the phrase "land reform." But it was not in a position to develop and publicize a systematic theory of political reform of sufficient scope to deal with the increasing problems of demographic growth, urban expansion, swelling unemployment, encroachment of the multinational giants and expanding foreign indebtedness. The ideology of *desarrollismo* was unable to indicate how it might be possible to get the rich and powerful to share more equitably with the poor and weak, either in terms of disparities between nations or of social classes inside of a nation.

Many of these issues were combined under the rubric "the noneconomic concomitants of economic development," and much of the stimulus for their study came from critics of the official economists, those who first became worried about the harmful aspects of the new industrialization. They said the current programs were based too much on calculation of growth rates in the average gross national product and paid too little attention to the human needs of the population. This feeling has recently been epitomized in the extraordinary remark of the president of Brazil, General Garrastazu Médici: "The economy may be doing well, but the majority of the people are still doing poorly."

This mood called for serious technical study of the trends in financial and political control over the industrialization process that shaped the distribution of its benefits. It called for reassessment of the relations between the advanced and the developing nations to seek some means of narrowing the distance between them. And it called for more attention to the needs of groups that were marginal to development: peasants, the many Indian communities, the throngs of city dwellers who did not have factory jobs and the unemployed and underemployed who grew in number and proportion to the total population simultaneously as the industrial sector boomed.

As these gloomy concerns were reaching public consciousness, they were met by a new trend that offered some hope for enlightenment: a worldwide surge in sociology based on the "scientific" method of studying social issues. The World War II years had brought considerable technical advance in the measurement of human attitudes and behaviors, especially in the United States. At the end of the war, sociologists were determined to make these techniques more meaningful by linking them in a systematic way to basic theories of social organization and change. Those theories took their roots from the great European thinkers who had originally created the noneconomic social sciences as means for illuminating the human consequences of the great transition from feudal to industrial society: Marx, Weber, Durkheim, Pareto, Freud.

Enthusiasm about a type of social science that combined formal theory with precise measurement spread quickly to Europe and Latin America. International agencies sponsored the diffusion of the new ideas: UNESCO was active in promoting the International Sociological Association, and various government agencies and private foundations that were beginning to extend aid to the developing countries included money in their budgets for research projects on the noneconomic aspects of growth. Some sociologists in the United States switched their own interests from the study of "social problems" at home to the study of "social development" abroad.

A few young Latin American scholars became involved in these international activities, they studied abroad, attended seminars and congresses and participated in comparative studies with those from other countries. The thoughtful among them brought home the new approaches with considerable reserve, for they feared that the issues raised were colored by the perspective of the advanced countries and might not be the most appropriate for illuminating the problems of the developing areas. They noted that much North American social science had an anti-Marxist slant that appeared to be an elaborate defense of the liberal philosophy of its practitioners, a philosophy to be expected in a society that felt it had solved its most fundamental problems and needed only minor reforms to make it function well. Such a view underplayed the role of conflict in social change, particularly in societies where interest groups faced each other in sharp contradiction, and it ignored the disparities among nations that might engender exploitation. Many Latins believed that the North Americans were biased by an ethnocentrism that regarded development as a process through which other societies would approach the "American way of life." To counterbalance these distortions, some Latin Americans acquired Marxist ideas from Europe, where they met with more enthusiasm than in the United States. Although these young scholars wanted to use the new research techniques that offered a greater empirical rigor to the study of society, they wanted to control them via a theoretical synthesis that would take what was valuable from both the emerging structural-functionalism of the United States and the neo-Marxism of Europe, recast in a form that was specifically oriented toward Latin American problems.

These scholars got some institutional support from government agencies concerned with plans for development, but they received even more from the expanding universities in their own countries. The new industrialization required many men and women with technical training, not only in engineering but also in economics, business and public administration. There already existed a middle class whose sons and daughters provided students—enough of them to force governments to expand the universities and create new ones. Enrollments grew much faster than the size of the general population, and various schemes for the modernization of the curriculum were put into practice. Professors in the social sciences were in demand, even before they were proper departments to train them. For example, faculties of philosophy, of economics and of law usually had one professor of sociology who was supposed to teach a broad view of society as part of the background training of the students. These isolated professorships or "chairs" existed long before there were departments of sociology that offered graduate training. The chairs were filled before the war by the *pensadores*; afterwards they were available to young scholars trained abroad as professional sociologists or the few who managed to get such training at home through various forms of self-study, occasionally aided by foreign visiting professors. By the mid-fifties, the demand was sufficient to support a special graduate training center in sociology in Santiago sponsored by UNESCO, which attracted students from all over the continent.

Once these young sociologists were appointed to the universities they immediately found an eager audience: swarms of students disenchanted with the direction of their societies and seeking new ideas. Many of these students expected bureaucratic careers and simply wished to prepare for them through training in social science instead of the more traditional path of law. But some were deeply committed radicals who were upset by an economic growth that combined industrial progress with widespread hunger. Of course, it was an old Latin American tradition for young people (often from establishment families) to use their university years as the opportunity for self-discovery through verbal rebellion against their families and their societies, but now there was an additional element: their universities had professors who claimed the ability to diagnose the ills of society in a scientific manner. These professors were pushed by their students away from minute and careful studies of limited situations into broad theories that would explain why the times were out of joint and how they might be repaired. This student pressure produced an enormous difference in mood from the North American departments of social science of that time, in which laboratory studies of small-group interaction seemed, to many, to provide the key to a scientific understanding of all social laws. Those who then traveled between the two types of universities experienced renewed culture shock at each end. Only by the late sixties did the political fervor of rebellious students in the United States begin to change their professors' directions in ways that brought some of them closer in spirit to their Latin American colleagues.

As sociology became established in the various countries in Latin America, it reflected some of these general postwar trends that had widespread influence. It also reflected two additional factors: the particular problems that were at the center of interest in each country and the special perspective of the key man who emerged as the leader of his generation in each local area.

The important social issues in Argentina could be phrased in two questions: first, Why had economic development gone stagnant after its early success in the first half of the century? The country had developed a "modern" economy before the others in Latin America, but instead of moving forward after the war it seemed to be stuck at dead center. The resulting political tensions dominated local thought and led to the second question: Why had Peronism first triumphed and then failed? Some believed that Peronism was a version of fascism, but others asserted that it was a genuine expression of the populist spirit of the working class and thus could not be considered a reactionary movement. At any rate, the failure of Argentine parliamentary democracy after several decades of apparent success and the new dominance of military rule had to be explained.

The academic social scientist who offered the most stimulating analysis of these issues was the sociologist Gino Germani. He was chosen for the only position in that subject at the University of Buenos Aires a few months after Perón was ousted from the presidency in 1955. Germani's central ideas were indicated by his key concept of *modernization* and by his emphasis on the use of scientific techniques to study society. Under the rubric of modernization, he developed a general theory of the social changes that accompany industrialization, sketched in terms of the existing advanced countries. For him, a modern society was characterized by a complex division of labor, with most men working in nonagricultural jobs and many of them earning high incomes as skilled manual workers, white-collar technicians and professionals. Everyone was literate, and indeed high proportions of the young people graduated from secondary school and university; social mobility from one generation to the next was high, via the educational system. Political participation expanded with literacy and urbanization, and universal suffrage was granted. The norms of the society shifted toward rational choice instead of prescribed, traditional rules and roles. Secularization, individuation and innovation triumphed over sacred, customary, collective values.

Germani suggested that much of the social tension in Latin America stemmed from the great speed with which it was modernizing combined with uneven rates in different spheres, which produced disjointed results. Since the region was industrializing late in history, it imported many huge factories in one sudden spurt, shifted peasants to the cities to work in them and tried to imitate advanced forms of mass participation in consumption and politics—but all of this without time to make the proper economic and social adjustments. Therefore, many elites still thought in traditional terms and resented the claims of the middle class and the workers for a share of political power. Those elites lacked an industrial mentality and were unable to generate government policies appropriate to the new circumstances that could keep economic expansion moving forward after the easier phase of early import substitution. While governments vacillated, the masses pressed for benefits that often were beyond the ability of the economy to provide. Furthermore, the new urbanites tended to express their needs through loyalties to charismatic leaders who promised much without having a clear policy for accomplishment, leaders who provided a symbolic link to the personal relations of rural life that were sorely lacking in big cities. This uneven late development based on imported models was offered by Germani as the underlying explanation for the notorious zigzag of Latin American politics, represented in Argentina by the shift from constitutional democracy, to oligarchical rule, to the populist dictatorship of Juan Perón, to military coup and back to free elections.

Although he rarely dealt with specific political issues or offered direct advice on policy questions, the implications of Germani's position were not hard to discern. He hoped for enough patience from various contending groups to allow the different aspects of society to come back into harmony after the difficulties of the abrupt transition from traditional to modern structures, and he recommended careful study of the rates of change to determine which spheres were moving "too slowly" in terms of the overall model. This led him to a series of empirical studies of Argentine society, probing in great detail census materials that had languished untouched in the archives, and he supplemented them with field studies using the techniques of the attitude survey being developed in the United States. He demonstrated that Argentina was changing faster than most people realized, that the shift toward urbanization and industrialization had already gone a long way and that subtle adjustments in family systems, status hierarchies, mobility rates, class-consciousness and political ideology were all well advanced. He hoped that when the governing elites realized the extent of the change that had already taken place they would stop relying upon old ideologies as guides to new solutions; thus, tensions between old and new aspects of society would be reduced.

In Mexico, the focus was not on political instability (as in Argentina) but rather its opposite: the signs of rigidity if not senility that affected the unfolding Mexican Revolution. That movement had torn the country apart in the decade following 1910, and by destroying the landed oligarchy and weakening its foreign partners, had created a society that was unique in Latin America. By about 1920 the regime was consolidated and began the task of reconstruction. It emphasized a profound agrarian reform that gave land to about half of the peasants, and then slowly began to industrialize. The nation achieved economic independence, or so it was then believed, when it expropriated the foreign oil concessions in 1938. During World War II the regime arranged a reconciliation with the United States, despite the expropriations, and it was an active partner in the stuggle against the axis powers. The years during the war and immediately after it brought a surge in industrial growth and a new feeling of national pride. Both local citizens and foreigners wrote books about "the Mexican miracle": rapid industrialization combined with a political stability based on reform policies that aided peasants and workers and produced national cohesion. The system was often held up as a model for other countries.

Some men, however, began to have doubts. They wrote about the weakening of the spirit of reform, about the growing strength of the industrialists and their ability to move government policies in conservative directions, and about the increasing ties between local and foreign business interests. Economists noted that the rates of growth were slowing down in the late fifties, that levels of foreign indebtedness were increasing and that unemployment was growing.

The man who developed a broad view of these trends and put them into political perspective was Pablo González Casanova, professor of sociology in the School (later Faculty) of Political and Social Sciences of the National Autonomous University of Mexico. In his teaching and research, González Casanova concentrated on a few critical issues concerning Mexico. He began by paying particular attention to the "marginals," or people being left out of development. At that time, most writers proudly reported various averages: the literacy rate going up, the proportion of children attending school going up, the infant mortality rate going down. González Casanova emphasized that despite those improving averages, the absolute number of people living in poverty was increasing. There were more illiterates, more children not in school, more babies dying each year than ever before, and he used census materials to quantify these trends. They were partly consequences of the population increase (which in turn was a result of earlier advances in social reform and economic growth), but in his view they were mainly a result of an economic expansion that was too slow and overly concentrated in certain areas of the country and certain sectors of the population. At first he implied that the marginals were forgotten people who were left out of development, but then he began to write that they were being "exploited" because the advances in the cities and dynamic sectors were in part based on an ability to squeeze an economic surplus out of labor in the backward zones. This process he described as one of "internal colonialism."

González Casanova then turned to the study of the political structures that shaped *exploitation*, insisting that the legal or constitutional system was a formal device that was usually ignored in practice. He noted that both political and economic elites were concentrated in the big cities where most of the investments in factories, hospitals and schools were made, and where most of the benefits of economic growth were enjoyed. Despite all the rhetoric of the Revolution favoring the peasants (especially the 10 percent of the population that was living in Indian communities), they were in fact stuck where they had always been while the urban part of the society was moving forward.

Further analysis of the political structure showed how the new industrialists were becoming more closely tied to foreign corporations as the emphasis shifted from mineral and oil extraction (now mostly nationalized) to manufacturing, which required foreign technology and capital. Indeed, the largest and fastest growing firms in the newest industries were precisely the ones with the greatest foreign participation and control. González Casanova showed how the indebtedness of the federal government to external banks, mainly in or controlled by the United States, reduced its ability to change financial policies. And he wrote about the lack of democracy and effective participation within the Mexican system, with decisions flowing from the top down through the federal bureaucracy and the big, official party that won almost all the elections and smothered political opposition. The president and a small group of close associates ran the country, despite legal structures that called for a division of powers and regional autonomy. And increasingly the president was allied with the big industrialists. González Casanova warned them that their policies restricted the size of the consumer market and were leading toward recession.

His later writings extended his view to the international system and described it as a set of layers of exploitation. Within the underdeveloped nations, the elites in local districts were sustained by their connections with the national political system, whose leaders were in turn strengthened by their ties to the international system dominated by the metropolitan or imperialist countries. This network of intertwined elites kept moving profits toward the center, thereby exploiting the periphery. And the nature of power made it difficult to change the system and make it more equitable, since local leaders were coopted to the point that their interests coincided with the metropolis more than with their own local constituents.

Although he is sharply critical of the Mexican political system, González Casanova never quite gave up hope; he considers himself "within the Revolution," although on its left wing. He advocates that the system be reformed from the inside by democratizing the official political party and by widening the participation of citizens in groups separate from the party, such as independent trade unions, student movements and other mass organizations. This puts him rather in the middle; many of the political bureaucrats think him dangerously radical, and many of the intellectuals feel that he plays the political game by not severing his ties with the establishment.

Brazil, unlike Argentina and Mexico, is not dominated by a single city and a single national university. This vast country is able to support several centers of influence, with two predominant among them: Rio de Janeiro and São Paulo. In Rio de Janeiro, Luis A. Costa Pinto introduced some of the innovative postwar trends in sociology while he served as director of the UNESCO-sponsored Center for Research in the Social Sciences. He cooperated closely with Germani in organizing an international, comparative study of stratification and mobility in four countries and served from time to time as visiting professor in Buenos Aires. Although Costa Pinto held a professorship in the University of Brazil in Rio de Janeiro, the university had no sociology department and did not provide adequate graduate training.

The major source of new ideas in Brazil was the University of São Paulo, which decided to renovate the social sciences with the aid of visiting professors from France. One of the young sociologists trained there emerged as the Brazilian whose voice was heard throughout Latin America: Fernando Henrique Cardoso.

Cardoso was at first caught up in the euphoria that gripped Brazil as a result of its unprecedented industrial boom in the fifties. All shades of public opinion, from the Communists to the conservatives, felt that the moment had arrived when the country was passing from a backward agricultural nation to an advanced industrial society, and most believed that the industrialists themselves were the main stimuli causing the transformation. The scholars at São Paulo established a Center for Industrial Sociology and began to study the entrepreneurs, using a perspective that came from the international literature that emphasized the creative role of businessmen in putting together new combinations of capital, technology and workers that would break through traditional barriers to change. However, the more Cardoso interviewed the industrialists the more he began to doubt. He noticed that once a firm had become established and sought to expand production, it tended to turn either to the government for help or to foreign enterprises, since its own resources of money and technique usually proved inadequate for modern production on a large scale. He realized that the structural conditions of the market and the rules and policies set down by government were more important than the personal skills of the industrialists in determining the direction of national evolution.

Furthermore, Cardoso noticed certain contradictions that weakened the political role of the industrialists and kept them from exerting their full potential influence on national policy. They verbally emphasized the individualistic values of free enterprise, but in fact had to keep turning to the government or the foreign monopolies for help. Consequently, they vacillated in their behavior and were unable to formulate a consistent set of nationalist goals and policies that could enlist the support of other sectors, such as the workers, and thus lead toward an effective consensus. The result was that the old political hierarchy, with close ties to agriculture, continued to operate, and government policy emerged as a series of confused compromises between the old and the new sectors. These conflicts impressed themselves on Cardoso's mind, and he foresaw a breakdown of the existing political arrangements and a threat to the prevailing prosperity. Events confirmed his fears, for in 1963 the economy suffered uncontrollable inflation and turned toward recession, while the political alliances that dominated the government began to unravel. As the situation approached chaos early the following year, the military assumed control.

Cardoso then moved to a job at ILPES, the Latin American Institute for Social and Economic Planning, a part of ECLA in Santiago, Chile. As he put it, this new experience turned him from a Brazilian into a Latin American, with the result that he expanded his particular analysis of Brazil into a general framework for all of Latin America. He realized that the various nations were not directly recapitulating the experience of the countries that had industrialized earlier and that theories of development based on the pioneer countries needed drastic revisions before being applied to the latecomers. He decided to focus on the political decisions that a nation had to make at each major stage of development before it could move toward a higher stage.

Since the Latin American economies had always been deeply connected with foreign markets, the interests of foreign investors, together with the local entrepreneurs who produced for export or were in other ways tied to foreign operations, had to be placed at the center of the political analysis. In some historical situations the foreigners and their local allies were the strongest power in the country; in other situations, they were but one element competing for influence with others. And the emerging factors that represented the "progressive" force of the moment, such as a steel or automobile industry, also involved foreign participation. Thus the local political decisions that shaped the flow of new investments and determined the direction the economy and society would take in the future were always the results of complicated political battles inside a country, and usually the role of foreign interests was a crucial factor.

Cardoso and his collaborator, Chilean historian Enzo Faletto, seized upon a phrase that was gaining currency in Santiago as a way to focus upon this continuous political process: *dependency*. They asserted that the Latin American economies were dependent upon outside forces, but in ways that varied from one historical situation to another. No simple theory of "imperialism" would suffice to predict the sequence of events despite the importance of imperialist interests. The theory of imperialism took the perspective of the metropolitan countries as basic and failed to elaborate the view from the dependent countries, thus oversimplifying the political process in the periphery; it was a theory of rape, instead of a more appropriate theory of seduction.

Cardoso and Faletto studied the political history of Latin America and found certain regularities. One pattern that was often repeated involved the insertion of "enclave" economies completely controlled by outsiders, such as the banana plantations of the United Fruit Company or the oil wells of the Standard Oil Company. Another pattern occurred when local entrepreneurs reshaped their economies for purposes of export and retained ownership, as happened when the grain and cattle ranchers of Argentina created new growth. The newest and most complicated pattern was being formed by the multinational corporations that responded to government policies of tariff protection by building their factories inside the tariff walls and producing for local consumption.

The work of Cardoso and Faletto suggested that an exit from the impasse facing Latin America called for a restructuring of political forces that would permit a redistribution of income and a widening of local markets, plus a more radical role for government in production and planning. The existing "national populism" had run out of momentum when international firms gained predominance, and a new ideology was needed to generate a new internal political alliance that would be strong enough to change policies. The greatest danger from foreign interests was not their external pressures but rather their abilities to influence internal decisions through local partners. That influence could only be counteracted by new pressures from the masses.

Cardoso returned to Brazil, and his focus shifted from general issues in Latin American development to the specific problem of mass participation in society and politics in Brazil. He became convinced that the construction of new theories on how to reorganize society by elitist means from the top down, even if based on Socialist or equalitarian goals, would not suffice. Instead, more direct knowledge was needed of how the masses spontaneously organized themselves—be it in churches, community improvement groups, labor unions, peasant leagues or political parties. Only by helping the masses to organize better on their own terms and thus become more confident of their possibilities for influencing events could the intellectuals fulfill their mission and contribute to a more just society.

Cardoso belongs to the school which believes that social science must be infused with ethical and political goals. He acknowledges the need for disciplined and "objective" research, but says it must be based on theoretical problems chosen in terms of the practical requirements of a more humane society. In Latin America this means deep reform, more democratization and much greater equality in the distribution of the benefits of economic development.

These brief sketches of the work of Gino Germani, Pablo González Casanova and Fernando Henrique Cardoso, which will be expanded in the chapters that follow, are sufficient not only to suggest some influences and perspectives that are common to them all but also to indicate a few points of difference. The most obvious theme that unites them is their shared sensitivity to the main social and political problems of their countries in the postwar years. They did not begin their careers with questions derived from unsettled issues in some abstract theory of society (the way many textbooks on social research advise), but rather focused on problems that were part of the public debates of their times. For Germani, the key issue involved the implications for Argentina of the rise and fall of Juan Perón. For González Casanova, the problem was one of a rigidity in the political institutions of Mexico that seemed to be leading away from the initial reformist impetus of the Revolution. For Cardoso, the central question concerned the political control of capitalism under contemporary circumstances that seemed to lead toward a loss of national autonomy and growing instability.

Each man felt that his nation faced certain profound inadequacies in social structure and that the superficial signs of those weaknesses were the particular political themes debated in the daily newspapers. A social problem is always defined in terms of ethical values which indicate that the observer is dissatisfied with the actual state of affairs and has in mind a model of a different arrangement that he would prefer. In order to discern the reasons why a given observer chooses a particular aspect of reality as the focus of his discontent, we must recognize the values he uses to filter the many alternative possibilities until he arrives at the one he decides is crucial.

Germani's values are those of liberal democracy. He had seen them collapse in the Italy of his youth, and he experienced a second shock when they were discarded in the Peronist Argentina of his early maturity. He yearned for a society that would respect the norms of constitutional government and grant full civil liberties to its citizens. As a student of history, he knew that such norms emerged only rarely and that they reflected particular social conditions. He realized that the middle-class style of parliamentary rule that spread through Europe in the nineteenth century and was imitated (albeit feebly) in Latin America could not thrive in the contemporary world without significant modifications, and he sought to specify the necessary adjustments. Most particularly, he saw that the transition to an urban society based on industrialization required a form of democracy that allowed the working class to have its proper share in the polity, and he believed that much of Argentina's continuing crisis stemmed from its inability to find a legal and legitimate channel for the full participation of the masses. This difficulty, in turn, he interpreted as being a consequence of the historical timing of that country's entry into industrial society and the disjointed rates of change of various aspects in the modernization process. Perhaps we can call Germani a realistic liberal: he values the type of democratic society that emerged in Europe and seeks to identify essential changes in order to adapt it to the Latin American situation. He believes such adaptation is possible, and therefore revolutionary approaches are unnecessary.

There is also a touch of nostalgia in the value perspective of González Casanova, not for a lost period of middle-class liberalism but rather for the reformist zeal of the Mexico of President Lázaro Cárdenas, which had prevailed when he was a youth. That had been the time of glory in the Mexican Revolution, the time when its promises of a better life for the masses were being put into practice through vigorous programs of land reform, support for labor unions and national control over foreign investments. Then came the industrialization of the forties and fifties, which brought economic progress but also a diminution in the spirit of reform, a growth in the influence of foreign investors, a widening breach between rich and poor and a host of unanticipated social problems. Finally, in the late fifties, even the previously steady growth of the economy showed signs of weakness. The economists, both local and foreign, agreed that the internal market needed stimulation through a redistribution of income, but their advice went unheeded because the powerful were not listening. Thus the central questions became not economic but rather political: What is happening to the power structure? Why is the Revolution turning away from its own ideological spirit? How can it be revitalized?

González Casanova does not phrase these political questions in terms of deviations from the norms of parliamentary democracy as most liberals would. He phrases them in terms of the content of the decisions that are made, emphasizing the trend toward conservatism in Mexico despite the recency of its Revolution. His country has never had a long period of liberal democracy, and he doubts that the usual norms of multiple-party parliamentary rule are suitable to its social structure. He accepts the inevitability of a strong executive backed up by a strong official party, but he wants to see them follow policies that benefit the masses instead of the elite. As long as the country is poor and suffers from stark inequality, internal and external, he values economic growth and the redistribution of income, education and culture more than the rules of liberalism. Furthermore, he believes that civil liberties for the individual and political participation by wide sectors of the population are possible even in one-party states, and finds clues to the further democratization of Mexico in its own history rather than that of Europe or the United States. He is the most profoundly nationalistic in outlook of the three sociologists under consideration.

Cardoso began with Brazilian problems but soon developed a continental view, perhaps because he lived for a time in a neighboring country. His most influential work concerns the larger trends that affect the entire region, particularly the evolution of the multinational corporation as an entity operating inside the various countries but controlled from outside. He related that trend to the decay of the national populist spirit with its support for local entrepreneurs, which was the political basis of the economic surge of the early postwar period. He showed how the internal dynamics of industrial growth led to new contradictions wherein the main currents of economic power were no longer expressed in, and regulated by, legitimate political channels, thus explaining the emergence of the technocratic military rule that succeeded the brief period of populist democracy in Brazil and several other countries. Cardoso is the youngest of the three authors and so is the least nostalgic for a golden age of the past. His values stem directly from his own experience and that of his generation, and many of his papers have a strong topical emphasis because they analyze events of the moment. He hopes to find ways of supporting sustained economic growth with enough national autonomy to permit a new internal political consensus leading toward socialism. Without that consensus, based on widespread mass participation, no government can force equalitarian policies on reluctant economic elites nor avoid a military take-over at a moment of crisis. But in a period of increasing influence of international capital and technology, he finds autonomy diminishing and the older nationalist slogans increasingly out of date.

Although each author derives his values and his foci of concentration from national questions, each seeks a way of interpreting them that goes beyond national idiosyncracy. There are differences in shading, but all three men combine a sense of local urgency with a broad view of worldwide change. All of these authors recognize the shared situation of Latin America: it is a part of the Third World attempting to industrialize late in the game and catch up with the early starters—in a world dominated by those early starters. All have studied the industrialization process in past history and seek to specify both the common aspects for all nations and the unique traits that arise from the particularities of time and place. All are grounded in the theories about the nature of industrial society that emerged during the period of Europe's modernization and became the base of contemporary sociology and political science, since all have studied in Europe and have absorbed its intellectual traditions. From those theories, Germani chooses liberal and functionalist models, whereas González Casanova and Cardoso opt for Marxist approaches. Yet all three follow with interest the development of empirical sociology in the United States, and all attempt to use the new quantitative methods wherever they can help to bring greater precision to theoretical insight.

These three men are among the most prominent leaders of the new sociology and political science in Latin America. They have been active in international scholarly organizations, and their books circulate in many countries. In addition, they have had direct influences as teachers and administrators. For many years Germani and González Casanova directed large teaching departments and research institutes in their own countries, and each had a deep impact on the formation of a generation of local students and investigators; Germani recently left Argentina and now teaches at Harvard University. Cardoso was forced to spend some years abroad, and when he was allowed by his government to return home, he was prohibited for political reasons from teaching university students. However, his connections with the University of Chile and with the international Latin American School of Sociology in Santiago have put him in contact with students from all over the continent, and his books are now in vogue.

Since social scientists in Latin America focus more on specific national problems and less on the attempts to build the abstract theories of society that preoccupy so many academicians in the United States, they speak not only to fellow professionals and students but also to the educated public. Therefore, the authors' books and articles have helped shape public opinion on the issues of development in their countries. These men have become public figures as well as cloistered academics. Their experiences in that difficult role will be illuminating to North American colleagues who are attempting to reshape their own work in order to answer the call of their students and their consciences for a professional style that fuses scientific restraint with ethical commitment and thus directs intellectual rigor toward issues that are relevant to public policy in the broadest sense of that term. C. Wright Mills reminded us over a decade ago that the highest purpose of sociology was to so illuminate the crises of the times as to help the enlightened citizen better understand his personal situation and devise appropriate social solutions. His message has been slow to spread in the United States, but is heeded more now than when it was first delivered. It is no accident that Latin American sociologists heard his voice from the beginning and immediately accepted the cogency of his view.

In order to appreciate the work of Gino Germani, Pablo González Casanova and Fernando Henrique Cardoso, it is necessary to grasp the close relation between personal biography and social context. Consequently, their writings will be interpreted in the pages that follow primarily from the perspective of their lives and careers; instead of evaluations from some outside criterion of what sociology ought to be, understanding will be sought from an inside view of how their work evolved in response to personal and national events. The best way to approach such a view is by asking the authors themselves; thus digests of their writings will be alternated with quotations from interviews in which they attempt to explain their purposes and methods. Only in the final chapter do I allow myself the full liberty of imposing my views as the framework for interpretation.

BIBLIOGRAPHY

References to works that offer background on the development of the social sciences in Latin America in recent years can be found in the bibliography. Readers who wish to explore the literature in English on the recent history of social science in or about Latin America will find these sources useful guides to the materials:

Werner Baer, "The Economics of Prebisch and the ECLA," in ed. Charles T. Nisbet, *Latin America: Problems in Economic Development* (New York: Free Press, 1969) and "Import Substitution and Industrialization in Latin America," *Latin American Research Review*, VII (Spring 1972): 95-122.

Susan Bodenheimer, "Dependency and Imperialism: The Roots of Latin American Underdevelopment," *NACLA Newsletter*, IV (May-June 1970): 18-27, reprinted in eds. K.T. Fann and D.C. Hodges, *Readings in U.S. Imperialism* (Boston: Porter Sargent, 1971) and "The Ideology of Developmentalism: American Political Science's Paradigm-Surrogate for Latin American Studies," *Berkeley Journal of Sociology*, 1970, pp. 95-137, reprinted as Vol. II, Sage Professional Papers in Comparative Politics, Beverly Hills, Calif., 1971. The first paper synthesizes the new writings by Latin Americans on dependency, and the second sharply criticizes the older writings by North Americans who ignored the problem; both have exhaustive bibliographies.

Albert O. Hirschman, *A Bias for Hope* (New Haven: Yale University Press, 1971) contains two of his wise essays analyzing the changing perspectives of economists: chap. 3, "The Political Economy of Import-Substituting Industrialization in Latin America," and chap. 13, "Ideologies of Economic Development in Latin America."

Rodolfo Stavenhagen, "Seven Fallacies about Latin America," in eds. James Petras and Maurice Zeitlin, *Latin America: Reform or Revolution?* (Greenwich, Conn.: Fawcett, 1968). An influential critique of some dominant themes in orthodox social science which give a distorted view of Latin American reality.

Charles Wagley, ed., *Social Science Research on Latin America* (New York: Columbia University Press, 1964). The book contains a series of papers evaluating North American studies of Latin America. It provoked a critical response by some Latin American scholars: Manuel Diegues, Jr., and Bryce Wood, eds., *Social Science in Latin America* (New York: Columbia University Press, 1967).

2

Gino Germani

Most writing in the social sciences takes its tone from its polemic thrust; by understanding what an author is *against*, we gain a clearer grasp of what he is *for*. Gino Germani has spent his life opposing what he calls *irrationalism*. As a youth in his native city of Rome, he refused to join the Fascist youth organization and instead participated in opposition activities, with the result that he was sent to jail. After he migrated to Buenos Aires in 1934 and became a university student for the second time, he remained aloof from the extremists of Right and Left who dominated student politics, and instead began to search for a scientific method of studying society that would lead to more reasoned discussion of social reality and political policy. Just as he was about to start a professional career dedicated to those ends the military dictatorship of Juan Perón was consolidated, and liberals like Germani were forced out of the university. For 10 years he lived outside of academic life but continued to educate himself in modern techniques of social analysis.

Finally the political tide turned, and in 1955 Germani won the competition for the chair in sociology at the University of Buenos Aires and simultaneously became head of the Institute of Sociology attached to it; he was 44 years old, and he strove to make up for lost time. He soon transformed his single professorship into a full department and turned the moribund institute into an active center of research on contemporary Argentine society. There followed a decade of extraordinary productivity with books and articles on Argentina; international conferences on the new trends in social research throughout Latin America; a group of young people trained in sociology, stimulated to study abroad for postgraduate specialization, and supported in professional careers on their return. Germani made Buenos Aires the center of activity for an entire continent.

However, the work produced fierce opposition. Reactionaries feared that the very study of society weakened its mystique and thus threatened national solidarity, while radicals insisted that cooperation with international agencies and use of North American research techniques meant submission to imperialism. Wearied by the constant battles, Germani accepted a professorship at Harvard University in 1966 and became an exile for the second time in his life. Shortly after he made his decision to leave Argentina the military assumed control of the country, and many of the sociologists Germani had trained were expelled or resigned from the university; irrationalism had triumphed once again.

Given a life dominated by such episodes, it is no wonder that Germani's stance toward sociology is intimately related to his search for personal and intellectual freedom and that his devotion to a social science based on objective rules of evidence serves for him as a quest for an alternative to ideological debate and emotional rhetoric. He wrote in *La Sociología en la América Latina* (1964): "Sociology is, as has been said so often, a science of crisis. It develops with the aim of offering a rational response to the problems created by the historical process. In other epochs, men sought that response in traditional knowledge or in revealed truth. But since the Renaissance Western society has moved in another direction: it has affirmed the legitimacy and the possibility of controlling its own destiny through reason . . . . That is the explanation that lies behind the growth of the modern social sciences" (pp. 104-5).

Gino Germani was born in Rome in 1911, the only child of an artisan tailor who earned a modest income from his own shop. Gino's mother was the daughter of a peasant family that owned a little land and lived slightly above the subsistence level typical of their village, but she was always worried about the threat of dire poverty. She was an ardent Catholic, and although unschooled she had learned to read and write. His father was a religious skeptic who had been an active Socialist in his youth, but by the time Gino was in school he had become a bystander to political activity; nevertheless, he read various newspapers and discussed with friends a wide range of current issues; this was a part of his son's earlier education.

Germani was not strong as a boy so was inactive in sports, and he rejected the *machismo* traits of Fascist youth culture. In addition, his family lived in a middle-class neighborhood but was among the poorest of the residents. Germani reacted to these circumstances with a mixture of shy withdrawal and rebelliousness; he says that he always felt different, like an outsider, and he was sensitive to snubs from class-conscious peers. He only attended his classes in high school for the minimum number of days a year required to pass (two-thirds of the total), and either stayed at home reading books or passed the time with a few friends inveighing against the society and everything in it. His family discouraged a formal study of music, which appealed to him, since they believed it impractical for earning a living, and urged him to learn something that would give him a career "better" than tailoring. He settled the issue by attending a technical school where he studied accounting. The courses he took qualified him for entrance into the economics (business) institute of the university, where he found himself to be one of the few students coming from a home of the shopkeeper or artisan class. This feeling again of being an outsider sensitized him to psychological matters, and he read books on the subject (including Freud's *Interpretation of Dreams*) in what he says would now be called "a search for identity."

In high school the boys were strongly pushed into joining the Fascist Vanguard, or youth organization. Germani (along with one friend) refused despite the pressures, and he continues to this day to wonder why; he recently spent some time in Italy studying documents covering that epoch, and published in 1970 a comparative study of Italy and Spain called "Political Socialization of Youth" that focused on programs for absorbing young people into authoritarian regimes. He speculates that any feeling of being different from average, regardless of the specific cause, was a basis for resistance, and he believes his own mood was reinforced by the anti-Fascist sentiments of his father.

Shortly after he entered the University of Rome in 1930, he was caught distributing anti-Fascist literature. He spent five months in the local jail, then he was shipped to a prison island for "confinement" for about a year. "I remember the first day I was put in jail—what was impossible to understand, even to conceive, was that someone should be put in jail because he *thought* something. The central question for me became freedom." Yet he says he was lucky, for if the authorities had discovered more about the anarchist group he was associated with, or if the police had not been reluctant to severely punish very young people since they wanted to maintain the facade that all youth supported Mussolini, he would have been in much greater difficulty.

He learned two specific lessons from the prison experience: First, that working-class culture had a coherence and vitality of its own. (His lower-middle-class background had not exposed him to the true proletarian culture before.) For example, there were songs and codes for sending messages through jail walls that originated in social-protest movements a century earlier; all the workers knew them and were astonished that Germani did not. Second, he was exposed to both Marxism and the Communist party. Many radical intellectuals, "some of the best people in Italy," were on the prison island, as were many leaders of the party. He found the latter to be rigid and uncompromising, unwilling to take seriously anyone who was not both a member of the proletariat and a true believer. He began to distrust their dogmas at the same time that he became interested in philosophic discussion about Marxism and the meaning of modern history.

He was paroled back home under "admonition" and was permitted to attend university classes, but he remained under constant supervision by the police. He did not find economics courses very interesting and explored other parts of the university. He attended lectures in various subjects and began intensive reading in history, literature, philosophy, psychology and sociology. He studied the works of Kant and Hegel and others who helped in understanding Marx. He read the Italian sociologist Vilfredo Pareto, considered to be the precursor of fascism. "I was trying to understand him because I was convinced that there was a general crisis of democracy, that even if fascism were overthrown we would never recover, and if democracy were re-established it would probably be a very different kind of democracy from what we had known before."

He found by chance an introductory book on sociology that discussed Emile Durkheim, who was not ordinarily studied in Italy, and Germani was able to follow that up by reading the original works in French; Durkheim in turn led him to Spencer and other English writers. Germani had learned good French in high school, and enough English to read adequately. Indeed, he said a lot of people read English in those days in order to follow the London newspapers that gave more news of Italy and Europe than could be found in the Italian press.

"There were a few people I could talk to, those who tended to be anti-Fascist, but it was difficult for me to have friends because of this admonition question; it could get them into trouble. I also used to go to the meetings of the young Fascists, in order to see what was going on, and I read their cultural journal."

At the end of 1934, just before he finished the university course (and after his father had died), he and his mother decided to go to Argentina where she had many relatives who had migrated earlier. For three years after arriving in Buenos Aires, Germani was unsettled; the business depression made it hard to find work, even with the aid of his mother's relatives who were well established, and he found that economics at the university consisted of mainly a course in business administration, which did not interest him. He kept imagining a return to Italy. But in 1938 he registered as a student in the Faculty of Philosophy, and his life changed:

"It was a great difference, even the first day; my isolation disappeared completely. I became active in the Student Union, and found an entirely different society, a big contrast to Italy. In Buenos Aires anybody could go talk to the dean like an equal; you did not have to be from a family of intellectuals or professors. In Italy, the professor was someone you saw from very far, but he didn't know about your career; maybe you talked personally to him once, for 10 minutes. In general, the social stratification in Argentina was much less evident.

"I took philosophy, which meant Greek, Latin, humanities. However, I hardly ever went to class; I read books, and I had a job. I was supposed to be working 10 hours a day in the Ministry of Agriculture, in the board that controlled the marketing of *mate*—a job an uncle who was a landowner got for me. But after a while I invented ways to do the work much quicker, and I only went there in the morning, since it was very dull, just routine clerical work. And when I went to the university I spent my time in the Student Union, discussing politics. There was some repression of the students (not like later, after 1944, when it got much worse) because the Conservatives were ruling the country through fraud and repression. The Student Federation was in opposition, and within it there was a struggle for power between the Communists and the others, a sort of reformist faction. They knew I was not a Communist, but I cooperated for unity of action.

"There was one professor of sociology in the Faculty of Philosophy, Ricardo Levene, although he was really a historian who had done studies on the economic history of the May Revolution of the past century. He had the idea that studies should be done on contemporary Argentina, so he organized an Institute of Sociology. He called on various students to do little projects in the institute; there was no money, we didn't get paid. The institute was just a bare room, without books. About that time I came across an introductory text on research methods in the United States, and tried to find some more books with practical suggestions about research. I had earlier in Rome learned a little about American sociology from reading *Année Sociologique* which the Durkheim school in Paris put out, with book reviews and critical articles about sociology in different countries. Then in the Institute of Philosophy of the University of Buenos Aires I discovered a treasure; the man who ran it had somehow gotten interested and he had 40 or 50 books by American sociologists, and I found Bogardus and Lundberg on methodology, and I found Parsons, *The Structure of Social Action*, and a collection of the *American Sociological Review* from the first number, and the *American Journal of Sociology* starting from about 1935. And for Europe I found the *Annales de Sociologie*, a revival of the *Année Sociologique*, which had been suspended during World War I. Nobody else read those books, except maybe the professor, but he wasn't a sociologist, he was a philosopher. I had nobody to talk to about them.

"In the other institute, the one supposed to be doing sociology, the professor would assign some subjects, like a study of the middle class, but he gave no orientation and the students did it their own way. I read a little about studies of the middle class in France, looking for models, and for the United States there was the research on Middletown. My first article used that, and some old references going back to a congress that was held in 1900 or 1901, and a little from Marx, and I said we should try to get empirical data to compare the statistics on occupations in different countries. I got something from the U.S. Bureau of Labor Statistics, and compared Chicago and Buenos Aires; I found the American material in the library of the Ministry of Labor, almost by accident. I also found there that big 10-volume study of London done many years earlier by Charles Booth. I was just searching for models; I didn't have any formal methodology at that time. Then a little later we prepared a questionnaire, and did one of the first surveys in Argentina (actually there had been a kind of survey that a journal of political science had done in 1910, but people didn't remember it). These articles on the middle class got published in the annual *Boletín* of the Institute of Sociology. I began to put out a lot of articles and book reviews in that *Boletín*.[1] The professor wanted a kind of annual review of what was happening in Argentina, and I remember commenting that 1942 was the first year in which the share of industry in national income was higher than that of agriculture. We also wrote about statistics on crime and education, and were somewhat involved in planning the questions for the next national census.

"In those years I was doing many things simultaneously. I was learning sociology, doing my first statistical research and also finishing my studies in philosophy; I received my degree of Professor of Philosophy in 1943. At the same time I kept working in the Ministry of Agriculture to make a living, and was active in the Italian community in the anti-Fascist movement. Of course the Spanish war and then the general European war were very important to us, and through our discussions I learned something new about nationalism. I saw that nationalist sentiment was strong among people who were leftists, although at that time they did not use the word. At first it seemed strange, since in Argentina the nationalists had always been linked to the conservatives, just as fascism in Italy had always been linked with diffuse nationalism there. You see, if you were anticapitalist you were supposed to be internationalist, because capitalists were all the same whichever country they came from; in Europe, the Left were internationalists. But in Argentina there was a sort of nationalist, antiimperialist Left."

Germani continued his part-time association with the Institute of Sociology until 1945, and developed three themes simultaneously: (1) descriptive studies of contemporary Argentina, using as much statistical material as possible; (2) a theory of modern society that could be used to synthesize the descriptive material; (3) a methodological stance that would be philosophically viable.

The theory of modern society came from several sources. Emile Durkheim's concept of *anomie* was of central importance, and Germani knew the writings of Durkheim both in the original and in the interpretation of Talcott Parsons. He also was acquainted with the studies of social disorganization that had been done in the United States, such as the vast documentation in Thomas and Znaniecki, *The Polish Peasant in Europe and America*, which used life histories to show how the process of migration affected personality and values. He knew the theory of ''secularization'' of society as the basic long-term trend of modern life, discussed by Max Weber and Ferdinand Tönnies and elaborated in the works of Howard Becker. And he was familiar with the views of Karl Mannheim and Erich Fromm, who probed the crisis of modern society and the effects of the weakening bonds of tradition and community on the psychic equilibrium of men.

Germani put these ideas together into a general view that linked the social processes of urbanization, secularization, migration and mobility with the social-psychological processes of individuation and ego-centered rationality. He also dealt with the pathologies that sometimes accompanied these processes, especially during the epochs of particularly rapid change, as shown by symptoms of instability, stress and irrational response. His theoretical emphasis was more on the universalities of social *process* than on the historical particularities of social *structure*, although he saw process as historical (that is, sequential) in form.

As a student of philosophy, Germani was concerned about the epistemological bases for an empirical social science. The predominant perspective at that time in Latin America came from the German thinkers (often via Spanish intermediaries) who stressed a sharp distinction between the sciences of nature and the sciences of man. The latter were presumed to be rooted in cultural traditions that had to be approached through philosophical insight rather than empirical observation, and the idiosyncracies of different national cultures were stressed rather than the regularities inherent in all human interaction. Germani says that the complete separation of the social from the natural sciences was a view that had developed in reaction to the excesses of positivism in the nineteenth century, and unfortunately it was accepted uncritically in Latin America. Philosophy and sociology used an inadequate form of literary essay that eschewed all need for verification of its statements; the style even rejected the nonquantitative but systematic analysis of history that was used by the German antipositivists. Germani found important support for his own critique of the predominant methodology in Latin Ameria in *Sociología, Teoría y Técnica*, published in

Mexico in 1942 by the Spanish *émigré* sociologist J. Medina Echavarría, a man well trained in German thought. The book presented an intermediate view that linked empirical data to philosophical concepts and justified the study of society through techniques that, from the broad methodological perspective, rested on the same ground as those used in the natural sciences. It also presented examples from North American sociology to show how it could be done. The book helped Germani articulate a position that emphasized the philosophical possibility of an empirical, scientific approach to social analysis.

In 1944 and 1945 the Peronist dictatorship was consolidated and nonconformist thinkers were forced out of the university; this situation prevented Germani from receiving the post of assistant professor that had been arranged for him by Levene. Instead, he concentrated on various tasks outside the university. He continued for two years in the Ministry of Agriculture, but switched to a job in its library that demanded little time and attention. He took advantage of the opportunity and read a lot, simultaneously beginning to plan and edit a series of translations of European and American books in the social sciences for a new publishing house, Editorial Abril, owned by Italian-Jewish immigrants who were friends of his. When he lost his job in the ministry, he became a member of the publishing firm and gained managerial experience that he says was useful in his later years as an academic administrator. Eventually the social science series was transferred to another publishing house, Editorial Paidós, and Germani was associated with Enrique Butelman as joint editor. The authors Germani translated or supervised included Erich Fromm (*Escape from Freedom* became a best-seller), Harold Lasky, Karl Mannheim, Margaret Mead, George Herbert Mead, Bronislaw Malinowski, Raymond Aron, Kurt Lewin, David Riesman and J.L. Moreno. Most of these authors were then unknown in Argentina and the rest of Latin America, and the appearance of their books in Spanish opened new perspectives in the analysis of society and created a clientele interested in the contemporary social sciences.

Germani was invited in 1946 to give some lectures in the Colegio Libre de Estudios Superiores, or Free College of Higher Studies, an organization of independent intellectuals, which gave him his first chance to disseminate his ideas about sociology and social psychology; he later became a regular professor at the college. The Buenos Aires branch was closed by the government in 1952, but he continued the lectures in the branch in the city of Rosario. He also participated in a seminar of scholars from philosophy and the natural sciences that met in a private home. They read Marx, Parsons and others who attempted to analyze modern society. These men returned to the university and became its leaders after Perón fell in 1955, and Germani believes that their earlier interest in the social sciences as a tool for reaching personal understanding of the Argentine situation led them to give valuable support when he established the department of sociology. However, his association with these men, some of whom were leftists, made him suspect as a Communist despite his long-standing personal rejection of the party; later attacks against him were led by conservatives who used these earlier associations as weapons.

Germani's reactions to Peronism were mixed. At first he was frightened because of the parallels with Italian fascism: the support of the Nazis; the suppression of freedom in the universities and the mass media; the marching groups in the streets. Then he began to notice differences: the organized workers supported Perón as they had never supported Mussolini; and the middle classes could organize protests and get away with them. The intellectuals in the Colegio Libre and in his private seminar were militant anti-Peronists because they focused completely on the issue of intellectual, or what he calls "formal" freedom. Germani pointed out to them that the workers were not too concerned with that issue, but they were vitally interested in freedom in the factory, that is, the opportunity to have workers' organizations that would protect them against the bosses and give them dignity and strength as laboring men. Compared to their very weak position in earlier years in Argentina, this was an important advance for them which they credited to Perón; in a sense, they were achieving substantive citizenship for the first time. Germani attended various street demonstrations and afterwards went into workers' bars to talk with the men. Increasingly he began to feel that Peronism was not just a repetition of European fascism but was something new, based on peculiarly Argentine conditions. In 1950, he gave his first lecture on the subject at the Colegio Libre and set forth the basic ideas that were developed in later researches.[2]

The year 1955 was a fortunate one for Germani; for the first time in his life, his timing was perfect. In the early part of the year, his first book was published, Estructura Social de la Argentina (The Social Structure of Argentina). It grew mainly out of his interest in the census of 1947, the best one that Argentina had yet experienced. He used to stay around the census offices while the various data were being tabulated, copying interesting results. He calls this a completely "private" research, something he was doing on his own. He compared the new data with earlier census results and added bits and pieces of information that he had collected earlier at the Institute of Sociology, producing a general treatise on demographic and social trends. It included sections on the absorption of immigrants from Europe, on internal migration from rural to urban zones, on the transformation of the labor force and on the system of social stratification and its expression in voting patterns. There was some delay in getting the book published, since the law prohibited the printing of any data that might compromise "national security," even if they were taken from official sources that were already public, but finally the book came out. It had an immediate impact in Argentina, becoming the prime example of how an empirical approach could be used to analyze contemporary society. The reputation of the book eventually spread to other countries and it is now accepted as a landmark in modern Latin American sociology.

In the fall of 1955 Perón was ousted by the military, and the next day the students took over all the universities in the country and demanded the resignation of those professors who had collaborated with the regime. Most professorships or "chairs" were declared vacant, and competitions had to be organized to refill them. There was something of a problem however: each competition required a panel of three experts to make the decision, and since so many professors were in disgrace, it was hard to find judges. But flexible criteria helped solve the problem; one of the judges for sociology in Buenos Aires was a psychoanalyst, and another was a Paraguayan exile temporarily in Argentina.

Germani lacked confidence in the system for making selections, so he applied for four chairs in as many different cities. To his surprise he won them all, in large part through the presentation of *Estructura Social de la Argentina* along with materials in the two books about to be published in Mexico. He accepted the one in Buenos Aires, and thus took over the very professorship of sociology where more than a decade earlier he had served his apprenticeship. Along with the chair came the institute, though by then it was nothing but a name, having lost even the one room where the assistants sat in those earlier years.

Expansion of activities began immediately. At first, Germani did not propose a separate sociology department but merely responded to the exploding student demand for more courses. Classes were given in the university to regular undergraduates, others were organized by the institute around research topics and some were offered in the reopened Colegio Libre. He needed colleagues to share the teaching responsibilities, and he began to give a special graduate course for what we colloquially call "retreads," that is, mature men who had graduated from other fields (economics, philosophy, psychology, history and even one from architecture). They became teaching assistants, supervising the discussion sections for undergraduates that accompanied the formal lectures by the few professors, and some quickly advanced to the senior staff.

Pre-eminent among these new sociologists was Jorge Graciarena, formerly an economist, who became Germani's right-hand man in administrative as well as scholarly activities. Another important associate whose writings soon earned him an international reputation was Torcuato S. Di Tella, who had studied earlier at the London School of Economics. In addition, foreign professors were invited to help fill the gap in instructors and research supervisors: Ralph Beals, Aaron Cicourel, Rose K. Goldsen, Irving Louis Horowitz, Albert Meister, David Nasatir, Luis A. Costa Pinto, Kalman H. Silvert, Frieda Silvert and others.

The first researches were done outside the university before the institute had time to get organized. Shortly after Perón fell, the temporary military junta ruling the nation called in Germani and a few other men to do some quick surveys on public opinion that would forecast the results of a proposed new presidential election. The surveys indicated that few people were willing at the moment to label themselves as Peronists and that about a third were undecided about the direction of their votes. So Germani checked their answers to other items indicating their political attitudes and correctly predicted that in fact they would be sympathetic to a Peronist candidate. They later voted for Arturo Frondizi, the candidate most active in courting the supporters of the deposed dictator. Germani indicated to the military junta that the bulk of the working class did not feel they had been "cheated" by Perón, as the new government was claiming, and that some method had to be found of channeling them back into legitimate politics instead of attempting to suppress them.

As the department and the institute became organized, a series of research efforts began. One was a study of a shanty-town district where university students were engaged in a form of social service, helping the residents improve the district. From that grew more extensive researches on the integration of rural migrants into the life of Buenos Aires.[3] Another effort concerned social history and united sociologists and historians in the study of the evolution of Argentine society and its class system. They also conducted projects in demography and in regional variations in rates and styles of development.[4]

Two years after the renovation of the university this new activity in sociology, social psychology and social anthropology had grown to the point where it was organized into a separate department of sociology. Its development was strongly supported by the rector of the University, Risieri Frondizi, a philosopher who was the brother of the nation's president. He was a vigorous leader who promoted a wide variety of attempts to modernize the university and raise its level of teaching and research. He helped Germani cut through the red tape of traditional procedures to establish many innovations. Germani himself was so energetic and task oriented that he generated resistance, and he now recognizes that some people thought he was too authoritarian. Yet in the first years the successes were so pronounced and the new opportunities for younger staff were so great that he feels they more welcomed than resented a strong "father figure." Furthermore, the younger people were held together by a firm sense of group solidarity that had emerged from the earlier anti-Peronist underground activities, in which most had participated.

One of the big steps forward came in the form of a grant of almost a quarter of a million dollars from the Ford Foundation. It was used to pay foreign visiting professors, to help build the library, to provide fellowships for doctoral candidates to study in the United States and to support some of the research activities.[5] The Rockefeller Foundation gave a much smaller sum to cover research expenses, as did UNESCO; furthermore, the Argentine National Research Council (founded by Germani's former associates in the private study seminar and the Colegio Libre) gave money to the institute that was used for research salaries to supplement the part-time pay of the teaching assistants in the department, permitting the staff to have full-time careers combining teaching and research; this combination was rare at the university and created resentment in some of the departments of humanities that lacked similar support.

In 1957, Germani finally got a traveling fellowship that allowed him to visit the United States for two months. He talked with the authors of many of the books he had been reading during his solitary years of self-education: Talcott Parsons at Harvard, Robert Merton and Paul Lazarsfeld at Columbia and many others. He visited the social research centers at the universities of Columbia, Chicago, Michigan and California, and collected various internal manuals that explained how to draw samples, conduct interviews, code data and do practical statistical analyses. Some of these were translated and served as guides for the early research projects in Buenos Aires. He even met a few people who were already familiar with his book on Argentina. He then traveled to France and Italy, making contact with various scholars. The whole trip gave him the invigorating sense of moving out of the library to join an international fraternity of scholars.

The next few years involved a great deal of activity that connected the work of Argentina to that of other Latin American countries. Germani remarked that Buenos Aires was the most cosmopolitan city on the continent, and his original international perspective as a European was constantly reinforced. He was active in the group that developed international teaching and research centers in Santiago (FLACSO) and Rio de Janeiro (CENTRO) with the assistance of UNESCO and was one of the leaders in organizing a comparative study of stratification in four Latin American capital cities, which the center in Rio sponsored.

However, by the early 1960s Germani sensed that the bloom in Buenos Aires would soon fade. The first troubles came from some small but strong right-wing forces in Argentina that espoused an orthodox Catholic perspective buttressed with falangist, pro-Franco, corporative sentiments (an ideological movement that had a brief moment of power under General Onganía a few years later). They falsely accused Germani of being a Communist, and they attacked empirical sociology as a threat to national traditions and solidarity. Germani says, in a tone of disbelief, "Why, even priests would give sermons against us on Sunday." Later extreme left-wing spokesmen got into the act by denouncing the acceptance of grants from the Ford and Rockefeller Foundations as representing submission to imperialism (some of those who joined the attacks had earlier been happy to accept fellowships from the foundations for study abroad or for research projects in Argentina).

"I had taken this habit of leaving the country from time to time for a sort of rest, a psychological defense, and to keep in contact with other people. In 1959 I was visiting professor in Chicago; in 1961-62 at the University of California at Berkeley; in 1964-65 at Columbia in New York. The first real trouble inside our department came when I returned from Berkeley. Now, there is one thing which is universal, maybe the universal social law. Even when you have plenty of jobs, the younger people have to do something different from the older ones, to rebel, to get their freedom. I always got along well with the first generation of sociologists, those who joined me at the beginning. But then came another generation of younger ones, many returning from study abroad and I was not so close to them. I became tired of being director of the department, and thought it was time for someone else. And also the political scene in the country was getting worse: President Frondizi was thrown out by the military, and I began to feel insecure about the general situation. I suggested that to avoid a repetition of the bankruptcy of the 1940s we should protect ourselves by forming alternate institutions, separate from the government. But at first the members of the department concentrated on only one problem. Who would be the leader? There were various factions. I made way by resigning as head of the department, and I also gave up the big required introductory course on systematic sociology, but stayed as director of the institute, doing research and giving graduate seminars.

"By then the department had grown a great deal; there were 2,000 students, although most were just in the first and second years. Up to then we had been very strict in the courses and examinations, and only had graduated a small number with the Licenciatura or first degree—even by 1966 there were only between 40 and 50 graduates. The students and the graduates had half of the votes on the governing board, and the professors the other half; in the earlier days when I was director, the personal contact was close, with lots of discussion, and my views usually were accepted. But now the students started demanding courses on Marxism, 'anti-imperialist sociology' and so forth. We had staff members with certain Marxist leanings, but there really were no outstanding scholars with a firm Marxist orientation available in Argentina. We invited the men the students asked for, and they lost their reputations with the good students when their incompetence became evident. In any case, some of the students were impossible to satisfy; even such a fine scholar as Paul Baran was rejected by them. Those students were looking for some kind of ideology, a personal solution to social problems, and were not serious as social scientists, as researchers. I think we made a mistake expanding so fast at the undergraduate level.

"And with the staff, there was a structural problem: over 100 teaching assistants, and not enough opportunity for promotion to professor. So I organized the Center for Comparative Sociology as an independent unit in the Di Tella Institute, which was a private foundation entirely separate from the University or the government. It would be able to give jobs to some of the people and would be protected from university and national politics. I could see another military coup coming, and after Mussolini and Perón, I felt two dictatorships were too many, I didn't need another.[6] To tell the truth, I was getting tired of Argentina and the local psychological problems. It was frustrating to see the tremendous intellectual potential of those people go to waste. I really wanted to go to Italy, where sociology was being built up (partly by a man who had discovered it in Argentina), but the Italian academic scene was even more chaotic than the Argentinian. In 1965 I was offered a professorship at Harvard to start the next year, and I accepted. Just after that, when it was too late, I was invited to compete for a chair in Italy, but they had been so kind to me at Harvard, I could not withdraw."[7]

Having sketched the sequence of events in the life of Gino Germani that influenced his scholary outlook, I wish now to turn to an analysis of his major writings. The appropriate place to begin is with his papers about the possibility of and indeed the necessity for a scientific sociology as an alternative to the type of ideological debate that leads to *irrationalism*.

In a collection of essays written between 1957 and 1963 entitled *La Sociología en la América Latina: Problemas y Perspectivas* (*Sociology in Latin America: Problems and Perspectives*), Germani discusses the transformation in the social sciences in the southern countries that has taken place since World War II.[8] Not only has a scientific approach come to challenge the older literary and philosophical style, but higher levels of professional skill tested by international competition have begun to push aside various pomposities of the past.

"Irrationalisms of diverse origin used to offer an excellent opportunity to cover up a complete lack of ideas or knowledge with a torrent of words," he wrote on page 2. But because the new styles were imported from abroad, they faced dangers. Some of their advocates were not properly trained and promised too much, and in fact, substituted the new simulations of false science for the old ones of false philosophy. Even those who are properly trained must fight against attacks from those who fear objective research.

"From the Right, the opposition comes on the one hand from a demand for 'national authenticity'—a nationalistic rejection of anything foreign (which, incidentally, was not applied to German irrationalism, accepted by the nationalists of yesterday). On the other hand (and this is the true motive), the rightist opposition stems from a perception that the new theories and methods of North American sociology represent a revived positivism, and that, as is well known, is the name of the Devil. Often the methods of empirical research and quantification are seen as expressions of 'materialism', and thus scientific sociology comes to be identified with Marxism, a paradoxical and amusing result since the other wing of the opposition, coming from the Left, attacks scientific sociology in the very name of Marxism. Of course, the leftists see 'Yankee sociology' as a mere penetration of imperialism, and all of sociology as a 'bourgeois' science whose purpose is justification of an extant social order. To these two wings of opposition can be added those who are influenced simply by the emotional connotations that stem from dependency, from the sentiments of inferiority in the face of the powerful American nation, which makes everything American subject to intense resentment. The task of scientific sociology in Latin America is precisely that of overcoming these emotional and ideological deformities that are part of the process of adopting the advances of a univeral sociology, regardless of where that sociology comes from" (pp. 7-8).

Germani believes that such a universal sociology exists and is based on the same basic canons of procedure as natural science, with necessary modifications to adapt them to the needs of the sciences of man. Further, he believes that modern sociology is crucial to the understanding of industrial society, which is also becoming universal in the contemporary world. He therefore urges that Latin American scholars adopt the new sociology and join the world community of social scientists.

Germani is a good polemicist; he has the sharp wit and pointed pen of a rebel, and he likes being in opposition to and tossing barbs at whatever happens to be the orthodoxy of the moment. He enjoys himself when he is playing the role of critic. But he is also a serious man, and he realizes that his major obligation is not to attack but to demonstrate by example. Instead of creating caricatures of various styles and then demolishing them with clever phrases, he has felt the responsibility of showing how cumulative social research based on strict international standards can in fact be organized in Latin America.

The necessary conditions for establishing scientific sociology are revealed by its own concepts. "Scientific knowledge can only develop in societies in which the process of secularization has gone far enough. In particular, the social structure has to include, at least as far as science itself is concerned, the institutionalization of change, the style of operating by rationally determined choice rather than tradition, the existence of free examination and permanent scrutiny of scientific propositions. The general process of specialization has to have reached the point where science is distinguished from other activities by its values, its social organization, its system of status and role. Indeed, there must be differentiation within science to have identified the social sciences as a special activity with autonomy and a legitimate function" (*Sociología en América Latina*, p. 40).

The Latin American countries have many obstacles to overcome before they can attain a full flowering of the new social sciences. The material conditions in most of the universities do not support full-time careers, so the style of the amateur predominates. For example, a lawyer in alternate years lectures on jurisprudence, philosophy, sociology, history and government. In some countries, chairs of sociology (but not departments or organized research institutes) were established as long ago as the past century, and the traditional style, modeled on Auguste Comte, is thus well entrenched and bolstered by vested interests. The beginnings of the new empirical research are examined with suspicion even in the daily newspapers, which find that a questionnaire survey is reminiscent of police interrogations and invasions of privacy, or else it must surely be the overt sign of CIA spying.

Germani kept urging his fellow social scientists to recognize all of these difficulties and to strive to overcome them. He saw attractive possibilities in international cooperation and sent students to study abroad in the most advanced departments of sociology. He asked them to apply up-to-date methodologies in their researches when they returned home, even though some simplification might be required because of the limitations of funds or the lack of background data. He has not feared to accept outside funds for his institute in Buenos Aires despite attacks on him as a tool of imperialism. And he has urged the critics to be more fair and stop taking the most extreme examples as typical of what foreign sociology is all about. Those who stress its weaknesses emphasize either the style of research that approaches mindless empiricism—fact-gathering without theoretical purpose—or else abstract and empty theorizing without factual base. Yet the best of American and European work avoids those extremes. It has learned from Durkheim and Weber and the other great masters of the past how to combine theory and research; it has developed a general perspective on industrial society that leads to hypotheses that can be tested by empirical procedures; it has refined those procedures so that new data can be collected for specific purposes (often, but not exclusively, by the sample survey) to combine with extant data from official sources.

In the interview, Germani acknowledged that his articles on scientific sociology were written as arguments against the older Latin American styles of work that used rhetoric instead of research and admitted that he may have underestimated some of the difficulties in applying the scientific method to social reality, although he had raised them in various publications. "As Parsons says, repeating other people, a fact is not a fact; it is the theory or idea which selects the fact, and the criteria of selection are so varied. It's true in the natural sciences as well, but they have somehow been able to agree on what perspective to adopt. But in the social sciences, you look at a certain process from one perspective, and the other fellow looks at it from a slightly different perspective, and he calls it by another name. And in a sense he is right because he is seeing something slightly different, so it is different.

"I have always insisted that we should choose the problem in terms of its own importance, and not get stuck in a form of methodological perfectionism or inhibition. Of course, if you restrict the number of variables and study only small groups, you can be more rigorous. But even in studying history, where there are so many facts or variables to be taken into account, you can make some progress. You can limit your study to particular historical types, similar to Weber's ideal types, which I did in defining the stages of development in Latin America. This allows more careful testing with empirical data than the completely intuitive or holistic approach of some of the German philosophers. Recognizing the complexity of the problem, the limits of social science, I have nevertheless tried in my own work to reach the best possible compromise, believing that the criteria of evaluation should be based on the usefulness of the content, accepting it if it provided theoretical insight into an important theme and was based on the best procedures possible within our present techniques and in terms of practical conditions.

"History is not completely determined—even leaving aside the question of human freedom, of freedom of will. It is in the making; you have a different range of possibilities, and you can say that several different orientations are possible. And once one of them starts, it becomes built into the process and influences the outcome. And of course the psychological and social determination of the observer, the ideological component in his work, shapes his selection of variables. Now what do you do? You try to be as scientific as possible, but you know you cannot be completely. You don't simply reject or ignore those subjects or theoretical problems which are outside the line of standard techniques or beyond the present limitation of the application of a strictly scientific method. You apply the method as much as possible, you make a kind of self-analysis in terms of your social and psychological condition, and you can, up to a point, go beyond that condition. You use the quantitative approach as much as possible.

"But maybe I give more importance to the historical method, because of the kinds of problems I am trying to look at, studying fascism. At the same time that I was reading Pareto trying to understand the roots of fascism, I was reading a great deal of ancient history, constantly trying to make comparisons between modern Italy and the fall of the Roman Republic. At a certain moment, a political system cannot resist the other changes taking place in society. The society keeps changing its social structure and therefore its political system. The problem then is to maintain some continuity in values as structures change. To me, the basic value was freedom, and I wanted to find out how to protect it, even enlarge it, in the changing social and political environment."

Germani discusses freedom in the context of two other concepts used in his conversations and in his writings—rationality and secularization. Both involve a double polemic: first, against the uncontrolled theorizing of the earlier social scientists, especially in Latin America; and, second, against the general political trends that culminate in one form or another of fascism.

"In both cases there is emotional content. It is clear that rationalism or rationality is related to a certain structure of the character in which one tries to understand everything intellectually. And with secularism, it is the question of having a great belief in progress and evolution—despite the Fascists and despite the way in which the Stalinists went wrong even though the ideals of progress are basic to Marxism.[9]

"You must remember that Italy is the country of the counterreformation, where even before the Fascists people were taught not to think on their own, but to believe and to accomodate. I never accepted that; oh, at first I had a religious formation; my mother was very Catholic and my uncle was a priest. I went to Sunday school, and once to a retreat for 10 days where they taught children, even using terror—I hated that terror. But I was already reading positivist books and an anarchist journal that some friend sent my father. So one day I said no, I don't believe any more, and I tried to do the kind of things which should provoke the revenge of God, and nothing happened. I had a physical revulsion against the priests. At first my mother was upset, but my uncle was broad-minded and said 'don't worry,' and when she saw later how the Church supported the Fascists and how the priests rejected her when I was in jail, she did not go to mass for years. She was deeply religious, and that was a tremendous step for a woman.

"Yes, you are right. Freedom is really a part of secularization. It means separating the Church from all parts of society and specializing it. It means individualism and individuation."

Germani does not start out to write a book *de novo*; he collects his essays between book covers. He takes articles that have been written for various purposes, such as outlines for classroom instruction, reports on research projects and statements for international congresses, and combines and edits those which have overlapping themes. He is restless and rewrites as he goes along, and occasionally he publishes the same material several times with new data and refined ideas. Because he is multilingual and travels a great deal, his pieces often bounce about in no particular sequence from Spanish to Italian to French to English to Portuguese.

His most important volume is typical. Its definitive edition is *Política y Sociedad en una Epoca de Transición (Politics and Society in an Epoch of Transition)*, which appeared in Buenos Aires in 1963. It began many years earlier as journal articles and mimeographed material to be used in the classroom, then part of it was published in Brazil in 1960 with the Portuguese title *Política e Massa* followed three years later by the Argentine edition. The first section is a didactic overview of the structural-functional theory of social organization and change based on such writers as Talcott Parsons, Kingsley Davis, Pitirim Sorokin, Karl Deutsch, Ralf Dahrendorf and George Herbert Mead. Germani attempts to integrate the views of these authors in a way that permits the study of both conflict and stability in order to avoid the conservative bias of some functionalist writings. Although this section is clearly oriented toward beginning students, it also shows the historian of ideas the basic sources of Germani's thought. The second section is a theoretical analysis of the transition from traditional to industrial society; the third section applies the theory to Latin America and the fourth contains specific studies of Argentina. Germani returned to many of the same themes in 1969 in *Sociología de la Modernización (Sociology of Modernization)*, and in the discussion that follows I shall combine materials from both books.

The perspective that dominates Germani's work is one which sees Latin America as passing from "traditional" to "mass" or "modern" society, but in jerks and spasms rather than in a smooth and harmonious process. His goal is to enhance comprehension of particular aspects of the current social scene, especially the noneconomic concomitants of economic development, by placing them in the context of the larger transition.

Germani uses a double approach to contemporary reality: first, he constructs "ideal types" of two polar extremes of traditional versus modern society, recognizing that any real situation involves a mixture of elements of both poles; and, second, he analyzes in detail the processes of transition towards modernism that are operating in the historical scene. He is much more interested in the processes than in the structural characteristics of the abstract types, but he needs the latter as a framework for discussing the former. And Germani always pursues the analyses of social process down to the level of the individual; he is as much a social psychologist as a sociologist. The result is a rather complex theoretical design that weaves together large historical trends (economic, political and social) with smaller-scale social interactions that incorporate individuals into the larger patterns of change.

His technique begins with the construction of the contrasting models of traditional and modern, that is, theoretical simplifications that are logically coherent. He then complicates the explanation by adding details of reality which show that any given historical moment is full of contradicitions because of the frictions of fact that keep real societies from precisely matching any theoretical type. Those frictions arise from many sources: societies modernizing today do not exactly repeat the transition that occurred a century ago when industrialization first reached full flower in Europe, partly because the new societies can borrow and do not have to invent; internal aspects of society do not change at equal rates, thus there are important "cultural lags" that often lead to conflicts; various groups in society have different interests and thus are trying to speed up or slow down the general transition to benefit themselves.

The purpose of showing the ideal types of traditional and modern is to help the observer grasp the complexities of real societies by comparing them with the orderly coherence of the models, which are deliberate creations of the imagination—generic abstractions designed to show some similarities among concrete forms that appear at first glance to be dissimilar. Many critics of this style of theory-building mistakenly attack it by showing that no society was ever an exact copy of the abstractions; since the model-builders were not trying to create descriptive patterns that come as close as possible to the concrete facts, but rather analytic tools that interpret those facts, the criticism is wide of the mark.

The approach followed by Germani was formalized by Max Weber, but it has certain parallels to the work of Karl Marx. It seems that most authors, wishing to rise above their own particular societies and seeking general principles or even laws of social development to aid them in understanding the particular historical circumstances in which they live, follow somewhat similar paths. They create evolutionary models to indicate that the present emerged from a past that had certain typical features that allow predictions (by opposites) of what the future will bring. Marxists speak of the transformation of society from "feudal" through "bourgeois" to "Socialist" forms, while others describe a movement from "traditional" through "transitional" to "modern" structures. Yet in both instances abstract or idealized models are being created. When the dynamics of change in the model are explained by one or two key factors (especially those which indicate lines of action to speed the process), such as "industrialization" or "class struggle," the writing becomes dramatic and politically charged. By contrast, when the model is complex and states that many factors are interrelated and tend to hang together in a functional syndrome, an approach that denies any single cause, the writing becomes convoluted and academic. If the author adds, as Germani does, that the techniques of measurement and verification in the social sciences are weak and only permit us to say that the interrelations among the factors are statistical probabilities and not absolute certainties, then the writing moves even further from political drama and closer to intellectual truth. Gino Germani is an academic man and not a political activist; thus, as the social sciences become more radicalized in Latin America and more directly involved in debates over specific political policies, he loses followers from among those seeking prophets.

"Our epoch is essentially one of transition . . . . What is typical of transition, the coexistence of social forms that pertain to different epochs, imposes conflict on a process that is inevitably lived as one of crisis since it involves a continuous break with the past, a rupturing that not only tends to divide people and groups, but also penetrates into individual consciousness wherein reside attitudes, ideas and values that belong to different stages of the transition . . . . The impact of this transformation involves all aspects of human life: economic organization, social stratification, family, morality, custom, political organization. But it also involves substantial changes in the forms of thinking, feeling and action—that is, a profound change in the structure of personality (*Política y Sociedad,* pp. 69-70).

Three aspects of this transformation should be emphasized:

1.   There is a change in the *forms of typical social action from prescriptive to elective*. Instead of tradition and custom dictating decisions, they are made on the basis of intellectual choice that weighs different alternatives and applies criteria of judgment based on efficiency and measurable self-interest. Thus action tends to become rational,[10] calculating, scientific and usually individualistic, although the actor

may identify with a group and thus blend individual and collective interest.

2. From the institutionalization of tradition we pass to the *institutionalization of change*. Religion tends to be superseded as the dominant institution by economic and political units that subsidize research and glorify development; youth and the future gain in prestige at the expense of age and the wisdom of the past; theoretical knowledge that permits new combinations and deliberate inventions replaces practical knowledge based on experience.

3. The old style consisting of undifferentiated institutions and roles that perform a variety of functions is changed to a new style based on *high specialization*. We even get to the point where we have specialized institutions of government whose jobs are to coordinate all the other specialized agencies. Coordination from long-accustomed ways of doing things that produced integration from historical experience is superseded by attempts at rational planning.

This whole process of transition, which can conveniently be called secularization or modernization, began with the Renaissance in Europe and reached its peak in contemporary industrial society.[11] "One of the essential problems of our times is to determine the minimum conditions for the functioning of an industrial society. Until the beginnings of the present century it was thought that the paradigm of England served as an answer to the question. But now it is perfectly clear that there are various models of industrial society and various styles of transition. The traits summarized above seem sufficiently general (although tinged with Western experience), but then comes the question of how far the process of secularization must go, and what are the necessary concomitants as against the accidental accompaniments of this process . . . . Discussions on this theme have occupied a considerable part of sociological interest in both the past century and the current one" (*Política y Sociedad*, p. 80).

Although some aspects of traditional society can continue into the industrialized stage there is always a basic secularization in science, technology and economic institutions, and there appear to be concomitant changes in stratification, family and politics. Ascribed roles, inherited and traditional, give way to achieved roles in which individual competition reigns. That competition takes place in secular schools and economic organizations, and leads to a relatively open status system with considerable upward and downward mobility and blurred lines between strata.

Furthermore, "there is a tendency for the lower strata to carry to their ultimate consequences the equalitarian principles implicit in industrial society" (*Política y Sociedad*, p. 85). Thus they want to participate in modern styles of consumption, to have equal access to education, to have a share in the political process. "In the countries which started to develop late this tendency toward total participation is manifested with particular intensity" (*Política y Sociedad,* p. 86). In those countries the masses are subjected to very rapid change (since the technology of development is imported), and they are aware of the new models of participation of their counterparts in advanced societies, both capitalist and Socialist. Therefore, they are likely to organize vigorous protest movements and subject the governments and economies of their developing nations to considerable strain. They want high consumption before there is advanced productivity, and they want political participation while elites still believe in traditional and exclusive values.

Secularization in the family leads it toward the nuclear form, free of binding obligations toward extended kin (but often linked with them in loose bonds of friendship and mutual aid). Within the nuclear unit, male authoritariansim declines, equality between the sexes and the generations grows and rational decisions are made about behavior that was previously thought to be beyond discussion, such as the spacing of births. These trends were illustrated in a study in Buenos Aires completed in 1958, which interpreted the data in terms of contrast with the rural family system.[12] In that rural structure, the old traditions lingered but in fact lost effectiveness; there was a gap between behavior and norms. About half the families were not legally married and there was much instability and illegitimacy. Interestingly enough the legal system, which reflected Catholic traditions, completely prohibited divorce, but the facts of life led a very large number of people to ignore the law. In Buenos Aires behavior more closely approximated norms, but these were the new norms of urban life. There was a clear scale: the longer the couple had lived in the city, the more likely it was to be legally married, but also the more likely it was to restrict the number of children through deliberate means. Traditionalists said that the use of birth control indicated a disorganization in family life and a weakening of the bonds of social solidarity. Germani argued that it was true that the norms were changing, but the data showed that urban families were more likely than rural families to follow group standards and less likely to show signs of severe disorganization such as abandonment of children or psychic distress. What had happened was a successful transition to the altered necessities of urban life—a new integration into a new normative system with a wider range of elective choice.

Another concomitant of development involves political reorganization. The local community fades as the main focus of personal identification when experience with the larger society, particularly the nation, grows. New forms of nationalism emerge to provide the necessary motivation for social cohesion, hopefully of a legal and rational nature but occasionally with irrational elements of charismatic leadership, particularly when change is abrupt and the uprooted masses seek security.

The process of secularization spreads to all aspects of society, but not evenly. As a result of unequal rates of change there develop "asynchronous" tensions, disequilibria among parts of society and among personal values. These disequilibria may be geographical, as one area moves faster than another. They may arise in the stratification system, as some strata develop more than others. They may even exist within individual consciousnesses, as persons keep old ideas and values while they also accept new ones that are not entirely consistent.

Two significant forms of disequilibria are produced by the "demonstration effect" and the "fusion effect." In the first instance, people compare themselves with others around them, particularly those a bit higher in the stratification system, and judge their situation by relative standards rather than absolute ones. Thus the desires for development are constantly growing; it is not a question of reaching a certain point and then relaxing but rather of always demanding more, since new wants are always being created by imitation of those above who have more. This is true of social strata within a country and even of comparisons between countries. In that relative sense, the backward countries will always be "underdeveloped," since it is unlikely they will ever catch up with those who started earlier.

"The fusion effect consists of the fact that ideologies and attitudes that emerge in an advanced stage of development are often transferred to a backward area with many traditional characteristics, and the new attitudes are then interpreted not in terms of their original context, but in terms of the traditional framework which uses the new symbols to reinforce old ideas" (*Política y Sociedad*, p. 104). Thus aristocratic groups take over some of the new phrases of development and use them to reinforce their leadership; the new nationalism can be used to strengthen old hierarchies.

In general, the most important disequilibria occur when the basic processes of "mobilization" proceed faster than those of "integration."[13] The first process involves the awakening of sectors of the population from traditional passivity through contact with stimuli from the more advanced parts of the society or through structural changes in their local environments. There may be a spread of new means of communication from the city outward to the country, or from the upper strata downward to the lower. There may be economic changes that produce new types of jobs. New wants are created, new means for satisfying wants through greater economic efficiency or through political favors are suggested and strong demands are placed upon the system. The powerful elites who control the system must then respond. They can attempt to repress the new demands, which generates conflict and instability, or they can accept orderly channels for the expression of the new wants: labor unions to allow workers to bargain for higher wages or political parties that incorporate previously passive sectors into the active determination of government policies. Perhaps the key symbol is the extension of the franchise to ever larger portions of the population, although to be truly effective, the franchise must be accompanied by mechanisms for cumulating desires and turning them into appropriate policies. Above all, for the integration of the masses into the polity to work smoothly, these new mechanisms must be accepted both in attitudes and in law as perfectly legitimate and proper, not seen as subversive attempts to destroy constituted authority. The whole vision of authority and solidarity must adjust to include those who were previously excluded, and the old elites must prove flexible enough to take these basic changes in stride by opening the doors before they are battered down.

Thus nations that enter development late are caught in certain key contradictions. The masses demand high consumption and high political participation before the economy is well developed and before democratic institutions are fully legitimated; in other words, mobilization moves faster than integration, and demands grow faster than the ability of the system to meet them. "The lack of legitimacy can affect not only the popular classes that reject the existing social order, but also the directing classes that are not too secure in their sense of legitimacy. This presents a situation radically different from that which existed in the currently advanced nations at the time they first began to develop. The extraordinary channeling of forces that was required at the beginning of the process was only possible as a result of the coexistence of a ruling minority absolutely sure of itself and the validity of its task, with a mass that, in spite of protest movements, did not yet question the legitimacy of that task. Thus it was possible to justify the demanding sacrifices that were necessary for development (which, in fact, proceeded at a much slower pace than it does today)" (*Política y Sociedad*, p. 108).

England, Russia and Japan provide examples of how powerful leadership in early years was able to get development going. However, the Latin American nations are having more difficulty repeating the process under current conditions, and they face constant political turmoil as a consequence.

It is evident that Germani is concerned not just with the transition from traditional to modern but also with the pace and sequence of various aspects of that transition. He notes that the specific historical context in which a country begins to modernize creates quite a difference because existing world markets and available technology set the framework of possibilities for any industrializing nation. He is particularly sensitive to the relative speed of various aspects of social change inside a nation, since most tensions and problems arise from the fact that the thrust of progress in one part of society cannot be smoothly absorbed by another part. But how do we decide that certain changes are not proceeding in a smoothly integrated fashion?

"When we speak of disequilibria or 'lag' we are not indicating a lack of change but rather the existence of some changes that are not congruent with a certain model" (*Política y Sociedad,* p. 101). The crucial theoretical decision faced is the selection of the model to use as a standard of judgment. "A basic question not yet theoretically resolved is the definition of the 'equivalencies' to be used for making comparisons of the sequences and rhythms of partial processes observed in different historical transitions. Some criterion of comparison is needed that is independent of the historical data themselves which would allow us to define what can be considered equivalent or expected among diverse partial processes. Generally two different procedures have been used: (1) the historical experience of the Western countries is taken as the model; or (2) statistical indicators from many countries can be averaged or intercorrelated to produce the model. Both procedures are useful but theoretically inadequate if the results are used as a universal norm for transition" (*Sociología de la Modernización*, p. 26). The danger, of course, has already been pointed out: history cannot repeat itself in a linear fashion because each epoch faces unique conditions set by earlier historical trends and by external contexts.

Germani suggests that the tentative answer to this problem is a set of stages in development stated so it is sufficiently general to cover a large geographical region yet restricted to that region and to defined periods of world history. He told me that such an approach was inevitable if one teaches a course on Latin America and not on the development of a single country, for without some generalized model of stages the discussion of the different countries has no common story or general perspective. He worked out a stage theory some years ago with Kalman H. Silvert, and he has modified it from time to time as he tries to make it more complex and thus closer to reality.

Each stage represents a rather long period of time that shows a certain stability of social structure; there is functional integration of various parts of economy, polity and society. Within this integration, certain decisions have been made that condition the range of possibilities for action, and only rather startling circumstances can shake up the equilibrium and cause the new decisions that initiate a new epoch.

The economists at the United Nations Economic Commission for Latin America in Santiago, Chile, who have had so much influence in the postwar

TABLE 1
Stages of Growth: Latin America

PRINCIPAL STAGES AND EXTERNAL STIMULI	ECONOMY	SOCIETY	POLITY
I. *Traditional Society* Discovery, conquest, colonization	Isolated regional economies; local subsistence with minor export trade	Traditional structure based on hacienda; landowners and peons	Colonial government
II. *Weakening of Traditional Society* French and U.S. Revolutions	Transition to dependent economy, with export of primary products	Persistence of traditional structure, but some signs of weakening; local or creole elites replace Spanish and Portuguese	Wars of Independence; anarchy alternating with *caudillos*; slow emergence of central governments
III. *Dual Society* Industrial revolution in Europe and U.S.; European migration to some parts of Latin America; liberalism (British) reigns	Export economy expands; internal communications to support it developed, often via foreign investment; sharp cleavages between subsistence and export sectors	Primate cities grow, with some modernization and consequent gap with countryside; middle classes expand; mobilization spreads near central cities	National power consolidated; central bureaucracy grows; in some countries middle classes admitted into polity via ''representative democracy with limited participation''
IV. *Mass Mobilization* Great Depression; Second World War	Industrialization and import substitution; foreign investment; first wave often followed by inflation and stagnation; directing ideologies are ''developmentalism'' and ''nationalism''	Rate of urbanization accelerates; death rates diminish and ''population explosion''; mobilization accelerates via internal migration to cities and new mass communications, dissolving dual society; proletariat emerges	Transition toward ''total participation'' including lower classes; populism; unions & welfare state measures sponsored by government; middle-class liberalism weakens under mass pressures, producing crisis of integration

Source: *Sociología de la Modernización*, pp. 51-58.

years, usually speak of two basic stages: *crecimiento hacia afuera*, or growth toward the outside, and *crecimiento hacia adentro*, or growth toward the inside. They refer to the fact that until about 1930 most of the region's countries responded to external markets as the major stimulus for economic growth. They exported minerals or agricultural products, and when the markets for those products grew the internal economies enjoyed prosperity as a direct consequence. In more recent years, investments in industries producing goods for local consumption have provided an impetus for growth that is less directly tied to the conditions of the export trade. As the internal economies develop, they produce changes that speed up alterations in the social system that began earlier: cities expand, middle classes grow and a new industrial proletariat emerges. Germani takes these ideas from economics and elaborates them into a series of stages of growth by inserting details about social and political changes that occur as concomitants of economic diversification. His scheme is presented in very condensed form in Table 1.[14]

Germani himself points out that this scheme is not a tight "theory of stages," but rather a common-sense condensation of Latin American history that highlights some characteristics shared by most of the countries of the region. In his concluding remarks concerning the scheme, he says that certain features of one stage may tend to continue into the next, producing anachronisms. For example, many countries continue with a mentality oriented to the export of primary products, unable to plan their industrialization in ways that will produce efficient manufacturing firms that can compete in world markets and thus overcome the tendencies toward stagnation inherent in import-substitution phases. In this case the landed oligarchies may no longer completely dominate but they retain influence and their perspectives persist in national thinking. Germani also emphasizes that some countries were still in a typically "dual society" stage even as late as 1970.

In various publications, Germani has bolstered this general approach by collecting comparative statistics from the different Latin American countries and arranging them in the form of parallel scales according to the degree to which each nation approximates the norms typical of the last or industrial stage of development. He showed that industrial countries like Argentina and Chile had, in 1960, reached a level or urbanization that put half or more of the inhabitants in cities of over 20,000 people, whereas countries still based on primary exports like Ecuador and Nicaragua had a quarter or less of their population living in such cities. Similarly, the industrial countries typically had a third or more of their population engaged in urban occupations at the level of the middle class (clerical, supervisory, technical) contrasted to a fifth or less in the export countries. Figures on high school attendance, birth rates, political participation and other social facts supported the notion that there was a syndrome of modernization in which economic, social and political trends tended to hang together in a consistent way, despite all the variations from one country to another. Therefore, a ranking of countries on any one of these indicators usually produced an order from "traditional" to "modern" that was roughly equivalent to the sequence produced by any of the other indicators. The obvious conclusion is that modernization is a single overall process, with each aspect reinforcing the others in a pattern of complex multicausation.[15]

This emphasis on the consistent patterning of modernization is what places Germani among the ranks of the "structural-functionalists," in the school of social science that found its most powerful voice in Talcott Parsons. However, Germani differs in mentality from orthodox members of the school because he is not interested in deducing interconnections between one aspect of social organization and another via chains of logic starting from stated premises (such as the "pattern variables" of Parsons). Instead, he discusses loose patterns that are observed empirically—noticed more by induction than deduction. He gathers available national statistics comparing one Latin American country to another (and he was doing this as an isolated scholar long before many of the newer compilations of data were made available by the United Nations and by the computers in U.S. universities) in order to connect historical trends with hard data, and then he organizes them, to use his own phrase, in a "common-sense" manner. Theoretically, he seems more interested in deviations from the usual patterns than in conformities to them; he concentrates on those "asynchronous" forms of change, involving lags between some thrust forward and the resistance to it, which produce the tensions and problems that keep Latin America in perpetual turmoil. He writes most vividly when he is analyzing what goes wrong with the modernization process, but in order to understand the difficulties he must be able to compare them to some model of "expected" congruence.

Germani recognizes that a structural-functionalist approach emphasizing the tendency for different aspects of society to hang together in congruent patterns within each stage of history suffers from a key theoretical weakness: it lacks a prime mover, a motor that explains why one stage dissolves and another commences. The Marxists portray the accumulation of capital and class conflict as the motive forces; many North Americans emphasize the inexorable growth of technological invention; and the *dependentistas* see new forms of intervention of foreign capital as the thrust that keeps the process going.

In the interview Germani said that he was well aware of the problem but felt that there was no satisfactory solution. He said that if one looks to technology, then one must explain why technology creates changes in some situations and not in others. Indeed, he wondered if each historical epoch might not have a unique force that at one point creates the fundamental change that sets the rest in motion. It might be the impact or diffusion of ideas from the outside; it might be demographic growth and pressure from within; it might be flaws in socialization that keep people from being completely "adjusted" to the current scene and their roles in it. Marx himself always emphasized that men, not abstract forces, make history and that the scholar must find, within a given context, the elements that are most disturbing to the system's equilibrium and most conducive to its alteration. He further indicated that he had always had an emotional reaction against the use of "imperialism" as the key factor. "In *Política y Sociedad en una Epoca de Transición* I did not go much into the question of imperialism. Why? Because I was looking at another side of the question. I was more interested in internal problems, and this was due to a reaction against nationalism. Of course, I recognized that in Argentina nationalism was partly a popular movement, but the implications were shocking. So often it becomes an aggressive movement, a Fascist movement, like in so many places in Europe. There is a connection between antiimperialism and xenophobia. Besides, even if it is true that there is no other way than some form of nationalism for a given country, it is really a kind of suicide for the human race, because if the nation-state is not abolished somehow, we won't have any more humanity. I am of the generation that believes in 'one world'. The multinational corporation is an expression of the kind of economic and technological structure which we now have that cannot be reduced to the limit of a nation, either capitalist or Socialist, and that structure is the enemy, not the United States. Now, it is true that in the present situation the political lesson is that the poor countries are defenseless, not so much because of imperialism but because of the positive feedback that Gunnar Myrdal writes about so well, which helps the rich get richer. But you don't solve that problem by more nationalism. For Latin America the solution would be to have a Latin American Union; you could start it through technological cooperation. Some say that Latin America as a working entity does not exist; well, then it should be invented, otherwise you will have Brazilian imperialism, which is very real. It may be too late to have this kind of union; the diagnosis for the present situation is very negative, very pessimistic, in my opinion. The speed of change is so fast that new political arrangements might come too late. But I see no alternative."

He added that he was also responding to certain specific national conditions when he turned away from a detailed analysis of imperialism. In the first place, Argentine industry was somewhat more local in ownership and had a longer tradition of independence than in the other countries. Furthermore, he was always most afraid of the right-wing forces in Argentina that would be tempted to use antiimperialist nationalism as an ideology for uniting the people in a xenophobic form of Fascist integration.[16] This became clear in the attacks that were made against sociology in general and against his Department of Sociology at the University of Buenos Aires. The critics picked up the fact that empirical studies of the family were underway, and they loudly asserted that national unity depended on Catholic traditions of the family and that anyone who questioned them was a dangerous Communist. Such irrational and antiscientific views have always been Germani's greatest fear and greatest enemy; consequently, he found it hard to make a scientific analysis of imperialism, since that concept seemed to him more an ideological weapon than a proper tool of sociological research.

Obviously, much of Germani's professional life has been a reflection of his desire to understand authoritarianism, first in Italy and then in Argentina. He has been particularly concerned with authoritarianism among the working class, since he noted that in Italy the proletariat mostly rejected Mussolini, but in Argentina they welcomed Perón.[17]

Accepting the usual observation that working classes tend to identify with leftist ideologies, Germani looks at various shades of difference within this general tendency. Classic leftism in Europe in the nineteenth century included strong ideas of liberty (even libertarianism and anarchy), and also of internationalism, since national states were seen as oppressive instruments of the bourgeoisie that would be destroyed by the emerging worldwide proletarian movement. By contrast, classic rightism was based on the strength of local cultures, and it called for internal solidarity among all social strata within a community, led by its traditional elite.

However, the clarity of these positions has constantly faded since World War I. Leftist movements began to embrace nationalism and ideas of totalitarian leadership, and rightist movements adopted some ideas of social welfare for the masses, using slogans of "national socialism." Thus both right- and left-wing movements showed authoritarian tendencies and attempted to incorporate the masses.

Germani specifies further the typical ideological commitment of various strata within the working class. In the countries that industrialized first, the working class as a whole tended toward leftism, but the lower strata within that class adopted a more authoritarian version of it and the upper strata a more libertarian version. In the countries industrializing at a later period, he found that the ideology of the masses as a whole become more nationalistic and more authoritarian.

That upper segments of the masses in the classic situation were more libertarian than the lower segments is explained as a form of diffusion. The ideas of personal liberty began among the elite, filtered to the middle classes,

and then eventually to the masses—always moving slowly down the stratification hierarchy and becoming stabilized in local tradition. Thus they
reached the higher segments of the working class before reaching the lower
ones. Similarly, ideas of nationalism filtered down the hierarchy but were in
many ways less intense in the older countries than they are today; long
tradition had established a firm sense of ethnic identity that needed less
support from ideological symbols. Furthermore, the general ideological
climate in the nineteenth century was one of democracy and freedom, with
the expectation that it would slowly spread and encompass all groups and all
nations.

The disruption of World War I and the collapse of the world economy in
the postwar years weakened many of these convictions. The inevitability of
progress through liberalism was no longer taken for granted. Simultaneously, vast social changes were occurring and at ever faster rates. Huge
numbers of men gathered in new cities; secularization in the urban scene led
to depersonalization of human relations, and this was a particular shock for
those who had recently arrived from rural zones. The manipulations of
politics through deliberate propaganda intensified and the "mass society"
arrived. New ideas of irrationality based on such writers as Pareto and Freud
seeped into intellectual formulations. The old values of slow change and
steady democratization no longer seemed adequate.

Under these new circumstances, many elites refurbished the old authoritarian ideas that previously were based on ethnocentrism and localism,
developed new symbols of nationalism (especially in the newly independent
countries where anticolonial struggles had shaped history), added some
ideas about mass participation and social welfare and attempted to capture
the allegiance of confused masses that were seeking alternate forms of
security to replace the lost solidarity of local communities. Thus old forms of
traditional and local elitism were fused with new forms of authoritarianism
based on explicit nationalist ideologies. A generalization applies to this
process: "The popular classes of a country—or subgroups within them—
will be more likely to support authoritarian movements (of Left or Right) the
more recently that those classes have been integrated into national politics,
and the more traumatic has been their transition from preindustrial to
industrial society. In those countries in which democratic mechanisms began
to function earlier and with full support of the general world ideological
climate, appropriate values were incorporated into political traditions and
were able to maintain themselves even under new and disturbing circumstances" (*Política y Sociedad*, p. 143).

Under modern conditions of mass society all nations have bureaucratic
structures that restrict freedom and limit the development of a truly democratic personality and life style. Thus the practices of political freedom as

formulated in parties and elections may not be fully supported by everyday experiences. "Here we discover another contradiction of the modern world: from one side political democracy requires men who are able to exercise freedom and take responsibility, while on the other it reduces them to the condition of mere objects during most hours of the day" (*Política y Sociedad*, pp. 237-38).

These general ideas are applied by Germani to the specific case of Argentina under Juan Perón.[18] Argentina "modernized" early in the twentieth century, creating all the formal aspects of a secular, industrial and highly urbanized society. But the social changes necessary to transform those formalities into daily realities for the masses were much slower in developing. "High politics" remained an activity in which only a small elite was actively engaged; the masses had a legal opportunity to vote, but it was rather empty because they lacked choices rooted in their real interests and supported by their own active political organizations. The ideas of democracy were not put into practice in the local community of residence or in the work place. Culture was divided into a cosmopolitan, European version for the elite and a cheap commercialized version for the masses who had little access to higher education. "The difference between democracy—or what should be democracy—and totalitarian forms rests on the fact that while the first tries to base itself on genuine participation, the second utilizes an *ersatz* participation, creating the illusion in the masses that at last they are the decisive element, the active force in public affairs. And for that part of the society which remains separate from this pseudoparticipation, totalitarianism uses successful means of neutralization . . . . In Argentina, the originality of Peronism consists of a form of fascism based on the proletariat which faces a democratic oppostion from the middle classes, a reversal of circumstances that would have been considered absurd by earlier European observers of classic and petty-bourgeois fascism" (*Política y Sociedad*, pp. 239-40).

Germani's explanation for the peculiar Argentine situation is based on the history of its rapid transition to industrial society.[19] "As a consequence of the speed of this process, the popular classes became urban masses recently and lacked long union experience tied to political parties representing proletarian interests. Furthermore, the middle classes (partly due to the extraordinary rate of immigration) were of recent formation and lacked the traditions of prestige which characterized European stratification—they did not fear proletarianization, but rather enjoyed their recent ascent" (*Política y Sociedad*, p. 241). It was thus the newly urbanized workers, inadequately integrated into city life, who formed the potential base for a mass movement; they were already waiting for a charismatic leader when Perón offered himself. Their goals were not revolutionary, but rather reformist; they wanted greater participation for themselves in the existing system.

In Europe, the leader promised vindication to the declining middle class through restablishment of hierarchy and order and through national grandeur and domination. The proletariat was asked to submerge its special interests into those of the national community, or was threatened with repression. But in Argentina, "the Fascist slogan of 'Order, Discipline, Hierarchy,' was changed to one of 'Social Justice and Rights of Workers' . . . . Although carefully avoiding any real changes in the social structure of the country, the movement offered itself as an expression of the working class in its struggle with the 'exploiting oligarchy'. . . . The usual explanation of this phenomenon is erroneous; it says the people sold their liberty for a plate of beans. However, the effective part of the dictator's demagoguery was not material advantage but the act of giving to the people the experience (real or fake) of having achieved certain rights. The workers who supported the dictatorship, far from feeling cheated of liberty, were convinced that they had achieved it. Not an abstract liberty of constitutional rights, but a concrete liberty against foremen and owners, the right to elect union representatives, win complaints in labor tribunals, to feel more in control of themselves. All of this was, for the ordinary worker, an affirmation of personal dignity. . . . To understand it, one must remember the state of inferiority and insecurity that was the usual lot of the urban worker, especially in Argentina, where in recent years there had been few free elections, where union activity had been persecuted and mass political parties acted with difficulty. Furthermore, the rapid industrialization beginning in the thirties had moved large rural masses, without political or union experience, into greater Buenos Aires and other large cities. For these masses the pseudoliberty of the dictatorship was the only direct experience they ever had that affirmed their own rights" (*Política y Sociedad,* pp. 244-45).

The middle classes that turned to fascism and nazism in Europe were completely irrational, since they were asking that the calendar be turned back to the nineteenth century by the elimination of large bureaucracies, the rights of workers and other effects of contemporary technology; they projected their frustrations but could not reverse social change. The Argentine working class was also somewhat irrational, writes Germani, in that basic changes in the structure of capitalism were not obtained, and many of the immediate gains in wages and welfare benefits were wiped out by mismanagement of the national economy and the resulting inflation followed by recession. But the masses did gain a major point, both in their subjective feelings and in objective fact: they demonstrated the power of the proletariat and showed that it could no longer be excluded from public life.

There are two issues in Germani's analysis of Peronism and working-class authoritarianism that continue to be debated, one empirical and the other theoretical.[20] The empirical question concerns the exact amount of weight to be given to the new urban migrants, the "mobilized but not integrated" sector, as a source of Peronist support. When Perón won the crucial election of 1946, much of his strength came from the old working class that had long been organized into unions. He afterwards reached out to new workers of other backgrounds, greatly expanded the size of the union membership and developed more emotional symbols of a populist nature. Most of the research that Germani did involved ecological correlations, indicating that electoral districts with high proportions of working-class residents were most likely to vote for Perón, but we do not have detailed studies at the individual level that indicate exactly which workers turned toward Perón for what motives and at what moment of his changing political career. Nor can we fully reconcile Germani's views of *ersatz*, irrational participation connected with charismatic appeal with his material on the ease with which most migrants adapted to the urban scene, getting jobs in industry or the services and reorganizing their personal and family lives to fit their new circumstances.

The theoretical issue is related to those empirical questions, and concerns the criteria for judging the rationality of behavior. Germani wrote, "It is true that rationality is a central problem, but I always used, implicitly or explicitly, the difference between instrumental and final or essential rationality. Modernity is based on instrumental rationality only . . . . There exists no way to find the ultimate rationality of ends, the *summum bonum*; but there is a low level way to find it, and that is to try to discover the real goals of a social group. This is, for example, the argument in the comparison between the behavior of the European middle class under fascism and the working class in Argentina."[21]

Radical critics assert that writers who analyze working-class politics as pseudorational and authoritarian impose a value judgment which implies that only classical forms of middle-class party politics achieve full rationality. Such a view underplays the possibility that both old and new members of the working class who supported Perón were acting quite rationally when they viewed the circumstances of the times and concluded that only a sharp break from pseudoliberal forms of establishment politics could possibly bring them real substantive gains. Germani's statement concerning method is a good guide, but it is difficult to follow without bias; we must combine a true understanding of the "real goals of a social group" (which demands great empathy) with a convincing analysis of its objective situation and various practical alternatives before we can evaluate the rationality of group action in relating means to ends.

Connected with his interpretation of authoritarianism is Germani's long-standing interest in a set of intertwined social processes: urbanization, migration (external and internal) and social mobility (that is, movement up and down the stratification hierarchy). The combined thrust of these processes produces a vast movement of people toward the cities and usually up the status ladder. Under favorable circumstances, the social-psychological consequences are mainly toward integration into modern society and satisfaction with it. However, there are times when the flows of people are greater than the capacity of the urban society for absorbing them, and the results are "marginal" groups on the fringes of the cities (often literally as well as figuratively) who are prime targets for charismatic leaders with a populist message.[22]

Germani emphasizes that Argentina, in proportion to its population, has absorbed more European immigrants in modern times than any other country in the hemisphere: "to the 1,000,000 estimated population (in 1850), 3,500,000 immigrants were added in the early decades of the flow and 8,100,000 in total. The proportion of the foreign born was always much higher than in the USA. The maximum in the USA was reached in 1910, with 14.7 percent foreign born. In Argentina they formed over a quarter of the total population in the last decades of the nineteenth century, then increased to more than 30 percent in 1914, and at present they still account for 12 percent of the total population. It has been estimated that in 1960, without the contribution of the immigrants and their descendants, the population of the country would have been 55 percent of the actual figure (which was about 21,000,000). The consequences of the high proportion of foreigners were further reinforced by the fact that they mainly resided in urban areas. Among the adult population of both sexes the foreign born amounted to 70 percent of the total population of Buenos Aires between 1869 and 1914" ("Social Modernization and Economic Development in Argentina" [1970], p. 37).

The migrants mostly came from Spain and Italy. Although some became agricultural laborers, the bulk went to the cities, and the natural growth of the rural population provided much of the needed increase in agricultural labor. Efficient large-scale farms produced cattle and wheat for export, and the immigrants worked in the auxilliary industries of construction, commerce and transport that were supported by agricultural production and profit. The anticipation of that profit induced foreign investors (mainly British) to send vast sums to the country for the construction of railways, port facilities and urban public utilities. Around the turn of the century, Argentina was absorbing almost half of all British foreign investment. The result of the movement of both people and capital meant that in a very short time the country became one of the world's major exporters of foodstuffs, and simultaneously a country dominated by urban centers; by 1900, over half of the population was engaged in nonagricultural activities and Buenos Aires was a great modern metropolis. The gross national product per capita almost tripled between 1850 and World War I (and has grown very slowly since then, increasing only an additional one-third by 1960).

The immigrants found it easy to adjust to the Argentine scene. The Spaniards already knew the language, and the Italians learned it without difficulty. People from both countries found that family life and other aspects of social organization followed familiar Mediterranean traditions. The growth of the economy meant that good jobs were available for the newcomers and the lack of rigid norms of status in the new country meant that those who succeeded on the job were accepted in the community. Many began as laborers and became either skilled workers or entered the non-manual or middle strata, which increased from 11 to 30 percent of the work force between 1869 and 1914, and reached 40 percent by 1947. As Germani had noted personally when he first entered the University of Buenos Aires in 1938, Argentina was an open society in which movement was the expected thing rather than the exception. "The rapid expansion of the middle strata caused a high rate of *structural* upward mobility (mobility due to the increase in the number of available positions at the nonmanual level). *Exchange* mobility also was probably high, and the two forms combined should have originated a very high rate of total mobility. In any case, taking into account structural mobility only, it may be estimated that the middle strata included at least two-thirds of upwardly mobile people (i.e., whose fathers—or themselves—had had manual occupations). Among the foreign population, this porportion was higher, since the great majority of immigrants had first been laborers" ("Social Modernization," p. 42).

The subjective consequence of the high rate of mobility was a double one: a raising of expectations among the successful who moved into the middle class and a general wave of satisfaction, even euphoria, since expectations were usually met. The newcomers demanded reforms to admit them into political action, and the oligarchy granted universal male suffrage in 1912. Four years later the middle-class Radical party won the presidency. Its supporters were easily satiated, however, and the party made only mild reforms; as the years passed, it became defensive of privileges and worried about growing proletarian demands.

But these early successes were not maintained. By World War I, Argentina had become a modern nation with high standards of living, far ahead of her neighbors in both economic and social development. And although the formalities of constitutional law suggested that the political system had also modernized, the realities of power were not adequate to the rapidly changing situation. "The establishment of the modern national state and the broad plan of economic and social transformation of the country originally envisaged was, in fact, made effective under the leadership of the landowning class. However, the program was conducted within the limits of its own social and economic interests, and this involved not only structural consequences for the society and the economy, but also a progressive increase in rigidity and a loss of capacity for change. In the first place, the landowning class and its politicians were not ready to accept the consequences of the transformation of the society induced by their own policy when it threatened their economic and political power, and, secondly, they became captives of their own economic success and continued in the same trend even when it had ceased to be the best available alternative. This limitation of the capacity for innovation and adaptation to new circumstances was linked not only to economic interests, but also to the prestige value attached to land and agricultural and pastoral enterprise over industry" ("Social Modernization," p. 33). In 1930, the oligarchy reversed 70 years of constitutional government with ever-widening participation and supported a military coup. Political instability has continued ever since.

The possibilities for expansion *hacia afuera* via export of agricultural products had pretty well become exhausted by the end of World War I and suffered total collapse during the Great Depression. Massive foreign immigration ended, but it was replaced by internal migration. In the first half of the present century death rates fell dramatically, the expectation of life doubled (from 30 to 60 years) and excess rural population moved toward the cities. They found a high standard of living and hopes of economic progress and social mobility based on past successes, but those hopes were somewhat soured by the new realities. In Germani's view, the dominating elites did not realize soon enough that agricultural development opportunities had ended and did not consciously switch to a new form of industrialization with export of manufactured products; instead, they allowed an unplanned industrialization for local consumption behind the spontaneous protection created by the Great Depression, reinforced by deliberate protection through tariffs after World War II. But industrial growth soon ran out of momentum and inflation, cyclical crises of foreign exchange shortages and stagnation were the results. Yet social change continued and put increasing pressure on the economy. By 1960, almost 60 percent of the population lived in cities of over 20,000 inhabitants; 45 percent of the work force was in the nonmanual or middle and upper strata; half of the teenagers were attending high schools and 10 percent of the youths between 20 and 24 years of age were in universities; the proportion of male adults who voted had reached almost 80 percent (compared to 10 percent 50 years earlier); trade union membership had reached 4 million. Social tensions increased steadily, and the Peronist dictatorship was followed by only the briefest periods of constitutional democracy between long interludes of military rule.

From a country with boundless optimism and faith in itself, Argentina has become a frustrated and bitter nation in a state of permanent crisis. Neither the military nor the civilian governments can find a way to reconcile the conflicting demands of the defensive middle and upper classes versus the aggressive new proletarians. The economy does not expand with enough energy to provide a surplus to divide among the claimants, and the perpetual political crisis makes it impossible to reorient the economy towards paths of new growth.

Having used social mobility as an important concept for the analysis of the specifically Argentine situation, Germani widened his interest and studied mobility in other countries. His procedure was typical of his style of work: he read all the latest materials in various languages, emphasizing empirical and quantitative studies wherever they were available, as well as the attempts by various authors to synthesize those studies into theoretical frameworks that grew out of the comparisons of one research to another. He then presented his synthesis of the other syntheses at an international meeting of experts in San Francisco (where I happened to participate as the commentator on Germani's paper). This was part of a long series of conferences because the International Sociological Association had for a decade been promoting mobility studies as an important step in the creation of comparative sociology.[23]

A research-review paper of this type is necessarily complex and pedantic; it must attempt to include within its scope a wide range of studies. The author is tempted to make an interesting generalization such as, ''high rates of mobility incorporate people into their society with a high level of satisfaction, which makes them politically conservative.'' Then he looks at another study and has to add, ''but it depends on the historical circumstances.'' A ''high'' rate is largely defined by what people expect, and it stems from what customarily has existed in *their* society for *their* stratum; thus, it is defined in terms of specific reference groups. A stratum accustomed to a lot of mobility that experiences a small reduction in rate will respond with dissatisfaction and often reactionary revolt. Yet, another stratum accustomed to slight mobility may experience a small increase in rate that generates euphoria, and both may occur simultaneously in the same society. Since Germani is both a structural-functionalist seeking theoretical generalizations based on comparative quantitative studies and a man who reads a lot of history and believes that the particular context within which a process occurs gives it its meaning, he is forced to qualify most of his statements with, ''but it all depends.'' When discussing Latin America, he uses the stages of growth as a framework to help him specify the historical circumstances serving as the defining context for particular propositions connecting mobility rates with social-psychological and political consequences. The totality of his scheme is too complex to be summarized here, but a few of its more interesting propositions can be indicated.

"In Latin America, the groups whose ascent was partially blocked by the persistent rigidity of the stratification system promoted revolutionary or reformist movements. That was customarily the situation of the rising middle strata created by the modernizing effects of economic expansion during the third stage of transition, that based on exports. Their recently acquired identification as a class, and their efforts toward participation in the political order and in positions of high prestige, led them to oppose the political (and at times, the social) order which gave the traditional elites a virtual monopoly of power and prestige. Supported by the recently mobilized lower strata that habitually lacked political experience and their own leadership, the intellectuals, professionals and industrialists organized the typical 'liberal-popular' or 'national-popular' movements that appeared at the end of the last century and during more recent decades. One can give as examples the APRA in Peru, the National Liberation party of Costa Rica, the Democratic Action party of Venezuela, the MNR in Bolivia, the 'Radical' parties of Chile and Argentina and in its earlier days the PRI of Mexico. One can also include in this broad classification the parties of Perón in Argentina and Vargas in Brazil to the degree that they included blocked sectors of the rising middle class . . . . The typical evolution of these movements has been from a revolutionary opposition to the political and social order to a much more moderate stance. This change appears to correspond to the level of integration of the middle strata" (*Sociología de la Modernización*, pp. 96-97).

Germani goes on to point out that a group which experiences downward mobility usually becomes reactionary. This mobility can involve an actual slippage of individuals down the status hierarchy or a relative loss of prestige and power of an entire stratum vis-à-vis a newly rising stratum, such as the sense of weakening status experienced by the lower middle class in Europe between the two world wars as a result of the growing power of the industrial proletariat.

He further emphasizes that a firm class-consciousness among the proletariat only appears as a result of a long period of isolation from the rest of society, an isolation that can be defined in several senses: rigid social hierarchy that makes sharp distinctions between various strata; concentration of many workers in large factories; tendency toward stable residence through time in special working-class districts; social clubs and political parties of their own that develop a leadership structure. The miners and factory workers in European countries developed that isolation and class-consciousness during the slow process of industrialization, but the comparable workers (except for some mining groups) have not done so in Latin America. For one thing, the pace of change has been too fast; there has not been enough time for such traditions to evolve. Furthermore, the geographical mobility of the population, which in Argentina brought so many foreigners to the new factories in the early years and which brought so many people from the countryside to the city in all the industrializing countries, has inhibited the emergence of homogeneous class feelings. Finally, the very high rates of upward social mobility have meant that the majority of the workers' children rise into skilled or white-collar jobs; the proletariat as a whole has not felt locked into a special status that makes them permanently "different" from established society. Consequently, protests are mainly demands for more opportunity to get a proper share—higher wages and more access to the schools and jobs and social respect that typify the middle strata. There have rarely been protests of a truly revolutionary variety calling for an overthrow of the total system. Geographic and social mobility have whetted appetites, and development has been sufficient to suggest that with a bit more pressure those appetites could be satisfied.

One might ask: If the process of transition from traditional to modern society occurred in a manner that reduced radical protest in Latin America, why has there been so much political instability? Germani's answer seems to be a double one; first, the elites lacked sufficient confidence in their mission to be able to properly handle the protests that did arise, so they failed to move fast enough in the creation of legitimate channels for political opposition and the full incorporation of newly mobilized sectors of the population into the mechanics of the system (except perhaps for the unique Mexican system, which does coopt new groups into its structure whenever they get strong enough to demand entry and which has achieved political stability). Germani tells these elites, as he earlier told the generals in Argentina, that they should not treat the workers as subversives but rather as men with legitimate requests. Second, there is constant trouble because the Latin American countries came into the industrial world late in the game, which means that the middle sectors grew faster than the industrial base, and their consumer demands grew faster than economic output. When the proletariat became politically active it faced resistance from defensive middle strata. The solution to this difficulty is less obvious than the first one, and Germani has no clear advice to offer.

Since he accepted a professorship at Harvard University in 1966, Germani has kept in contact with activities in Buenos Aires by trips to that city once or twice a year. He has a continuing relationship with the Center for Comparative Sociology in the Di Tella Institute, particularly with its program Population and Society, which he organized before leaving Argentina. Originally, its purpose was to produce an updated version of his early book *Estructura Social de la Argentina*, but it has expanded in scope with the addition of several young demographers who are publishing a series of monographs using census data from various years.

When he first left Argentina, he was involved in many controversies about his work as a scholar and administrator, mainly because of attacks from the extreme Left. As the years have passed, tempers have cooled. Germani himself recognized that some of the questions raised were at a high level of intellectual criticism, such as indications that certain aspects of Latin American reality stemming from the "dependency" relationship of the region to the "imperialist" power of the United States were not given much attention in his publications, or that his writings emphasized the "superficialities" of stratification instead of the "basics" of social class in the Marxist sense of the term, and he was willing to debate such scholarly issues. But he resented other criticisms that he considered to be low-level attacks coming from ideological commitments, such as claims that he was a tool of imperialist interests controlling the development of sociology according to their wishes.

Despite the controversies, he does not feel that his work in Argentina was in vain, for several competent and dedicated men were trained and are still able to follow their careers, if not in the University of Buenos Aires then at least in the Di Tella Institute or in some of the provincial universities where scholarship appears to continue in a more tranquil environment. "There is not the vacuum that once existed; now there is teaching and publication in various centers."

Besides following the work on demography in Buenos Aires, Germani has one other important research interest that currently occupies him: the comparative study of the socialization of young people into Fascist-type regimes.[24] Much of his concern with this problem stems from reminiscences about his youth in Rome, and it has been stimulated by his new friendship with Kenneth Organski of the University of Michigan, who also grew up in Rome. They now have a research underway, in cooperation with several Latin American scholars, comparing national development and authoritarian trends in Italy, Argentina and Brazil.

An evaluation of the work of Gino Germani can well begin by noting his impact as teacher, academic administrator and publisher. He was a crucial figure in the revitalization of the University of Buenos Aires after the fall of Perón, and for many years he served as the most influential spokesman in Latin America for a sociological approach that combined the classic European theoretical tradition with the newer North American methods of empirical research.[25] These traditions were known at the time only in piecemeal fashion. Although a few of the main authors had been translated into Spanish, the style of sociology that stresses the necessity for stating one's theoretical perspectives in the form of propositions that are presumed capable of test through the proof of numerical data was not widespread. Germani wished to divulge the theoretical perspective, tie it up with the new research techniques and offer the package as an alternative to what he considered to be either useless or dangerous ideological polemics. Within the university, he wanted to establish sociology as an accepted scientific endeavor, and outside of academia he hoped to see the ideas of the discipline used as guides to policy and its techniques adopted as practical tools in social planning.

The ideological arguments of that period were usually presented in extreme fashion: the right wing spoke of the mystical unity of society to be gained from traditional and religious premises and from a reaffirmation of order and authority, and the left wing spoke of the necessity for fundamental revolution to reorganize society according to a Marxist blueprint. Germani entered the debate by suggesting that what was happening to Latin America in general, and Argentina in particular, was a recapitulation (with local variations) of a general process that had occurred in other countries. When people understood the process, their polemic passions presumably would be calmed because they would realize that many facets of their personal experience were the inevitable results of society's modernization.

Germani conceived a model of what the typical modern society was like, which was, by implication, what Argentina should be like. Hindsight suggests that his model contained a somewhat more specific political commitment than he was willing to admit. His abstract style of writing stressed general scientific comparisons, but they were usually marshaled to support the goals of the political Center. Germani's own experiences in Fascist Italy and Peronist Argentina had made him a crusader for individual freedom and a man who stressed the procedures of restrained, constitutional government and the necessity of total civil liberties. He assumed that in the long run those procedures, if conscientiously applied, would lead to wider participation of both middle sectors and proletarian masses in the decisions of government and thus in the benefits of industrialization.

Toward the right wing of the debate Germani took a reformist stance and attempted to convince it that the Peronist movement (which, according to the elections that finally took place in 1973, represented half of the population) was not a wildly revolutionary force but a means of expressing the demands of the newly mobilized masses of the population. Since most of those demands were appropriate to the current stage of development of the society, they had to be met even though their mode of expression often seemed to include irrational and charismatic elements. Indeed, he implied that the irrationality was a momentary and passing phase produced by the recency of mobilization.

Toward the left wing of the debate, Germani took a developmentalist and gradualist stance and appeared to argue that Argentina was already too far along the route to modernization to have appropriate conditions for revolutionary action. Its society had achieved middle-class domination and its workers had experienced so much mobility from farm to factory to office (if not in one, then in two generations) that they lacked a truly revolutionary consciousness. He hoped that a new stability would be attained at a higher stage of social integration that would institutionalize worker participation in the polity.

In the preceding paragraphs, words like "imply" and "assumed" and "appeared" were deliberately introduced, not to invoke academic caution and irresponsibility but to indicate that Germani's style causes a problem for the critic. He belongs to the tradition of "scientific" sociology that stresses the obligation of the writer to keep personal ideology and social analysis in compartments that are separated as much as possible. Consequently, he does not openly state his political convictions as necessary components of his analysis (as do González Casanova and Cardoso) but attempts to keep them apart. He admits that complete separation is impossible, but nevertheless he strives to maximize the distinction. In recent years I have become increasingly skeptical of this approach, since I find that it tends to deepen the influence of personal values on sociological analysis because it hides their impact.

There are connections between facets of Germani's life and work that are best made explicit: his personal commitment to individualism and libertarianism; his interest in the psychological or subjective side of modernization; his use of a functionalist theoretical framework that emphasizes universals of process over specifics of structure and describes them in sets of statistics that correlate variables that hang together to define a stage of development. Now, all of these approaches are not so tightly linked as to completely explain one another, but they do relate in ways that produce a coherent view of the modernization process as well as a model of the typical modern society.[26] The implied result of that general view is an ideology of gradualism and a concentration on the political procedures within a nation that are thought to be appropriate to a given historical stage, such as that of "total mobilization." This interpretation of contemporary reality deflects attention from contrary trends that lead in the direction of international domination, widening disparities within and between nations and new forms of manipulation that distort the legal equality of individuals and the sovereign equality of nations. In short, this approach underemphasizes the possibility that nations which enter the path of capitalist industrialization late in the game may not recapitulate the stages of the earlier countries, and that their failure to do so may lead to sharpened conflict and sudden transformation instead of steady evolution toward "modern" integration.

It is true that Germani wrote extensively about exceptions from the model of progress, ranging from middle-class Fascist movements in Europe to working-class authoritarian movements in Latin America. But the total effect of his writing was to interpret the exceptions as disequilibria, as undesirable deviations from the basic model. The functionalist tone implied that the difficulties would disappear through time as equilibrating processes took effect, although Germani's personal views (expressed more in conversation than in writing) often suggested more pessimistic predictions. At any rate, the model's logic lead one to think of disequilibria, not of built-in dialectic trends that contradict the model itself.

As a result of these ambiguities, Germani's books are often read without full understanding, and he is criticized without justice. Some readers assert that he is a tool of United States imperialism, instead of recognizing that he is a spokesman for a European brand of liberalism that antedates, and in its deepest meaning is incompatible with, contemporary imperialism. Some call him a conservative who views the working class as frighteningly authoritarian, when in fact he is a centrist who has spent much of his life fighting the authoritarianism of the right wing. Some assert that he is a Communist who favors dissolution of the moral standards that unify society, yet he indicates that full modernity implies new norms and willing submission to their legitimacy because they are suited to the needs of an orderly, advanced society. These confusions show that readers of social science are not "neutral" or "value free," and that writers of social science cannot avoid the ideological implications of their work by refusing to make them explicit.

There is another aspect of Germani's approach that is worth discussion, namely, his belief in a form of science-making that takes its inspiration from the natural sciences and requires relatively small adaptation when dealing with the human sciences. He aspires to a set of abstract theoretical laws that can be tested by empirical data, yet he also recognizes the significance of historical specifity. But the precise role of history is not clear. Is it part of the circumstance that must be specified to make "all other things equal" so that the relationships between independent and dependent variables will hold true? If so, the laws will only be useful within one homogeneous historical epoch and will not have the transcendent quality of physical laws. If, on the other hand, historical change is part of the explanatory system itself, then comparison and generalization becomes difficult if not impossible. Reflecting this problem, Germani is hesitant when handling the scheme of stages of Latin American development. He needs the stages and yet writes disclaimers that they represent an adequate form of theory. I suspect that the problem cannot be solved within the framework of a science that aims at general laws. However, since this issue recurs in the work of González Casanova and Cardoso, a full discussion of it is best postponed until the concluding chapter.

NOTES

1. Those articles attracted the attention of Lucio Mendieta y Núñez and J. Medina Echavarría in Mexico, and the former invited Germani to collect them and other essays in two books published by the National Autonomous University of Mexico in 1956: *La Sociología Científica* and *Estudios de Psicología Social*. See bibliography at the end of the chapter.

2. His first article on this key theme was "Algunas repercusiones sociales de los cambios económicos en la Argentina" (1952).

3. See "An Inquiry on the Social Effects of Industrialization and Urbanization in a Working Class Area" (1961).

4. See T.S. Di Tella, G. Germani, and J. Graciarena, *Argentina: Sociedad de Masas* (1965); and T.S. Di Tella, *La Teoría del Primer Impacto del Crecimiento Económico* (1965).

5. In response to my question, Germani replied that the Ford and Rockefeller foundations never tried to dictate policy concerning research or teaching. He said that his only problems with "cultural imperialism" came from certain inferiority feelings among some Argentines toward foreign professors when the activities in Buenos Aires were first getting underway.

6. It arrived in June 1966.

7. For Germani's written account of the rise and fall of sociology in Buenos Aires, see his "Sociology in Argentina" (1967), perhaps more accessible in the Spanish version in *Revista Latinoamericana de Sociología* 4, no. 3 (1968).

8. An earlier book, *La Sociología Científica* (1956) covers some of the same themes. It in turn includes material from a still earlier volume written in 1945-46 that was circulated in mimeographed form but not published, *Teoría e Investigación en la Sociología Empírica*.

9. Actually, Germani feels a need for faith in secular progress, but not much hope that it will triumph; his observations of life in the twentieth century, combined with a pessimistic aspect of his personality, usually lead him toward gloomy predictions.

10. On reading the manuscript, Germani added this footnote: " 'Rational' in the instrumental sense—that is, rationality of *means* not of *ends*. I have always used this essential distinction."

11. For a careful analysis of the concept, see Germani's "Secularization, Modernization and Economic Development" (1967).

12. See *Política y Sociedad*, ch. 10.

13. The concept of *mobilization* appears extensively in the writings of Karl Deutsch, but Germani uses it somewhat differently, referring not to a transfer of population to urban settings but to social changes with psychological consequences.

14. For more details, see 'Stages of Modernization in Latin America'' (1970) or *Sociología de la Modernización*, ch. I. For an application of the scheme to Argentina with considerable historical and statistical documentation, see "Social Modernization and Economic Development in Argentina'' (1970).

15. See *Sociología de la Modernización*, ch. 5.

16. Recent events, as Eldon Kenworthy reminded me, suggest an opposite interpretation: military governments, closely allied with the right wing, moved Argentina toward closer integration with the U.S. dominated international economy. See Cardoso's similar observations concerning the Brazilian military regime in ch. 4.

17. Germani's ideas on "working-class authoritarianism" were maturing in the fifties simultaneously with those of Seymour Martin Lipset; the two men maintained contact and influenced each other.

18. See "The Transition Towards Mass Democracy in Argentina" (1965), "The Consequences of Social Mobility" (1966), and "Mass Society, Social Class, and the Emergence of Fascism" (1967).

19. The reader unfamiliar with Argentina may wish to consult these books for background information: Imaz (1970) and Scobie (1971).

20. See recent discussions in English by Smith (1972) and Kenworthy (1974).

21. Germani (1972): personal communication.

22. See "The Strategy of Fostering Social Mobility" (1963); "Assimilation of Immigrants" (1965); "The Consequences of Social Mobility" (1966); "The City as an Integrating Mechanism" (1967); and the "Introduction" to his *Modernization, Urbanization, and the Urban Crisis* (1973).

23. See "The Consequences of Social Mobility" (1966); the paper became ch. 3 of *Sociología de la Modernización* with a more elegant title that would read in English "The Impact of Social Mobility on Consensus and Acceptance of the Social Order."

24. For a preliminary report, see "Political Socialization of Youth in Fascist Regimes: Italy and Spain" (1970).

25. On the theoretical side, his task was not without parallels to that of Harvard University's Talcott Parsons for the English-reading public; both emphasized the same European authors, and both searched for the key convergences of industrial society. Germani's perspective had been formed before he discovered the work of Parsons, but upon reading *The Structure of Social Action* (1937) in the early forties he immediately recognized a kindred soul. As teachers, both emphasized the unity of the social sciences, and as administrators, both tried to keep sociology, social anthropology, and social psychology under one roof.

26. The lack of full predictability from theoretical perspective to political opinion (or the reverse) is shown by this interesting contrast: González Casanova starts from explicitly different theoretical grounds from those of Germani, yet he too is a gradualist reformer with respect to national politics in his country and he also talks of a model with stages, such as late welfare capitalism leading toward socialism.

Bibliography of Gino Germani

Books

1955   *Estructura Social de la Argentina*. Buenos Aires: Raigal.
1956   *La Sociología Científica*. Mexico, D.F.: Universidad Nacional Autónoma de México.
        1962   Second edition.
1956   *Estudios de Psicología Social*. Mexico, D.F.: Universidad Nacional Autónoma de México.
        1966, 1972 Enlarged editions, *Estudios de Sociología y Psicología Social*. Buenos Aires: Paidós.
1960   *Política e Massa*. Belo Horizonte: Universidade de Minas Gerais.
1963   *Política y Sociedad en una Epoca de Transición*. Buenos Aires: Paidós.
        1964, 1966, 1968, 1971, New editions.
        1972   Portuguese: *Política e Sociedade*. São Paulo: Mestre Jou.
        1972   French: *Politique et Société*. Gembleux: J. Duclot.
1964   *La Sociología en la América Latina: Problemas y Perspectivas*. Buenos Aires: Editorial Universitaria de Buenos Aires (EUDEBA)
        1965   Second edition.
1965   *Argentina: Sociedad de Masas*. With Torcuato S. Di Tella and Jorge Graciarena. Buenos Aires: EUDEBA.
        1966   Second edition.
1969   *Sociología de la Modernización*. Buenos Aires: Paidós.
        1971   Italian: *Sociologia della Modernizzazione*. Rome: Laterza.
        1972   Portuguese: *Sociología da Modernisação*. São Paulo: Mestre Jou.
1973   *Modernization, Urbanization, and the Urban Crisis*. Editor. Boston: Little, Brown. A reader, with an introduction by Germani entitled, "Urbanization, Social Change, and the Great Transformation."

Articles in English

1959   "Development and Present State of Sociology in Latin America." In *Proceedings of IV World Congress of Sociology*. London: International Sociological Association, vol. 1.
1959   "The Process of Urbanization in Argentina." United Nations Seminar on Urbanization in Latin America (Doc. E/CN/12/URB/9).
1961   "An Inquiry on the Social Effects of Industrialization and Urbanization in a Working Class Area." In *Urbanization in Latin America*. Edited by P. Hauser. Paris: UNESCO.
1961   "Politics, Social Structure and Military Intervention in Latin America." With Kalman H. Silvert. *Archives Européenes de Sociologie* 2: 62-81.

1963   "The Strategy of Fostering Social Mobility." In *Social Aspects of Economic Development in Latin America*. Edited by E. de Vries and J. Medina Echavarría. Paris: UNESCO.

1963   "Problems of Establishing Valid Social Research in Underdeveloped Areas." In *Industrialization and Society*. Edited by Bert F. Hoselitz and W. E. Moore. The Hague: Mouton.

1964   "Social Change and Intergroup Conflict." In *The New Sociology*. Edited by Irving L. Horowitz. New York: Oxford University Press.

1965   "The Transition Towards Mass Democracy in Argentina." In *Contemporary Culture and Society in Latin America*. Edited by D. B. Heath and R. N. Adams. New York: Random House.

1965   "Assimilation of Immigrants." In *Handbook of Urban Studies*. Edited by P. Hauser. Paris: UNESCO.

1966   "The Consequences of Social Mobility." In *Social Structure and Social Mobility in Economic Development*. Edited by Neil J. Smelser and Seymour M. Lipset. Chicago: Aldine.

1966   "Mass Immigration and Modernization in Argentina." *Studies in Comparative International Development* 2, no. 11: 165-82.

1967-68 "Mass Society, Social Class, and the Emergence of Fascism." *Studies in Comparative International Development* 3, no. 10: 189-99.

1967   "Secularization, Modernization and Economic Development." In *The Protestant Ethic and Modernization*. Edited by S. N. Eisenstadt. New York: Basic Books.

1967   "Sociology in Argentina." In *La Sociologia Contemporanea*. Rome: Instituto Luigi Sturzo.

1967   "Urbanization in Latin America." In *Political, Social and Economic Role of Urban Agglomerations in the States of the Third World*. Brussels: Institut International des Civilizations Différentes.

1967   "The City as an Integrating Mechanism: The Concept of Social Integration." In *The Urban Explosion in Latin America*. Edited by Glenn H. Beyer. Ithaca, N.Y.: Cornell University Press.

1969-70 "Stages of Modernization in Latin America." *Studies in Comparative International Development* 5, no. 8: 155-74.

1970   "Political Socialization of Youth in Fascist Regimes: Italy and Spain." In *Authoritarian Politics in Modern Societies*. Edited by S. Huntington. New York: Basic Books.

1970   "Social Modernization and Economic Development in Argentina." Geneva: United Nations Research Institute for Social Development. Report no. 70.6

Articles in Spanish and Portuguese
Not Listed Above in English
nor Included in Books

1942   "La Clase Media en la Ciudad de Buenos Aires." *Boletín del Instituto de*

Sociología (Faculty of Philosophy and Letters, University of Buenos Aires) 1: 105-26.

1944   "Métodos Cuantitativos en la Investigación de la Opinión Pública y de las Actitudes Sociales." *Boletín del Instituto de Sociología* 3: 85-107.

1950   "La Clase Media en la Argentina." In *Materiales para el Estudio de la Clase Media en la América Latina*. Washington, D.C.: Unión Panamericana, vol. 1.

1952   "Diez Años de Discusiones Metodológicas." *Ciencias Sociales* (Unión Panamericana) 2: 67-86.

1952   "Algunas Repercusiones Sociales de los Cambios Económicos en la Argentina." *Cursos y Conferencias* 20: 559-78. Also in *Ciencias Sociales*.

1955   "Sociología e Investigación Social en Francia." *Ciencias Sociales* 6: 12-27.

1955   "Indices de Movilidad Social en Algunos Grupos Urbanos en la Argentina." *Revista Universidad de Guatemala*.

1958   "La Enseñanza y las Investigaciones en Sociología, Economía y Ciencias Políticas en la Argentina." With Jorge Graciarena. Santiago de Chile: Instituto de Sociología, FLACSO, Publication no. 3.

1963   "Antisemitismo Ideológico y Antisemitismo Tradicional." *Comentarios*.

1963   "Urbanización, Secularización y Desarrollo Económico." *Revista Mexicana de Sociología*.

1963   "Autoafiliación a Clase e Indicadores Objetivos de Estratificación." Series "Datos" (Institute of Sociology, University of Buenos Aires).

1963   "La Movilidad Social en la Argentina." In *La Movilidad Social en la Sociedad Industrial*. Edited by S.M. Lipset and R. Bendix. Buenos Aires: EUDEBA.

1965   "Regularidad y Deserción en los Estudiantes Universitarios." Series "Datos" (Institute of Sociology, University of Buenos Aires).

1965   "La Clase como Barrera Social: Algunos Resultados de un Test Proyectivo." *Revista Latinoamericana de Sociología* 1: 431-34.

1967   "Crecimiento Demográfico y Desarrollo Económico y Social." *Revista de Sociología*, no. 4.

1968   "Sociología en Argentina." *Revista Latinoamericana de Sociología* 4, no. 3.

1970   "O Profesor e a Cátedra." *América Latina* 13, no. 1.

1972   "Aspectos Teóricos de la Marginalidad." *Revista Paraguaya de Sociología* (March).

1972   "La Estratificación Social en la Argentina y su Evolución Histórica." In *Argentina Conflictiva*. Edited by Juan F. Marsal. Buenos Aires: Paidós.

Other References

1942   Echavarría, J. Medina. *Sociología, Teoría y Técnica*. México, D.F.: Fondo de Cultura Económica.

1970   de Imaz, José Luis. *Los Que Mandan–Those Who Rule*. Translated by Carlos Astiz. Albany, N.Y.: The State University of New York Press.

1965   Di Tella, Torcuato S. *La Teoría del Primer Impacto del Crecimiento Económico*. Sante Fe, Argentina: Instituto de Sociología, Universidad Nacional del Literal.

1975   Kenworthy, Eldon. "The Function of the Little-Known Case on Theory Formation, or What Peronism Wasn't." *Comparative Politics*.

1971   Scobie, James. *Argentina: A City and A Nation*. Second edition. New York: Oxford University Press.

1972   Smith, Peter. "The Social Base of Peronism." *Hispanic American Historical Review* 52, no. 1 (February).

3
Pablo González Casanova

The motivation propelling the work of Pablo González Casanova is his desire to study Mexico in ways that will improve it. For him, the test of theory is practice, the purpose of social science is social progress. Yet he is by nature a reflective and cautious man who does not rush into action without a careful plan, so he seeks systematic guidelines for change that emerge from detailed studies of the existing situation. This approach is shown in his research by his attempt to gather a mass of historical and statistical materials and then interpret them from a theoretical stance with Marxist roots, and it is exemplified in his career in his shifts from periods of quiet, scholarly study to those of active administration of academic institutions that have political resonance. Most of that career has unfolded at the National Autonomous University of Mexico, the huge institution that dominates the intellectual life of the country, where he has been professor of sociology, dean of the School (now Faculty) of Political and Social Sciences, researcher and director of the Institute of Social Research, rector (president) of the university, and once again, researcher at the institute. He is a public figure in his country who is widely recognized as one of its most influential intellectuals.

González Casanova wants to modernize Latin American social thought by leading it toward a reconciliation of European Marxism with North American empiricism. He maintains that Marxist theory must first be brought up to date by moving its reference from the relations between the owner and the workers in a factory to the relations between the advanced capitalist nations and their semicolonial hinterlands; then the theory should be subjected to the discipline of orderly statistics and hard facts. In conversation he sometimes refers to the need to inject some cold Anglo-Saxon empiricism and pragmatism into the emotional discussions of Latins engaged in radical rhetoric. But he also wishes to make empirical research more "relevant" by directing it toward the grand themes of development and conflict that engage political attention in our troubled times. Toward the end of the 1960s this approach became fashionable among many students and even some professors in the United States; because González Casanova has been practicing it for a long time, he can serve as mentor to the newly engaged.

He does not propose to test the modernized version of Marxism-Leninism in the hypothetical-deductive manner so fashionable in North American social science (imitating the laboratory manuals of natural science), since he believes that we derive our fundamental perspectives on society from our historical experience and our practical goals rather than from rational theory. He insists that "we are all political men." However, once a perspective is chosen it can be refined and chastened by the use of theoretical logic and contemporary research techniques, even if that process falls short of laboratory proof.

González Casanova is acutely sensitive to ideological conflicts and seeks to discipline his thought within them rather than pretend that they can be pushed aside by a "value-free" social science. Like all Latin American intellectuals, he lives in a highly political environment; the universities are centers of controversy, and thoughtful men within them must develop a coherent position in order to communicate with students and colleagues. They do not live in a situation that permits the luxury of "scientific" social research that is supposed to be nonpolitical in inception and purpose. Latin American countries are going through a sharp transition and social science is expected to speak to the dominant problem of the epoch—rapid economic and social development. The nations are faced with two models of development, capitalist and Socialist, and must choose between them or find new and appropriate ways to combine them. Social analysts are faced with two theoretical models of social thought, Marxism and liberalism, each with its own techniques of analysis and research. They cannot rest comfortably upon decisions made by earlier generations, as do so many writers in the United States and in the Soviet Union, and spend their energies on minor refinements of accepted models. The models themselves are at issue, the future of their countries rests upon the choice and thus science and action are intimately intertwined.

González Casanova is the first Mexican to have received a doctorate in sociology and is the man who reshaped the national pattern for professional careers in that subject. Born in 1922, he came from a landowning family of the old upper class in the state of Yucatán. His father finished advanced studies in philology in Germany, and after the Revolution had a successful academic career as a linguist. The son first attempted to write poetry, then turned to the study of accounting, then attended classes in law for two years; finally, he found his main interest in history. In the interview he said:

"I was attracted to the new professional career in history that was being established in the early forties cooperatively by the School of Anthropology, the National University and the College of Mexico. My father studied Indian languages, and my house was full of books; the idea of being a researcher fascinated me. I did not want to study history as an art, but rather as a science. Some of the institutionalist perspectives, or the view of history as philosophy that occupied some of my professors, did not interest me. The fashion then was to study the eighteenth century, but I was interested in contemporary history. Looking for more modern studies, I did some work at the Institute for Social Research at the university, and began to connect history with sociology—especially the history of ideas and the sociology of knowledge.

"The political atmosphere of the time showed all that mixing, that heterogeneity of ideas that is so typical of Mexico. Through the stories of our Spanish *émigré* professors we relived the fall of the republic, and also received from them a lot of German academic ideas in history and the social sciences. Influenced by the ideas of Lázaro Cárdenas, the president in the preceding decade, there was an ideological return to the countryside, a concern for the Indians and an awareness of the issues in agrarian reform. We also were close to the repercussions of the expropriation of the foreign-owned oil industry in 1938 under Cárdenas.

"After finishing work for the master's degree in history, I received in 1947 a scholarship to study for the doctorate in Paris and stayed for three years. Although there was no degree-granting department of sociology at that time at the Sorbonne, all my courses and seminars were in sociology or philosophy. I did not study history any more. I studied Hegel and French existentialism, and under Gurvitch and Friedmann and others delved into sociology. My thesis *French Ideology toward Latin America* concerned the ways in which the Europeans in various epochs saw America in terms of their own changing perspectives, such as the need for a utopia, and projected those ideas onto the American reality whether they corresponded or not; my thesis supervisor was Fernand Braudel.

"On returning to Mexico I began to teach at the university and to do research both at the Institute of Social Research of the university directed by Lucio Mendieta y Núñez, and with the group of historians at the College of Mexico led by Daniel Cosío Villegas. But I realized that my training was very defective, and I tried to find time to study the newer methods of field work and statistical analysis. At first I did not have financial support for full-time research, so I started my long career of moving from administration to research and back again. After a spell as secretary-general of the Mexican Association of Universities, I became a full-time researcher at the Institute for Research in Economics of the national university and wrote my book *North American Ideology on Foreign Investments*, which analyzed documents from U.S. congressional hearings and other sources that expressed U.S. perspectives.

"Then from 1957 to 1965 I was director of the National School of Political and Social Sciences at the university. At that time it was dominated by lawyers, and my goal was to stimulate new approaches, leaning at first on economists and anthropologists because we had no trained men in sociology. Through a plan of scholarships for foreign study we created a young generation of sociologists. We all studied some of the newer empirical methods (I think my earlier training in accounting was very helpful), and sought to link them up with classical problems and classical methods. Making that linkage has been my obsession."

While directing the school and teaching in it, González Casanova wrote his first major work and the one that continues to have most influence: *Democracy in Mexico*. From that he went on to write theoretical works on the abstract categories used in studies of development and on the concepts of "exploitation" and "internal colonialism." In 1966 he moved a few hundred yards from the school to the university's small Institute for Social Research, where he became its director. Besides stimulating a major expansion of its activities, he continued his own research. He finished a large-scale investigation, based on both qualitative interviews and a questionnaire survey, of social stratification and political attitudes in Mexico City—a project begun earlier with the collaboration of Professor Ricardo Pozas using students in the school as interviewers. This was a follow-up of an earlier comparative series on several Latin American cities that had been inspired by Gino Germani. He also organized a technical project with Víctor Manuel Durand and Enrique Contreras using factor analysis of macro-statistics to study regional inequalities in Mexico.

During the 1960s González Casanova traveled widely, especially in Latin America, participating in the movement to create a regional consciousness among social scientists, something quite lacking before World War II and before jet airplanes and international foundations. He was a member (and for a time president) of the board of directors that supervised the Social Science Research Center in Rio de Janeiro and the graduate school in Santiago, Chile (FLACSO) that served all Latin American countries, both initially subsidized by UNESCO. He encouraged several of his Mexican students to go to Santiago to obtain master's degrees in sociology at FLACSO, some of whom have continued their doctoral studies in the United States or Europe. And he invited foreign social scientists to lecture at the School of Political and Social Sciences in Mexico City in order to broaden the intellectual perspectives of the students. Yet there remains a nationalist base to his thinking: "In the postwar years Mexican sociology has followed lines similar to other Latin American countries, and we have close contacts with our colleagues, but perhaps there is a shade of difference in our approach. We are fortunate to have a growing group of young, well-trained men and women, and we have conditions that allow them to work steadily and securely. The majority think within theoretical frames that reflect our own history and our own ideologies; what we are trying to do is to turn those perspectives into empirical studies. I think in the next few years you will see much originality in Mexican sociology."

In May 1970, González Casanova was elected rector of the national university and remained in the post until the end of 1972. They were stormy years, reflecting the changes taking place in the larger society. The size of the student population increased rapidly to close to 100,000 (plus 70,000 in preparatory schools administered by the university), as more and more young people demanded the kind of training, or at least the certification, that would lead them to professional careers. In his desire to democratize the university, González Casanova sympathized with plans to reform entrance requirements, modernize the preparatory schools, increase student participation in governance, build branch campuses to accommodate more students and otherwise connect the university more closely with the needs of the society outside its gates. But the pressures to expand and change outran resources of money and professors, outraged conservative vested interests and led some students to commit excesses in the name of progress. At one point the offices of the rector were occupied for several weeks by students (and outsiders pretending to be students) who insisted on imposing their own views concerning entrance requirements to the law school. Wishing to avoid violence, as well as to reiterate the principle of university autonomy (which had been violated in 1968 when military troops occupied the campus), González Casanova refused to call in the police or the troops to evict the occupiers. Eventually they quietly left the building, but the "authority" of the rectory had been weakened by the incident. Shortly thereafter a long strike of nonacademic employees began, stimulated in part by outsiders who wished to embarrass a rector who was identified with the reformist wing of the new national administration of President Luis Echeverría. After the university had been closed by the strike for most of the fall term in 1972, González Casanova resigned in order to open new possibilities for compromise. He then returned to the Institute of Social Research as investigator with plans to resume his interrupted research activities, particularly a project for the study of Latin American history through the use of comparative statistical time series.

As rector, he had learned some new lessons about the difficulty of channeling protest into peaceful and constructive dialogue. His own stance as a man who supported the type of progress that would aid the masses instead of the elites had raised expectations around him. For instance, he had backed a substantial increase in wages and fringe benefits for the university employees just a year before they went on strike for the first time in the university's history; one labor leader then told him that they knew the next rector would be less sympathetic, so they had to push as hard as they could while he was in office. Similarly, radical student groups expected him to be completely on their side, without recognizing that his job required him to balance the interests of many groups in the university community. Many of the radical students (and their allies among members of the faculty) were bitter and accused him of selling out to the establishment, at the very moment that the conservatives in the university and the public press accused him of weakness for failing to call in the police to repress the students. He knew that the university lacked legitimate procedures of governance to handle such tense situations, but said, "I believed in two principles above all else: autonomy from the ordinary forces of politics and the government so that we could keep our freedom, and nonviolence as an absolute necessity for settling academic disputes. Any violent act from one side promotes a violent response from the other. We had to begin somewhere to practice discussion and compromise even though we did not have traditional means of conflict resolution adequate for the problems we faced." When he resigned, he had kept faith with his principles. As a social scientist, he had also accumulated new data; he promises one day to give us a published account of his years as rector and of the interplay between university politics and national forces. Those who accept his call to combine theory and praxis await the book with considerable impatience.

During the early period of establishment of the new sociology in Latin America just after World War II, fads and fashions followed one another. González Casanova disagreed with those who were so nationalistic as to reduce all social theory to an expression of local culture, thus negating the possibilities of international communication, and he castigated those who denied the applicability of empirical procedures just because they may have been invented in the United States and were thus tainted with "imperialism." He was equally disdainful of those who adopted and imitated outside procedures in a mechanical way, revealing a "foreign-directed personality. . . . New forms of simulation, of magic and rhetoric characterize these imitative processes. Statistical analysis, 'matrices', electronic computers are turned into sacred entities and magical instruments . . . . A similar lack of a genuine and solid scientific attitude leads the imitators to posit 'evaluative neutrality' and 'scientific rigor' as metaphysical entities without indicating the possibilities and the necessity for a scientific rigor linked to values, to political orientation and commitment. The absence of a genuine scientific attitude and the failure to recognize the undeniable existence of the sociologist as a political man leads them to new forms of escapism, of a superficial objectivity or neutrality that avoids the great themes of conflict that can and must be treated with a scientific spirit.''[1]

In another context he introduced one of his works by saying; "This book is written especially for those students in Latin America who have adopted the false rigor of empiricism, so closely associated with the social sciences that are predominant today in the United States. It is also written for those who remain fixed within the slogans and pompous words of orthodox and dogmatic Marxism, renouncing the great Marxist traditions of high-level scientific investigation that have always complemented and accompanied research on the level of militant action" (Sociología de la Explotación [1969], p. 3). Thus he rejects crude empiricism and the apolitical stance that so often goes with it; he rejects a dogmatic Marxism that is so linked to momentary political action that it cannot participate in abstract and disciplined analysis; he rejects either immediate imitation of foreign models or chauvinistic disdain for an idea or a technique simply because it comes from abroad. He seeks a social science that can enlighten and guide the developing nations that are modernizing in a hurry, utilizing a framework that is based on philosophic and historical analysis but one that incorporates the latest technical tools of empirical research when they can be shown to be useful.

His own research focus is mainly on Mexican society, and he mines the census and other sources of fact seeking detailed descriptions of current reality. His theoretical framework is neo-Marxism, for he sees Mexico as existing in an early-capitalist stage strongly influenced by external imperialism and suffering from internal colonialism. His political goal is a peaceful transition through a stage of welfare capitalism toward one of democratic socialism, guided by a strong national state that strives to reduce both foreign domination and internal exploitation of one sector by another. These combined views guided him as he wrote La Democracia en México (Democracy in Mexico), which was first published in Spanish in 1965, then slightly revised and reissued two years later and published in English in 1970.

At the beginning of the book González Casanova commits himself to a value position: he is in favor of development defined not only as growth in per capita economic product but also as more equitable distribution of that product among all sectors of the population. He asks, "In what way does the structure of power in a country like Mexico condition and limit the decisions in the field of economic development or lead to decisions that correspond to simple growth of product? Up to what point is it possible to modify the structure of power in order to produce full development, including more equitable distribution?" (Sp. ed. 1967, pp. 13-14). He says he is tired of having economists repeat over and over again that the government should adopt policies leading to improvement of the purchasing power of the masses at the same time that they ignore in their analytic models the very reasons that have prevented the government from taking such steps for three decades.

He believes that a proper analytic model of development must include economic, social and political factors and must not be automatically borrowed from the experience of nineteenth-century Europe. "Our countries—underdeveloped, poor, colonial or semi-colonial—resemble each other more than they resemble the metropolitan countries. Therefore generalizations that encompass all countries should be replaced by generalizations that are deduced from the direct experience of the poor countries. It is necessary to put aside the last vestiges of intellectual colonialism, conservative or revolutionary, and attempt an analysis of the relations between political structure and social structure, using categories appropriate to underdeveloped countries, in order to arrive at a proper understanding of the political institutions of Mexico" (p. 17).

In looking directly at the power structure in Mexico, González Casanova immediately dismisses as irrelevant the legal philosophy lying behind the Mexican Constitution, stemming from the French and North American experience of the eighteenth and nineteenth centuries. True, there is a division into legislative, executive and judiciary powers; true, there are elections and new presidents succeed one another in peace; true, there is more than one political party. But the reality is more simple than the model. One party has governed Mexico for 40 years (and it is a direct successor of the group of generals who won the Revolution and governed for 10 years before they organized the party); it regularly wins some 90 percent of the presidential vote; it controls the labor unions and the confederations of peasants and most other major interest groups in the country; it dominates all overt political activity. Under the leadership of the outgoing president, the party chooses a new president to serve for six years and delivers into his hands almost complete power. The legislature automatically passes the bills and the budgets sent to it; the state governors do as they are told or else their funds are cut off or their powers dissolved by decree; the courts make minor corrections of bureaucratic abuses but do not have independent power to make major decisions. Local governments (*municipios*) are controlled by state governors and are too poor to complain because they have a very weak tax base.

Through the years the dominant party (now called the Partido Revolucionario Institucional or PRI, the Institutional Revolutionary Party) has succeeded in whittling down independent bases of power. It fought off or bought off the local chieftains or *caciques* who emerged from the decade of chaos following the outbreak of the Revolution in 1910; it has slowly reduced the proportion of the national budget going to the military and increasingly brought them under civilian control; it continued with the complete disestablishment of the Catholic church, a process which began in the nineteenth century (although the influence of the Church on some middle-class families may be growing at the same time that its direct participation in government remains small).

The one sector that has come to have major power outside of the official party hierarchy consists of the big businessmen. Before the Revolution, economic power resided with local landowners and foreign capitalists; since then, economic growth has produced a large number of wealthy industrialists and financiers. But the entrepreneurial sector is divided into groups that do not always have identical interests: there are thousands of small businessmen participating in local markets; there are some national corporations that produce and sell both within and outside of the country; there are a handful of giant enterprises owned and operated by the government, particularly in transportation, steel, oil, petrochemicals and electricity; there are branches of international corporations, sometimes owned partly by Mexican citizens in partnership with what González Casanova calls the "international monopolies." He quotes one study that gives an idea of the relative strength of these groups in 1960: of the 100 largest companies in Mexico, 39 were owned by foreign firms, 17 had a heavy participation of international capital, 24 were owned by the government and 20 were owned by independent Mexican capitalists. The various entrepreneurial groups each have their organized chambers of commerce and industry (established by law), and they consult very closely with the government on basic economic policy.

Unfortunately, González Casanova is unable to be very specific about the detailed processes of economic decision-making; he can only set the structural framework within which the actual decisions are reached. Thus he indicates that the government has a powerful, direct role in the economy, more in terms of the influence of its new investments on key growth sectors than in terms of its total contribution to the gross national product, which is only about 10 percent. However, its power is limited by its sources of credit, almost half of which comes from outside the country—mostly the United

States. "Therefore, the credits that are obtained in the exterior, especially from the United States, added to the power of the companies owned or partly owned by foreign corporations and supported directly or indirectly by the United States government, reduce considerably the power of the Mexican state, of its presidential regime, its productive and financial apparatus, and invites serious reflection on the proposition that if the Mexican state should diminish its economic intervention would not the result be a growth in the power and influence of the North American state? Thus it is necessary to analyze objectively national power and the factor of domination by the great power to the North . . . . Mexican history in the twentieth century is one of political, military and economic measures designed to limit American influence and increase the negotiating capacity of the Mexican state. It is a history of obstacles, advances and retreats which have not broken the dynamic of inequality. At different levels, and with a negotiating capacity much greater than we had in the past, the same problem continues, whether it be in the field of economics, of politics or of culture" (Dem. en Méx., pp. 58-59).

There follow many pages of descriptive statistics to support these assertions—data on investments, on the proportion of imports and exports going directly north, on the circulation of American magazines in Spanish translation within Mexico, on the sources of news of Mexican papers, on the distribution of American motion pictures—all of which show the extraordinary degree of influence on Mexican life of stimuli coming from the United States. The net impression gained by the reader is not one of conspiracy through which a few men in Wall Street and in Washington tell the Mexicans what to do, but rather of an environment that sets the stage and a collection of vested interests that guide the actors; the two together make changes in policy very difficult. Consumer tastes are shaped by advertising and by imitation, both flowing from north to south; continued economic growth is needed to provide jobs and tax revenues, and to maintain such growth it is necessary to promote "confidence" and "optimism" among investors (local and foreign) and among the international bankers and the tourists whose dollars cover deficits in the merchandise trade and also make it possible to pay the interest, royalties, dividends and principal on earlier borrowings. The government's own companies act like efficient businessmen seeking growth and profits; the large firms of the private sector follow similar goals. The capitalist mentality spreads. Progress comes to be measured by increases in the gross national product and by the soundness of the peso, which has been declared "hard currency" by the International Monetary Fund. Indeed, the nation's credit standing abroad has not been so good for many decades—since, to be precise, the days of Porfirio Díaz, the "efficient" dictator who ruled until toppled by the Revolution.

Summing up his views on the power structure in Mexico, González Casanova states that the important criteria for evaluation should not be based on the theory of representative democracy stemming from Montesquieu and Madison (yet that is the way most foreigners approach their judgments), but rather from the conditions that existed in Mexico after the Revolution: chaos, rule by local *caciques* (bosses) and self-proclaimed generals, domination of the economy by foreigners, combined with a lack of communications, education and the other features making up the infrastructure of a modern state. In the 50 years since the Revolution, great progress has been made and much of the credit must be given to the presidential regime. It has maintained the peace and has succeeded in building a mixed economy with sufficient government participation and control to permit increased power of negotiation with the United States government and American corporations. Local industries have grown; a completely new educational system was built, the power of the landlords was broken and a portion of the agricultural workers were granted their own lands to farm. Since 1940 the gross national product has increased at a rate of slightly over 6 percent a year, the best record in Latin America. Thus, within state-guided capitalism, the Mexican one-party government has been able to promote growth. Up to this point, González Casanova supports the system and its accomplishments; he is, to use the Mexican phrase, "within the Revolution."

But then he parts company with the official rhetoric. "This is the true problem which confronts the country, not the violation of the classic theories of liberal economics or representative democracy, but the inability so far to break the dynamic of external and particularly internal inequality typical of underdevelopment" (p. 71). That *continuing* and in some ways *growing* inequality is the focus of his description of the social structure lying behind the political system, and is the central problem to be explained by the theoretical concept, which he introduced, of "internal colonialism."

For many years the predominant statistical reports on Mexico stressed the progress of the averages. Illiteracy reduced from 67 percent in 1930 to 38 percent in 1960; the proportion of young children *not* attending school reduced in the same period from 49 percent to 37 percent; the Indian population (defined as those speaking an Indian tongue) reduced by assimilation from 16 percent to 11 percent; the rural population reduced by migration from 67 percent to 49 percent. All of these averages are interrelated, since the thrust of development has mainly come from the Spanish-speaking cities where the schools, industries and doctors are to be found. In 1960 the per capita income was 1,500 pesos in the rural areas and 6,300 pesos in the cities; the population of the country was split about evenly between the two zones.

González Casanova has been one of the few who kept pointing not just to averages but also to measures of distribution and to total numbers of human beings. From those points of view, "progress" seems more limited. In the same 30 years covered by the improving averages, the *number* of illiterate people has grown from 9 to 10.5 million; the number of children outside of primary school has grown from 1.7 to 3.1 million; the number of Indians has grown from 2.3 to 3.0 million; the number of people classified as rural has grown from 11 to 17.2 million. Since the standard of living of a considerable part of the rural, especially Indian, population has not improved, the absolute amount of misery in the country has markedly increased.

It is clear that the structure of Mexico's plural society continues to generate "marginality," which means that certain regions and strata are left outside of development: these are "internal colonies" controlled for the benefit of people who are not members of the local community. Furthermore, the gap between the marginal people living close to subsistence and the sectors benefiting from economic growth gets wider through time as some get richer and others remain as poor as before (just as the gap between rich and poor nations increases). The supposedly automatic mechanisms of dynamic capitalism and mobility of resources should operate to equalize income across regions, but they are blocked by the social structures of internal colonialism and external imperialism.

In the poorer agricultural zones of the country, the local inhabitants do the heavy work, but outsiders—*mestizos* or *ladinos* rather than *indios*—control commerce and credit and collect the profits. Capital is drained out; so is talent, for the successful *indios* often change their clothes and language and become *mestizos*. Individuals may climb and benefit themselves, but the community remains poor and backward.[2] And it remains politically impotent; the people are not organized into unions or pressure groups. They either abstain from voting or are herded by the PRI into an automatic vote for the official party (which gets its highest percentage in the poorest zones) without understanding the meaning of the act. They are unable to pressure the government or the businessmen into giving them adequate schools or better prices for their goods or their labor. The statistics on government investment show that funds tend to flow to the advanced regions in response to effective demand, instead of flowing to the poorest regions to help them move forward. The differences between states indicate a mortality rate twice as high in the poorest compared to the richest, one-quarter as many teachers per capita and twice the rate of illiteracy.

A combination of regional variations plus class differences within regions produces stark inequalities in income distribution. The 30 percent of poorest families receive only 7.4 percent of the total available income, whereas the richest 5 percent of families get 38 percent of the available income, and the maldistribution has gotten slightly worse in recent years as the urban upper-middle class has gained at the expense of the poor.[3]

González Casanova raises a basic question: In a country with an official policy of "revolution" on behalf of the masses, yet a country with such continuing and even broadening inequalities in income, life style and political power, how will the people respond? Will they rebel again and produce a second revolution? Not, he believes, as long as certain processes continue, particularly the high rates of individual mobility that produce "the hope factor," combined with the successful use of PRI-coopted intermediaries that channel the suppressed yearnings of the poor into the traditional methods of supplication for favors. But both depend on continuing prosperity, and the maldistribution of income threatens that prosperity.

In contrast to the slow rate of economic change that characterized Europe during its early industrialization (and which led to radical movements among the masses), the extraordinary speed of events in countries such as Mexico entering industrialization by borrowing it rather than inventing it has produced a sense of hope among wide sectors of the populace:" . . . that is, the idea that the individual can save himself, that he can solve his personal problems and those of his family within the channels of current development, without substantial structural changes or the need for radical attitudes" (p. 106). Of course, all individuals do not have to experience success in order to share the hope of it; if they see some neighbors getting ahead, and see a rate of change that indicates improvement for their children, they can cling to optimism and continue to accept the promise of the revolutionary slogans. The fact that the government organized a land redistribution that gave a small plot to over two million heads of families; the fact that the unemployed from backward farm zones can move to new areas of irrigated land or, even more, to expanding cities where they find a level of life that is low by urban standards but an improvement over rural misery; the fact that schools for their children become more readily available; the fact that a portion of the working class, that which is well organized in unions and attached to the more lucrative industries, manages to climb above poverty and that their children can aspire to the middle class—all of these create a circulation within the masses that raises hopes. As long as the economy keeps moving and avoids stagnation and crisis, the hopes will probably persist. Thus a society based on hierarchy, if it is expanding and modernizing, can avoid widespread radical protest without reducing inequality.

For the more than half of the population that is not benefiting from economic growth, there is another channel for desire besides the hope for personal advancement: the traditional patient supplication of the *peón* to the *patrón*, of the humble to the powerful. This is a deeply ingrained attitude that emerges from 400 years of subjugation and it is exploited by the present system through "intermediaries," specialists in taking petitions from the unorganized masses to the seats of power. Whenever a leader emerges in any subordinate group, he faces the system of organized power and petitions for something: a water well, an irrigation dam, a road, a school, an increase in the wage rate. If he does so *within* the system, accepting its values and its hierarchies, he has some chance of success. Open protest or conflict is not permitted; indeed, it is ruthlessly suppressed. The more adept he is, the more likely the new leader is to be coopted into the hierarchy itself; thus union organizers regularly end up as federal senators.[4] In this way the official structure extends its power through the unorganized masses, and they occasionally receive favors. While the economy keeps expanding, there is always a bit of surplus available for distribution: the best-organized segments of the population get wage increases, and the unorganized masses get favors or new fringe benefits. This system is far more flexible than the old dictatorship that kept grinding the masses to an ever-lower level of living by taking land away from them and forcing them into a form of debt servitude on the large haciendas; it can absorb and mollify tensions at the same time that it maintains differential privilege.

"With the previous analysis it should be relatively easy to understand how the decisions are made that concern economic development, and to see how the structure of power conditions and limits those decisions . . . . It should be possible to judge the viability of the technical works that are submitted under the name of programs or development plans, and that, elaborated by specialists in national and international organizations, do not get at the true problem of development or analyze the political obstacles that prevent its realization" (p. 129). The plans always suggest the same things: (1) greater equality in income distribution in order to expand the internal market, which would permit more efficient production by plants that now have underutilized capacity and would keep capital at home that now flows abroad for lack of opportunity; (2) diversification of external markets to end dependency on agricultural exports that have a declining position in international terms of exchange; (3) reduction of foreign participation in the economy to achieve more local control over decisions and reduce the outward flow of dividends; (4) more vigorous use of the government's taxing powers to collect money from the rich and use it to benefit the poor.

That is what the experts recommend, but what actually happens? "The average real wage for 1960 was 6 percent less than in 1940, and the minimum agricultural wage was 45 percent less; yet general productivity had gone up 120 percent in the same period, and agricultural productivity had gone up 100 percent[5] . . . . True, the fringe benefits that today constitute between 10 and 15 percent of the wage earners' income had expanded and the real wage rate had gone up in certain industries, such as electricity and petroleum, but these benefits had tended to go to the urban workers attached to the best-organized industries'' (p. 130). Furthermore, fiscal reforms have made little headway, with the heaviest burden falling on wage-and-salary earners and not on those who receive profits, much of which are not declared to the tax collector. Foreign trade has diversified somewhat in terms of products and countries, but it remains concentrated with the United States; thus, dependency continues.[6] Indeed, in some ways it grows, since an increasing percentage of government investment comes from borrowings abroad and an increasing percentage of dollar earnings comes from the precarious tourist trade. In recent years, the flow of corporate profits abroad has been greater than the flow of new investments into the Mexican economy.

"But it is relatively difficult to take measures to control foreign investments and diversify foreign trade which would change the economic structure and its secular tendencies when, from 1942 to 1960, North American banks have granted credits to government agencies in Mexico of 1.5 billion dollars, and year by year those credits have grown; when the balance of payments depends upon those loans, on foreign private investments (which reached 1.4 billion in the same period), on tourism and on the earnings of *braceros*. We have a heterogenous country, highly differentiated, in which the participating sector and the state apparatus cannot ignore political realities and vested interests. Only by accentuating a popular policy to benefit the masses and through it strengthening the state could the government undertake a national policy regarding foreign investments and the diversification of foreign trade that would bring us to a level of equality with the United States . . . . In all the cases we have seen, it is the political structure of the country more than the laws of the market that keeps the country from breaking out of the dynamic of inequality both internally and externally, and thus the political structure is the true bottleneck in the path of development'' (p. 134).

In the advanced countries that have entered a neocapitalist stage it is the political apparatus that has forced redistribution of wealth; trade unions and radically oriented political parties depend upon the labor vote. "To move in this direction will not necessarily bring Mexico a two-party regime, but it does require forms of internal democracy within the government party, and parliamentary institutions that can control the economic power even of the public sector and can bring 'decolonization' of groups within the country, including Indians. We need institutions that will promote periodicals representing minority points of view, and various new forms of government that take advantage of the national experience and carry forward acts of political creativity, even though the responsibility would remain in the control of the current governing class and particularly those groups within it most representative of the national situation. Until that occurs we can speak of decisions regarding economic growth, but not real development. . . . The slow rhythm of such development in recent years, the depressing conditions of the world market for raw materials, the limitations on the internal market, and the awakening of the masses in great sectors of the country demands one fundamental decision: the democratization of our national institutions. Whichever way we look we come to the same view, the need for an effectively democratic regime without violence, or else the danger of an economic contraction and an expansion of violence, which in the current conditions in Mexico instead of leading to a radical solution would necessarily produce a period of stagnation and dictatorship similar to that which exists in many countries in South America. But, what are the possibilites of a decision to move toward more democracy?" (pp. 136-41).

This question brings us to the final section of *La Democracia en México*; it is a *tour de force* that attempts a political diagnosis of the current scene first from the viewpoint of Marxism and then from the viewpoint of contemporary empirical sociology. Using different concepts, both arrive at the same conclusion, namely that the objective conditions for a radical revolution do not exist and that further economic development depends upon a political democratization that is, in fact, feasible.

According to the Marxist-Leninist model, classic capitalism and parliamentary democracy go hand in hand. The Mexican Revolution occurred before the country had fully reached either one. During its early years, through the regime of President Cárdenas, which ended in 1940, there was a natural alliance between incipient local entrepreneurs, organized labor and unorganized peasants against the reactionary tendencies of the large landowners and the foreign investors, who were mainly involved in monopolistic exploitation of land and minerals. The "national bourgeoisie" in the cities was progressive; it was part of the alliance against foreign domination and thus the "national task" took precedence over class conflict. Oil was nationalized; land was distributed.

But now the situation has changed. The national bourgeoisie has merged with the international capitalists and together they put primary emphasis on the expanding and dynamic manufacturing sector. There is no basic clash of interests between them. Furthermore, the working class is split into factions that make it impossible at this time for a clear class-consciousness "for itself" to arise. The skilled workers attached to modern industry are divided from the unskilled workers, and they from the marginal unemployed of the cities, and they from the peasantry. Stratification by status within the worker and peasant groups is a powerful counteracting force against unity, and thus there is no homogeneous proletarian awareness. Individuals attempt to climb one step at a time, and groups protect their own narrow interests.

Therefore, as long as the economy continues to grow, the workers remain divided and the government retains its vitality, there will be no Socialist revolution in Mexico. The political agility of the government follows the dictum of Marx: "The more that the dominant class is capable of absorbing the best men of the oppressed classes, the more solid and dangerous is its domination." Indeed, the Mexican government is characterized by its "counter-coup" capacities. González Casanova recommends that the tacticians of the Left stop wasting effort on subtle discussions of the timing of the uprising and recognize the facts of life as set forth by a proper Marxist-Leninist analysis of the objective conditions. He warns them of the ever-present danger from fascism and imperialism that would crush premature adventures.[7]

González Casanova believes that there is no independent national bourgeoisie of sufficient strength to lead a movement to free the country from external domination and that there is no chance under current conditions for class conflict of the scope that would lead to a successful Socialist revolution. Thus the radicals' task is to promote the democratization of the existing institutions, to support competitive and national capitalism rather than international monopoly, to organize the marginal workers in order to help them increase their share of national income, to constantly pressure the government to put into practice the democratic ideals that are already written into the Constitution and are repeated so often in the official political rhetoric and thus to slowly weaken the structures of internal colonialism. In this way, the evolution to mature welfare capitalism and finally to democratic socialism would be speeded up.

González Casanova then shifts perspective; instead of quoting Marx and Lenin on the objective conditions for revolution and warning adventurers on the left, he quotes Seymour Martin Lipset and Ralf Dahrendorf on the secular tendencies of neocapitalism and gives advice to the elite. Those sociologists use statistical indicators to compare nations across space and time and conclude that the countries with higher levels of economic development tend to have more democratic institutions. For the first concept, they use measurements such as the proportion of the working force in industry, the level of schooling, the degree of urbanization and per capita product. For the second, they use the percentage of the population that votes, the existence of opposition parties, the peaceful turnover of political power and the growth of institutions that legitimize and control conflict. They say that fascism (under its various names and guises) is a protest against modernizing trends from those who wish to maintain authoritarian solutions and antiquated economic powers. They point out that all societies have conflict, but that advanced societies organize the lower-status groups, admit them to full citizenship and then institutionalize the conflict; thus Disraeli, a conservative, was in favor of the working-class vote in Britain, and all contemporary industrial societies set up rules of the game for labor negotiations that lead to controlled pressures for wage increases that in turn constantly revitalize the economy by increasing market demand.

Since Mexico is modernizing its economy and moving in the same direction as the advanced industrial societies, the probabilistic laws of empirical sociology predict that it too will have more democracy. They also show that increases in the purchasing power of the masses are crucial to continued expansion of capitalist production. Thus the proper direction of political action for progressive capitalists as seen from this perspective is the same as that for sensible radicals as deduced from Marxism-Leninism: struggle for the democratization of political and industrial institutions simultaneously with economic growth. Each is vital to the other, and the advice to the government and the bourgeoisie is clear; their long-run interests are on the side of more popular participation in national life, not on the side of authoritarian repression that would lead to economic stagnation.

The mood of *La Democracia en México* (written in the early sixties) was rather optimistic despite the sad statistics on marginality, for it suggested that there was a good chance for steady evolution toward a more homogeneous society and thereby a more just society. In the interview, González Casanova said, "More than a denunciation, the book aimed at explaining the underlying political model of the system in an attempt to pin down our problems in a more precise way. My purpose was to discuss problems of conflict in an objective manner, and thus to disqualify the ideologists. The economists had already written of income redistribution, but did not emphasize sufficiently the political requisites for producing it. The main theme stresses that with more democracy there would be more development—not the other way around."

In the more recent writings of González Casanova, the tone shifts and becomes more pessimistic and, perhaps, more ideological. He explained the change by saying, "Well, in the 1960s we all felt a change in mood. The optimism of the early postwar years, the hopes of *desarrollismo* or developmentalism entered a crisis. The hope that the Third World would create a force strong enough to get free from the two great powers—led by Sukarno, Nkrumah, Nehru, the populist governments in South America—those hopes ended.

"But in many ways our history has been different from that of other Latin

American countries; I still have hope that we can escape some of the sad history we see around us. Even in the colonial period Mexico was the richest of the Spanish provinces; our middle-class farmers were stronger than those in other countries, and actively promoted the independence movement from Spain. They continued to struggle for social change through the period of the Reform led by Juárez, and they had links to popular movements as shown in the Revolution. Our state is not based on urban populism in conflict with the big landowners—which leads to great problems, such as inflation, when the oligarchy won't bend, won't compromise. Our populism is also rural, and our state has learned to participate actively in the economy, especially after the crucial oil expropriations of 1938. This state power makes it possible to guide and control private investments.

"We are also blessed with a political culture different from many South American countries, a tradition of restraint that keeps political arguments from reaching the point of breaking the system. My hypothesis is this: if we make the right decisions, based on our own history, which has social and institutional elements that offer possibilities—if we make them properly, taking advantage of the growth of the urban middle classes, then we will have a better situation.

"Many South American writers are now emphasizing the concept of 'dependency', which is interesting, but somewhat different from our line of thought. What you have to do is seek ways of reaching independence, to look for processes of decolonization, techniques of augmenting national power and negotiating capacity. That is a less ascetic way of looking at things."[8]

The theoretical essays that were written both simultaneously with and just after *La Democracia en México* deal with the concepts of internal colonialism and exploitation. In part they are polemics against liberal economics (but also against orthodox Marxism, which tends to underplay the relations between regions and countries); to make their point, they stress the ways in which the advanced areas get richer by taking advantage of the backward areas. Another theme concerns the degree to which social science concepts are reflections of the political interests of their authors. Thus they strike the reader as pessimistic, for they stress the continuing creation of inequality among men and the continuing self-interest of those who analyze society. Those themes are placed in counterpoint to the more optimistic tone of González Casanova's analysis of the specific Mexican situation, which discusses maldistributions and inequities of the present but mainly for the purpose of stimulating progressive political action to improve matters. Since Mexico is a post-revolutionary society, he can stress reform within existing institutions, something that cannot easily be done for Argentina or Brazil or Colombia. He recognizes that his belief in the possibilities for deep reform in contemporary Mexico is not shared by all radical intellectuals in his country:[9]

"Perhaps that is my most controversial position: I believe that we have to make every effort to reform the structure—e.g., to promote internal decolonization—and thus attain a higher level of development even though some forms of exploitation continue. Our history shows it can be done. If we fail, our friends who doubt this policy, who believe nothing can be done, will be right; but I think we should try.

"My work has its roots in the ideology of the extreme Left in the Mexican Revolution. Within that continuing social movement which we call the Mexican Revolution are positions very similar to mine, such as Cardenism, or groups once led by Lombardo Toledano, which recognize the need for more income redistribution, for state participation in the economy, for an increment in national power to negotiate with outsiders in order to speed development."[10]

González Casanova's theoretical essays are collected in a book called *Sociología de la Explotación* (1969) (*The Sociology of Exploitation*). The second half contains four articles on themes that parallel the descriptive material on Mexico in the earlier book. They deal with class, region, internal colonialism and external imperialism, and they represent an attempt to modernize Marxism and make it more applicable to the underdeveloped countries.

González Casanova points out that the original Marxist analysis of social classes was based on the directly observable relations between the English entrepreneur and his unskilled workers. The owner got richer through various forms of exploitation of his laborers, and they in turn often got poorer (or at least stayed close to the subsistence level). The inherent conflict was obvious. And through extrapolation from these observable realities, plus certain laws of economics that were adaptations of the prevailing theories of his time (such as diminishing returns to capital and overproduction leading to depression), Marx predicted the eventual crisis and demise of the system.

Contemporary liberal social science has claimed that since these predictions have failed, Marxist theory is wrong. Current writers emphasize these trends: increasing skill and income of the working class and its internal differentiation (rather than its pauperization); high rates of upward social mobility and the expansion of the middle class (rather than a sharpening polarization between bourgeoisie and proletariat); successful anticyclical policies by governments that depart from pure laissez faire; development of welfare measures by the state; the steady perfection of society. Marxist writers respond by dismissing these trends as superficial exaggerations by neocapitalist apologists, but González Casanova says that they are wrong. Although perhaps exaggerated in the telling, the trends are real, but to be understood they must be put in the context of worldwide development, which is producting increasing wealth among the countries of the metropolitan center but leaving the countries of the periphery in relative stagnation.

Part of the explanation of neocapitalist affluence comes from the technological sophistication and organizational skills at the metropolitan centers and the lack of those facilities at the periphery; part comes from low rates of population growth at the center and high rates at the periphery; but a very significant part of the explanation must be based on the *relationships between* center and periphery that permit exploitation or an unequal distribution of the fruits of development. To make this analysis, it is useful to add the abstract category of *region* to the Marxist category of *class*, and develop a complex model that combines the two. Regional differences involve the relations of city to countryside, of the advanced part of one nation to the backward part of the same nation, of an advanced nation to a backward nation.

The application of new technology plus a transfer of wealth through exploitation from peripheral to central regions have made possible the enrichment of the middle class and the proletariat as well as the bourgeoisie of the advanced nations, thus reducing the level of conflict. In addition, the colonialist wars of the center against the periphery have permitted anticyclical policies to be effective. But all the beneficiaries do not live in the metropolitan countries: internal colonialism has created in the cities of the peripheral countries classes which are allied to the exploiting classes of the metropolitan countries and share the rewards. Thus we see an international system that bolsters capitalism not only in the metropolitan countries but also in the colonial countries, always by pushing the exploitation outwards to a region further removed from the center.

"The underdevelopment of the periphery is an essential part of the neocapitalist system. There is no doubt that there is a growth in the means of production and in the consumption of the underdeveloped countries, which leads to optimistic predictions of lineal development until 'popular capitalism' reaches everywhere. But in fact, growth in the means of production and the expansion of consumer goods and services follows the same pattern it did in other parts of the world; it generates differences between and within classes, and the gap widens between the colonial metropolis and its own hinterland. The final and irreversible weight of the system falls on the rural peripheries of the Third World" (*Socio. de la Explot.*, p. 213).

The concept of *colonialism* has been used to deal with the control of one country by another, but it also can be applied within many countries to the internal relations between one region and another. A composite definition of colonialism would be: "(1) a territory without its own government; (2) a situation of inequality between that territory and its controlling metropolis; (3) control of administrative affairs by the metropolis; (4) inhabitants of the territory not electing their leaders, but finding them designated from the metropolis; (5) the rights of the local inhabitants, their economic situation and their social privileges regulated by the metropolis; (6) the situation of dominance not 'natural' but growing out of conquest or international concession; (7) the local inhabitants belonging to a race and culture distinct from that of the dominant people, and speaking a different language (a characteristic that does not exist in every colonial situation, but does exist in many of them) . . . . This definition is not sufficient to analyze colonialism, since it is legalistic, political. It does not include the object of the domination, phrased by Montesquieu in these terms: 'the object of the establishment of a colony is the extension of commerce' . . . . Always when there is a colony there is a condition of monopoly in the exploitation of resources, of labor, of the export-import market, of investment, of tax income" (p. 232).

Development of the colony is shaped so as to complement the economy of the metropolis; the colony supplies it with needed raw materials, absorbes its surplus production and supplies capital. The ability of the colony to negotiate with other centers is small or nonexistent, and its living standards remain below those of the metropolis. Of course, all of this is descriptive of the short run. The colonial process itself in the long run creates enough development and enough acculturation to produce an eventual explosion which breaks the bonds of dependency, as Marx correctly predicted for India.

There are important political and psychological consequences of colonialism that go beyond commercial exploitation. They include attitudes of ascription in social relations that classify people as being fundamentally "different" according to their position in the social hierarchy and that lead to the dehumanization of the lower ranks, who get treated as though they were "things" or "animals." Thus the people's backwardness is not really explained by differences in cultural values, as some authors would maintain, but by the system of stratification and exploitation that preserves or creates those differences in values.

"Colonial structure and internal colonialism must be distinguished from class structure, since they deal not only with domination and exploitation of workers by owners, but of domination and exploitation of one people (with its distinct classes of owners and workers) by another people (which also contains different classes) . . . . Internal colonialism explains in part the unequal development within the underdeveloped countries, in that the forces of the monopolized market and the lack of political participation of the inhabitants of the backward regions create a 'dynamic of inequality' that offsets the forces of equalization that come from development'' (*Sociología de la Explotación*, pp. 240-49).

In the interview I asked González Casanova which came to him first: the description of marginality (the term he uses to describe those being left out of progress, particularly landless peasants and underemployed urban slum dwellers) or the theoretical explanation of it in terms of internal colonialism and exploitation. He replied, ''I started some articles before *La Democracia en México* in which I posed the problem of maldistribution of income and culture and power. Perhaps I was influenced in those essays by Mexican economists who were then writing on the necessity of income redistribution. Those ideas then tied up with some more general discussions of marginality, for example in the meetings in Rio de Janeiro that were attended by C. Wright Mills. Then I remember starting to work on the article on plural societies (first published in *América Latina* in 1963) and moving on to the somewhat more general ideas of distribution that appeared in the book. Marginality seemed to me useful in describing maldistribution, geographically or by social strata.

''There was some influence from earlier writings on dual societies, such as Jacques Lambert on Brazil. Boeke who wrote on Indonesia in those terms was more reactionary. The concept of dualism has produced a strong negative reaction in some Latin American ideological circles. But for me it is only a descriptive term, not an explanatory concept. My explanation is in terms of internal colonialism. This was formalized in *Sociología de la Explotación* as a characteristic of contemporary society, which is integrated throughout the world in terms of metropolis and periphery, with asymmetrical relations between them, whether it be on an international level or on an internal level within a country. This explanation goes beyond what the economists do when they merely describe inequalities.''

González Casanova believes that the contemporary underdeveloped countries are now going through a process of development unlike the one the European countries experienced in earlier years. The new countries do not start from a feudal background and slowly develop an urban bourgeoisie. They start from a situation of colonial dependence, with plantations and mines established by outside capitalists for the purpose of supplying the international market. By completely controlling the labor force, the owners are able to establish a form of exploitation that is economically rational, and it succeeds by destroying pre-existing forms of communal life, subsistence agriculture, artisanship and independence. Under these conditions the local bourgeoisie never has a chance for full development, and when industrialization begins the local entrepreneurs become allied with international capitalists, who have more powerful sources of credit and technology, and permit the local industrialists to perform only subsidiary functions. Further-more, the local government never becomes powerful enough in its own right to initiate full independent development, as did, for example, the govern-ment of Japan at the end of the nineteenth century.

The semicolonial countries are, in fact, developing, but only in ways that complement the economies of the metropolitan powers. Their rates of development are not sufficient to absorb the growth in the labor force, and they remain in positions of inferiority and inefficiency. Improvements in productivity in the mines and plantations are not fully distributed as profits and wages to the local people but are partly transferred to the metropolitan countries through both profits and deterioration in the terms of trade. Native technology does not develop, artisanship is destroyed by factory competi-tion, and styles of labor-saving technology are imported that are profitable to owners but disastrous to the underemployed labor force. Local manufactur-ing expands in the form of subsidiaries of the international monopolies who make basic investment decisions that promote their own worldwide interests at the cost of the local economy.

In the earlier years European capitalism led to the impoverishment of its own working class, but now that impoverishment is transferred to the colonial countries. From time to time populist political movements arise in those countries, led by students and intellectuals, small proprietors and lower sectors of the bureaucracy. However, they soon discover the degree of dominance of the imperialist forces and their local allies among the "bought-out" bourgeoisie and the political-military hierarchy, and they fail to gain power or hold it for long enough to alter the basic structures.

The first half of *Sociología de la Explotación* consists of a long and recent essay that bears the same title as the book: "The Sociology of Exploitation." It is an ambitious attempt to deal with the tension between the empirical methods of North American social science and the historical models of Marxism. It will probably not be easy for proponents of either position to grasp or accept the anaylsis of González Casanova, for he asks them to stand outside of their own customary frames of reference and examine assump-tions and procedures that they usually take for granted. It is precisely the type of essay most likely to come from an intellectually marginal man, that is, one who stands between two powerful traditions claiming his allegiance and who seeks to understand them both in order to choose that which is useful from each without succumbing to a superficial eclecticism. It takes courage to produce such a work, since it is bound to leave enthusiastic believers of both traditions dissatisfied.

González Casanova states that the scholars of the Socialist countries usually look with skepticism on quantitative sociology; although it is used for planning purposes, it is not considered appropriate for the study of the classic questions of Marxist doctrine, which are debated using the methods of history and philosophy. And the experts in quantitative sociology in the capitalist countries do not apply their methods to the measurement of exploitation because they feel that the concept is evaluative or ideological rather than a scientific.

"The problem of the possibility of a sociology of exploitation thus presents itself in two senses. To demonstrate the value of such study to the Marxists depends upon showing the connections between empirical techniques and their theoretical model. But in the case of the empirical and neoliberal sociologists it seems necessary above all to invalidate the objections that lead them to reject the very idea of a scientific study of exploitation. For that purpose it seems useful to analyze analogous concepts that are used in empirical sociology and neoliberal economics that are also directly tied to values . . . .

"In the best scientific tradition of liberalism and empiricism one manipulates in technical language and with sophisticated methods the concepts of inequality, asymmetry and development. . . . But the measurement of inequality is inconceivable without the historic transformation that produced the society of the free market, the French Revolution and the Declaration of Independence of the United States" (pp. 11-12). In other words, the notion first had to be established of the independent individual free from a fixed status; only after it was believed that "all men are created equal" in some natural sense did it seem appropriate to measure existing social facts to demonstrate that some men were more equal than others and thus that current social conditions deviated from the natural order.

In some statistical work symmetry is assumed: variables x and y are related but the direction of causality is not fixed. In other work asymmetry is assumed: x causes y, but not the reverse. And in many studies of the distribution of a single variable (such as the model of the normal curve) neither assumption is involved.

Now, in plotting the distribution of a single social variable the underlying notion of the individuality or equality of men—or even more, the liberty of men—is present. When we turn to studies using models of the asymmetry of two variables, we come closer to notions of power, influence or dominion of man over man or nation over nation. Unfortunately, much empirical work sticks to the level of dispersion of single variables, which tends to treat men as isolated individuals and not as members of groups that have differing characteristics, particularly of the type that create asymmetrical relations, such as the power of one over the other. Thus many of the standard models of empirical sociology have great difficulty when they attempt to generate measures of groups or collectivities: they tend to merely aggregate individuals, which leaves out the asymmetrical relations *among* individuals.

Another standard concept of capitalist social science is that of *development*. This imples a constant movement in a desired direction, or progress, a notion quite foreign to the cyclical beliefs of the ancient Greeks, or the apocalyptical perspectives of the Judeo-Christian tradition. It accepts the basic form of society as given and seeks to measure its steady trends. It fails to remember that capitalism is a historical product, that its structure changes, and that depending upon the historical circumstances it does not operate the same way in different times and places.

"The lack of scientific rigor in empiricism comes from its renunciation of the study of its own values and its paradoxical affirmation that the social system is *natural* and that any values that deny the system are *unnatural*. Empiricism is thus less scientific and more ideological in so far as it renounces the scientific study of its own values and relegates them to an extrascientific realm . . . .

"In non-Marxist philosophies (including positivism and empiricism) the defining entities or concepts are metahistorical and coherent in the sense that they ignore struggle, conflict, irrationality. In Marxism the social relationship is the defining concept and it is historical, contradictory and concrete. It deals with a specific social relationship: 'It is always the direct relationship of the owners of the means of production with the immediate producers which reveals the deepest secret, the hidden base of all social structure.' (Marx, in *Das Kapital*)" (pp. 22-26). The tensions and conflicts in this relationship in turn generate technical progress, social change and eventually the destruction of the original relationship itself.

From this perspective, there are no independent and free men who voluntarily enter into competitive social relations; there is no natural order of equality that should emerge from such competition and that can be used as a benchmark for the measurement of inequality. Inequality is not an aberration to be measured and reduced but an inherent feature of a society of exploitation. It is inevitable as long as that type of society exists. Furthermore, it is inevitable in the relations among classes and among nations as long as those classes and nations are products of capitalism. And this is not inequality in the sense of one having a little more and another a little less; it is structured inequality in terms of conflict and domination. It is not to be measured by an ordinal variable that ranges individuals along a continuum, but by a relationship or a ratio indicating a constant state of conflict of interest between two individuals or two groups; when one party gets more, the other gets less.

By contrast, the difficulties or errors that create vulgar Marxism tend to flow from a slip into metaphysics that weakens scientific precision:

1. The tendency to expand the concept of exploitation to cover every-thing, making it a single cause, and failing to connect it to other related factors such as changes in the forces of production.
2. The failure to specify the historical context and make a concrete analysis of it, for exploitation is not everywhere the same.
3. The failure to remember that exploitation is the defining concept for understanding history and a consequent slip into objective or subjec-tive idealism. Exploitation is a basic perspective for viewing conflict and change, but it does not explain anything by itself without a detailed study of specific circumstances.

As a result of these errors, vulgar Marxism underestimates the changes in contemporary capitalism. It does not pay sufficient attention to the development of the productive forces through technology, modern forms of administration, advertising and so forth. It underplays the role of politics as an independent influence on the system that is able to shape and change the flow of events, thus it underplays the role of ideology and of the consciousness of man. It tends to repeat analyses that stemmed from the Europe of the nineteenth century, not recognizing the new facts of the late twentieth century. True, Lenin sketched some of the newer trends of monopoly capitalism and imperialism, but his ideas have not been followed up with systematic study.

González Casanova attempts to provide a quantitative model leading to a modernized and empirical Marxism. The mathematical formula for exploitation is simple: the ratio of surplus value to labor value. This is different from a proportion that merely attempts to allocate the total value of production into wages for workers and profits for owners. The ratio concentrates attention on the *human relationship* involved: of the value of what the laborer produces, some goes to him and the rest is appropriated by the owner in the form of surplus value. Depending on various circumstances, the ratio changes, and the study of those circumstances and changes is precisely what the sociology of exploitation is all about.

The level of abstraction used in the research can vary from the individual firm, through the firms in a given industry or a given region, through the total number of firms in a nation, to the relations of firms in one nation to those in another. When one grasps the complexity involved in the mechanisms of transfer from one firm and one region to another, one begins to understand the channels of international exploitation that make it possible for the surplus value produced by poor farmers in an isolated region of Mexico to end up in the pockets of merchants in Mexico City and bankers in New York.

A detailed study of a concrete situation would have to disaggregate the terms in the ratio into component parts. For example, the surplus value and thus the exploitation can increase without lowering the income of a firm's workers by means of improvements in technology, more efficient methods of administration or more effective monopoly control over prices. Or, on the contrary, the surplus value could remain constant, the income of the workers could increase through unionization or government laws about wages and thus the exploitation can decrease. But these changes in the situation within a given firm ignore the effects on others: if prices go up (either to increase profits or wages or both) the costs are passed on to some group of consumers outside the firm. A complete study would trace all of those effects.

González Casanova attempts to outline some of the logical possibilities through a series of equations, starting with the defining ratio of exploitation and then successively disaggregating its terms. The analysis is abstract and mathematical; the algebraic symbols are not turned into concrete quanitities based on measurements of specific instances. The exercise stands as a model to guide future research rather than an example of empirical method applied to neo-Marxist theory. Indeed, in the interview, González Casanova admitted that his own research team was having difficulties getting appropriate data and disaggregating them to fit the model.

For the study of development, the crucial question of course is the use of the surplus value by the owners. Some of it will go into luxurious consumption while some will go into productive investment, which in turn can be broken down into direct investment for expanding production and indirect investment through taxation for the building of schools, roads and infrastructure. And if one looks at the totality of surplus value within a given nation, one sees the seeds of conflict in its distribution (quite apart from the conflict between owners and workers), for there are opposing interests between monopoly capitalists and small, competitive capitalists, between one industrial sector and another, between the needs for taxes and the desires for profits.

On the side of wages, although the ultimate minimum is based on the costs of subsistence of the laborers, in fact many groups of laborers receive more than this mimimum. In the largest, most modern and most monopolistic industries, the workers are likely to share in some of the benefits of technical progress and receive higher wages. This produces a gap between them and the marginal workers (especially if there is a large "reserve army" of unemployed) that is maintained by unions and other institutional devices. A full analysis of the situation on the labor side of the ratio would also involve differences in the standard of living of workers in different regions, the length of the workday, the number of workers in each family and so on.

"Exploitation was first created when there was development without participation in its fruits by all of those who contributed to it, since the excess was appropriated by the owners as their property. Now there is a new form of it, and thus there are two definitions of exploitation: (1) Those are exploited who have levels of living that are at or below the minimum of consumption when there has been development or the creation of surplus controlled by private owners who use it for their own consumption or new investments; and (2) Those are exploited who despite living at a level above the bare minimum do not receive the full value of their labor, since their skills contribute to a growth in the rate of economic development that is greater than the growth in their wages, with the excess appropriated by the owners of the means of production'' (p. 74). The last 150 years have seen an economic growth unprecedented in the history of the world, so we must recognize the importance of both types of exploitation and not concentrate solely upon the first, which was prevalent in the time that Marx wrote.

And we have to recognize that the second type of worker will not only have a higher standard of living but will also have a different subjective perspective. ''He will have more free time, possess a greater knowledge of the political process of the society in which he lives, will have more organized political force at his disposal which, along with increased productivity, raises his income. His identification with other workers outside of his own group will be less than that with his own kind, organized into unions and even political parties, except perhaps in certain periods of crisis.... In the affluent societies of the capitalist world exist zones of misery; but in such societies the poor are in a minority, and their society appears more the result of waste of resources in ridiculous ways than of exploitation, for there is enough for all if it were properly distributed. It will only appear as exploitation if there is a crisis that produces unemployment among the technicians and the skilled workers as well as the poor....

''Today in the developed countries people are perceiving the waste, and perceiving the misery of the underdeveloped nations, but in the moment of analysis of their own societies they put all their emphasis on the waste, and when speaking of the misery of the workers in the poor countries they emphasize the necessity for development'' (pp. 77-80). But one must ask: When does the misery end? And when does the analysis recognize that part of the resources that permit waste are transferred to the rich countries as a result of the misery of the poor ones?

González Casanova recognized in the interview that his writing on exploitation raises questions he does not answer. ''The book is abstract, and attempts to show how one might deal rigorously with a value problem, that of justice. But the possibilities of moving to empirical studies are not easy. The data on profits are hidden, or else they are only available in global terms that cannot be disaggregated to fit the equations of the theory. If you tried to make up a questionnaire to get material on rates of exploitation, you would run into difficulties; you cannot ask such questions in the ordinary way and expect to get answers. Nevertheless, I hope the formalization of the theory will help us think more precisely and lead us toward new data. So far we have not really solved the problem of operationalizing those equations. We may have to depend on historical, qualitative studies of exploitation, or else on indirect measures of the effects of it on other variables that we can measure, such as inequality. It may look like an issue in economics, not sociology, but it deals with a problem the economists have neglected, even Marxists like Bettelheim, Sweezy and Robinson. To study it properly you have to include in the set of equations certain political factors, such as national power or the bargaining strength of labor unions, which are aspects of social structure. A factory worker is not in the same situation today as a factory worker in the nineteenth century, so although we keep the old concept of exploitation, we have to modernize it to include the new realities."

The study by González Casanova of the social and political realities of his own country led him toward a formalization of the theory of classes and regions, of internal colonialism and external imperialism. That position in turn took him to the next higher level of abstraction—an examination of the theory of exploitation. Finally, he arrived at an epistomological view of the basic categories that are used by proponents of various schools in the study of economic development, published in 1967 as *Las Categorías del Desarrollo Económico y la Investigación en Ciencias Sociales (The Categories of Economic Development and Research in the Social Sciences)*. It is the most elegant of his writings, a tightly composed essay of just over 100 pages with a coherence derived from mature reflection.

Noting the attempts in recent years to design practical research projects in the social sciences concerning economic development, he finds that they are either completely one-sided in theoretical perspective, or, if sponsored by international agencies such as the United Nations, they often fall into simple description in order to minimize the difficulties of theoretical and political tensions that arise when research teams are put together whose members represent different disciplines and different countries. In a somewhat melancholy introduction, he indicates that the ideological battle between capitalism and socialism engulfs the social sciences, and that there is no easy way out. "But if it is not possible to eliminate the struggle, above all in a critical moment in peaceful coexistence in which the social sciences are being used more and more for military purposes, it is necessary to think of models that include the struggle itself within the frame of scientific investigation seeking to be 'objective', that explicitly analyze the theoretical and political suppositions underlying the research, namely, the fundamental categories that determine the options of the whole project. That way one not only recognizes the struggle but tries to carry it to another level, the most aware and rational level that is possible within the social sciences leading to cooperation among divergent and heterogenous groups of specialists, until there appears the truly irrational element in cooperation. That is the purpose of the present work concerning the categories of economic development'' (p. 12).

Modern empiricists agree that all measurement depends upon certain qualitative decisions that precede the creation of quantitative operational indicators of the specific variables that are to be measured, and González Casanova quotes such eminent North American mathematical sociologists as Lazarsfeld and Coleman to support that statement. These preliminary decisions involve the perspective to be used to subdivide the infinite world of experience into smaller and manageable elements: the creation of the very categories of observation and description. These are mental constructs, specific dimensions that formalize an aspect of common-sense experience. Within the framework of these arbitrary dimensions—and they are arbitrary because they are imposed by us on experience and do not automatically emerge from it—we create specific hypotheses relating one concept to another, and then we attempt to find indicators that measure quantitative units that correspond to the underlying theoretical concepts. The final stage is to inductively relate these indicators to one another in the form of statistical matrices or other mathematical procedures. The ground rules of statistics then tell us whether our hypotheses are supported or negated by the data, always assuming that the indicators are indeed good measures of the underlying concepts.

"All serious researchers, including those who are most addicted to empirical procedures, would agree with that analysis; nevertheless, they themselves (to say nothing of a horde of followers), once recognizing these limitations of the research process, give special emphasis to the mathematical manipulations of the matrices of data and to the predictions that emerge from simulation. They dedicate their professional lives to the statistical part of the analysis and put aside to a secondary place in terms of effort and precision the original problem of the simplification of experience, the qualitative choice of the criteria that are going to serve as the bases for counting and calculating . . . . In general terms, one can observe that quantitative analysis is typical of North American sociology compared to that of other nations, and of young sociologists compared to older colleagues who tend toward impressionistic methods. It is a style linked particularly to empiricism and to the ideology of progress in the social sciences. Frequently, it is seen only in that light. But the quantitative style is also associated—in terms of emphasis, of perspective—with certain political positions . . . .

"It should not be said that all politically conservative positions lead to quantitative approaches, but in industrial society there is a high probability that the two will be associated. On the other hand, all emphasis on qualitative analysis is not radical, but when one finds a revolutionary position that desires to change the social system, it is likely that there will be an emphasis on qualitative methods" (pp. 23-24). This proposition now applies to the Soviet Union as it has for a long time in the United States, as quantitative methods are increasingly being adopted by Soviet social science technicians for the purpose of improving socialist planning and for perfecting aspects of the existing system, which is a conservative task.

Indeed, observation permits a listing of some of the characteristics that hang together within the quantitative style (and by logical opposites, in the qualitative style):

1. Emphasis upon the quantitative measurement of variables within the system (rather than comparison of systems).
2. Analysis of components of the system (rather than synthesis of its total pattern).
3. Study of spatial arrangement of parts of the system or changes in time of some internal elements (rather than change in the structure of the system itself.)
4. Reification of social relations and the search for natural laws (rather than the humanizing of social relations and the search for social or historical laws that determine the change of systems).
5. Nonhistorical view of the system itself.
6. Experiment as the ideal form of proof (rather than successful practical politics as the ideal form of proof).
7. Planning of internal resources to reduce contradictions and tensions in the system (rather than procedures to accentuate crises and force change in the system).
8. The system as a constant (rather than as a variable).

"In the contemporary world there are two systems for organizing human relations and only one for 'organizing' nature; however, it would be sufficient that the former are based on moral considerations to separate the social from the natural sciences. The loss of a moral sense in the social sciences in relation to the given social system takes them closer to the natural sciences in style and to a politically conservative position with relation to society. Thus the struggle between two styles in sociology, quantitative and qualitative, has a political root and is never based on propositions that are purely scientific, in the natural science sense of the term; the sciences of man cannot avoid being political sciences no matter how closely they approach the sciences of nature in the quantitative manipulation of social facts" (p. 30).

Current practice in the study of development tends to commit a number of mistakes. Lists are drawn up of the ideal characteristics that define underdeveloped nations—such as illiteracy, high infant mortality, a weak middle class—without recognizing the various levels of abstraction and the confusion of theoretical perspectives involved in the components of the list. Furthermore, the basic direction of explanation is often not stated: cause and effect are jumbled in correlation coefficients; spatial comparisons are turned into supposed temporal sequences; economic, social and psychological variables are confounded together. Only in the most recent years has this confusion of indicators begun to be sorted out into systematic schemes that attempt to theoretically explain the basic processes of development and that maintain clear distinctions between concepts that refer to geographic entities, individuals, real social groups and institutions.

The basic or "primitive" categories for the study of economic development are really quite simple, according to González Casanova. Underlying all the specific concepts that are used, we find four abstract categories: wealth, power, consciousness (or values) and exploitation. The first three have been used since ancient times; the last was added by Marx. "The originality of Marxism did not consist in the discovery of materialism, socialism or the dialectic, but of one of the basic categories of social analysis, which was not previously used as a modular concept in the study of social systems and which gave an original content and method to materialism and the dialectic. Marxism added to the classic categories this new one which is often confused by anti-Marxist thinkers and by vulgar Marxists with the category of wealth, from which it is distinct in its explanatory function. *Exploitation* is directly related to the appropriation of the means of production and the product—which fall under the category of wealth—but it is specifically a *human relationship* . . . .

"These four categories combine with units of data such as geographic entities, individuals, real groups, institutions and organizations, which in turn correspond to more abstract categories such as space, man, form" (pp. 51-52). They can be used as general organizing categories, or turned into specific variables. To give some examples: using *wealth*, we can classify *nations* as underdeveloped or developed (or turn the dichotomy into a variable that ranges along a continuum from poor to rich); using *power*, we can classify them in terms of degrees of dependence and independence; using *exploitation*, we can classify them in terms of imperial versus colonial states; and using *consciousness and values*, we can discuss degrees of national integration and solidarity. The same categories can be applied to units that are smaller than nations, such as regions within them, leading us to the analysis of internal colonialism that was given above.

The classification of *individuals* and *groups* would take us in the direction of social strata ranging from upper to lower, or from professionals to unskilled workers (*wealth*); to elites, masses and marginals (*power*); and social classes such as the bourgeoisie and the proletariat (*exploitation*); and to the phenomena of political sentiment and organization (*consciousness and values*).[11]

"Employing the term *system* one alludes concretely to the most general types of categories of human organization, such as the system of market economy or capitalism in contrast to the system of planned economy or socialism. Employing the term *structure* one thinks of numerical values that correspond to the specific weight of the relations between distinct aspects of the system . . . . Thus capitalist systems have different structures to the degree that there are variations in the relation between private and public property, between profit and nonprofit firms, between the free market and the planned sector" (*Categorías del Desarrollo Económico,* p. 56).

The definition of the basic categories of analysis and the basic units of data has to this point been static. The introduction of time to the scheme is necessary. The most common procedure, states González Casanova, is to treat the various categories as variables and see how they evolve through time; this produces a "semidynamic" analysis, since it assumes continuity of the system within which the variables operate. In this approach, one concentrates on the structures within the system and looks for alterations in the numerical weight of various of those structures. The procedure is summarized in Table 2, which cross-classifies units of data with basic categories phrased in terms of change through time. Thus change in the wealth of nations involves economic growth, capitalization and industrialization; change in the power of nations involves internal nation-building and external penetration; change in exploitation involves the evolution of the economic devices of imperialism (through international corporations, changes in the terms of trade etc.); and change in consciousness and values involves such processes as alienation and the growth of the sentiment of nationalism.

"The conception of time is indissolubly linked to action, and many of the concepts that refer to time cannot be explained without specifying, on the one hand, the relation of the authors to the political action that is explicit or implicit in their analyses, and on the other hand the general philosophies and theories of action to which they subscribe" (p. 65). Thus the empiricists see society as in a constant state of small changes leading toward progress; the system is constant but the structures evolve in quantitative and accumulative fashion; technical progress (including that in the social sciences) is seen to be the promoter of peaceful and rational development. The Marxists, by con-

TABLE 2
The Categories of Development
as Variables in Time,
by Units of Data

Units of Data	Basic Categories			
	Wealth	Power	Exploitation	Consciousness-Values
Nations	Economic growth Capitalization Technification Industrialization Urbanization	Nation-building Conquest and foreign penetration National liberation	Processes of Imperialism Evolution of anti-imperialism	Alienation, growth of nationalism Changes in values toward modernism
Individuals and Groups	Vertical mobility (inter- and intra-generational)	Political mobilization	Development of classes and class-struggle Development of colonial and imperialist groups Disappearance of classes and colonial groups (socialism)	Alienation Emergence of innovators
Institutions	Evolution of economic and social institutions	Evolution of political institutions	Evolution of institutions of exploitation	Evolution of ideological institutions

Source: *Las Cátegorias*, Table IV, pp. 62-63.

trast, see the system as well as the structures as changeable; they look to a specific historical moment in which a sudden qualitative change takes place via violent means that creates a new system, this being the outcome of a series of earlier quantitative structural changes that altered the balance of power of different classes. There exists a third view, an existentialist-Fascist perspective, that looks to the establishment of an irrational, perfect system through violent and heroic action.

"In empiricism the historical categories end with the current epoch; one tends analytically to isolate the capitalist system from time and from Socialist space. In Socialist theory one seeks to compare development in the Socialist and capitalist countries, using time categories to place the current Socialist epoch in the context of its capitalist past. Empiricism isolates capitalism in time and space as a form of preserving it, while Marxism relates it to time and space as a means of destroying it" (p. 69).

The fundamental political philosophy of a given author tends to lead him to emphasize in his research those factors or variables which he sees as open to influence through planned action. At the extremes, we get those arch-conservatives who do not favor development for the backward nations (or feel that it is impossible) and advise birth control and limitations on aspirations to keep them relatively quiet, and those arch-radicals who wish to avoid development in order to accentuate tensions and thus bring the revolution closer.

Between those two extremes, we get the range of positions that favor development but suggest different programs to foment it. "Within the more conservative pro-development positions are various versions of the theory of innovators as the basic factor: Protestants, entrepreneurs, men with high 'need-achievement' and, above all, men gifted with high creative mentalities (which often must be accepted as accidentally given rather than theoretically explained). Within the same political position there are explanations that are not psychological but rather depend upon the historical accumulation of capital, of technology, or of civilization. The more liberal and reformist views tend to stress as crucial factors in development a better distribution of wealth and income, the existence of a strong middle class, and a wide dispersion of political power throughout the society, which leads to studies of social strata, of marginal and participating groups. The ideologues of the Third World put in first place the explanatory categories of national independence and industrialization, of social justice and national integration. The Marxists conceive of development as a result of the class struggle and the relations of production within capitalist society, phenomena that are also the causes of the pauperization and impoverishment of the proletarian classes and the colonial countries" (*Categorías del Desarrollo*, p. 77).

Since the authors from the various schools tend to choose different categories as central to their explanations, they do not really confront one another in a theoretically meaningful way. Instead, they talk *past* one another. We must conclude that their senses of action, their feelings for the aspects of life that can and should be altered by deliberate and rational procedures, are the determinants of their theoretical perspectives—not experimental research of a purely scientific nature. Social scientists are political men before they are men of abstract science. And we must remember the point at which this analysis began: theoretical perspectives shape the choice of operational indicators and measurements, and thus predetermine much of the outcome of any specific investigation, regardless of the "objectivity" of the techniques that are used.

González Casanova ends his essay with a plea for wider intellectual cooperation across the Marxist-empiricist boundary, but with an admission that he is not very optimistic that it will come about. He sees several difficulties. "The crisis of peaceful coexistence, the intensification of the neocolonialist wars, the aggression—day by day more open—of imperialism, and the end of the Third World, are undermining the theme of economic and social development as it appeared in the United Nations and in a good part of the world consciousness at the end of World War II. The supposedly 'developing' countries, according to a variety of indices, appear today clearly to be countries on the road to impoverishment and military submission. Underdevelopment appears to be a dynamic and increasing process in that the terms of trade keep moving against the three poor continents, and they are losing more and more of the benefits of their productivity and even their technicians. At the same time, they have increasing populations and increasing hunger, and growing groups of protest—educated, literate, politicized—so that in place of 'underdevelopment' as the central theme we have 'conflict', 'subversion' and 'revolution' as the themes that begin to take first place in social research of the empirical school" (p. 103).

González Casanova says that under these circumstances some empiricists turn away from the study of development and become specialists in the defense of the status quo, as illustrated by those who worked with Projects Camelot, Colonial and Simpático of the U.S. Department of Defense (all aimed at systematic social research for purposes of counterinsurgency).

Others turn away from traditional styles of research when they realize that only a small proportion of the variance of major developmental trends is explained by the particular variables included in their models, since the models do not predict the failure of development, the internal military coups and the outside interventions that are taking place. These men face a danger: seeking more powerful tools, they are likely to turn to analogues of the key

Marxist concepts of exploitation, class struggle and imperialism, but may invent them all over again, failing to recognize their long historical existence. They will find it difficult to adopt concepts that have been associated with the Socialist and revolutionary tradition, and thus may devise ad hoc substitutes.

The social scientists in the Socialist countries, on the other hand, who wish to modernize their research techniques face a different temptation: the use of empirical methods to make minute studies of internal social processes in their own countries, repeating essentially the same investigations that have been done in the capitalist countries—a route being taken by the contemporary Polish sociologists.

Major social research demands institutes and resources. These now exist in the Socialist countries, creating the possibility of a new historically minded social science that takes the great themes of development as it focus, takes the great writings of the political leaders of the revolutionary countries as sources of working hypotheses and then applies the rigorous techniques of empirical analysis. But for such a style of research to succeed, it is necessary to modernize theoretical perspectives by relating them to the realities of the current world scene in which international dependence is a key factor. González Casanova concludes the book by writing: "Empirical techniques of research exist where there are organized states; in the nineteenth century all states were capitalist but in the twentieth century there are also socialist states with universities and institutes. Therefore there is the chance for a new and creative synthesis, just as much for the empiricist who decides to adopt the theoretical categories of Marxism as for the socialist who decides to apply the techniques of empiricism to the phenomena of exploitation" (*Categorías del Desarrollo Económico*, p. 108).

Having described the basic work of González Casanova, it is now appropriate to attempt a limited evaluation of a few of his key themes (with certain broader issues postponed until the concluding chapter). I shall concentrate on his analysis of Mexican society and politics and his use of the concepts of internal colonialism, imperialism and exploitation.

The strength of González Casanova's writings on Mexican politics comes from a firm grasp of the social structures underlying political behavior. He never forgets the heterogeneity of his country; he recognizes the emergence of the new industrial and financial bourgeoisie in the big cities, but he remembers the local men of power in the small market towns of the interior; he differentiates between the skilled workers in the strong unions attached to the technically proficient modern factories and the marginal workers in the construction trades and in the slums, yet he never forgets the rural origins of so many of those workers. He does not get caught in oversimplified abstractions such as the concept of "proletariat." Instead, he pictures a fluid society of constant mobility in horizontal and vertical dimensions. Political aspirations shift along with social status and reference group.

He sees power as something that must be continually grasped, not a gift from a written constitution. Through time it has passed from the rough hands of victorious generals who emerged as populist leaders out of revolutionary chaos to the manicured hands of professional party politicians. They are brokers between organized pressure groups, and their main goal is continuation in power through a balanced equilibrium of forces. Although they have ideological beliefs, their principles are continually adapted to pragmatic realities. It does little good to give them abstract advice stemming from moral axioms or from formal economic analysis if that advice cannot be linked to political forces that they can sense and manipulate. To predict their behavior one has to understand it, and the best understanding comes from continuous study of the changes in the relative social status of various groups in what is one of the most complex societies in the world: modern Mexico. And of course, the key to part of that complexity is the relation between various sectors in Mexico to groups in the United States.

This analysis allows González Casanova to explain the paradoxes of Mexican economic and political trends: growth more than development, in the sense that the total product and the productivity per worker increase and all the statistical averages improve but the gap between rich and poor widens as does the absolute number of people living in misery. The big cities modernize more quickly than the countryside; the rich become fabulously wealthy; the middle classes expand; even the skilled and comfortable segment of the proletariat grows; but so do the marginal classes that remain close to subsistence, located mainly in the rural (especially Indian) zones but increasingly shifting to the urban slums. Despite 60 years of the rhetoric of the Revolution, the political stability continues; the discrepancy between radical promises and conservative policies does not generate serious opposition and new revolt, since individual mobility and political cooptation serve as safety valves for protest. Perhaps the very promises of the rhetoric continue to convince the poor if not the intellectuals.

González Casanova startles us and awakens us by posing probing questions: Why don't the miserable ones revolt? Why doesn't higher productivity produce higher wages for the masses? Why does a government that professes a revolutionary ideology fail to promote redistribution of income? Why is it that the obvious and expected things (whether the expectations arise from Marx or from Lipset) do *not* occur? Thus he uses background theory in the most creative way: he confronts it with the negative fact, the null detail, the denial of the obvious. We are forced to reconsider.

There seems to me to be two major weaknesses in González Casanova's approach to contemporary Mexico: an inability to explain the specific routes of decision-making within the general power structure he describes and an inadequate formal analysis of certain economic and demographic trends. On the first point, the critic must admit the difficulty of the problem; data on decisons are notoriously hard to obtain, since the actors do not invite an audience. But his writing implies too much if it cannot be buttressed by specific examples. He writes of the growth in influence of Mexican industrialists and bankers and of the expanding influence of certain North American centers of power, but he does not illustrate the consequences with convincing examples. He might have enlightened us at least with historical examination of a series of crucial decisions on economic policy. Indeed, in reading *Democracy in Mexico* I sometimes wished his research assistants had gathered fewer tables of descriptive statistics (there are 65 tables) and spent more time on case studies of policy decisions. For example, on the government's policy after 1940 of holding wages under control and supporting large corporate profits: Was it reached through the influence of technical economic analysis on the need for capital accumulation? Was it dictated by Mexican financial powers? In what way did foreign corporations intervene? Why did this policy come just *after* Cárdenas and a populist period and *before* the growth of the huge fortunes? Or, another example: the decison in the mid-fifties to take major steps to reduce the inflation rate that during the preceding 15 years had benefited capital at the expense of real wages. Why the shift in policy? Did it not imply an increased strength of labor because it aided improvement in real wages, and thus did it not contradict González Casanova's view of the trend toward increasing power of the big industrialists? Why the decision to expand government borrowing from abroad, instead of taxing or borrowing more at home? How will the increased external debt limit the government's freedom of choice? Can it reverse the policy now if it so desires? Or, take a final example: How does economic policy change as foreign investment in manufacturing grows—do tariffs or taxes change? Do consumers suffer, or other producers?

We need much more specificity on these issues, since it is a major part of González Casanova's argument that the power structure that emerged in the country limits and shapes economic policies in ways that benefit foreigners and wealty Mexicans to the detriment of poor Mexicans. There is a gap between the structural analysis and the decisional outcome: the various human participants are missing; the struggles between interest groups are not made explicit; thus, it becomes too easy to imagine devious manipulations of power that may not exist.

In reply to these criticisms, González Casanova said, ''I think we may have to work more by analyzing general historical tendencies than by

studying case studies of decision-making, since details on specific government actions are hard to get. For instance, I've talked to some politicians
about decisions that were made 20 years ago, and they did not know how to
explain the process that led up to them. They could offer a synthesis of the
forces in play, but could not give an adequate intellectual description of how
the decisions were actually reached."

González Casanova condemns the Mexican power system on two
grounds: it perpetuates inequality and it leads to stagnation. On the first, all
recent history supports the charge. On the second, the last decade of
economic boom in Mexico negates the charge. The gross internal product
has not slowed its long-term expansion, despite some bad years in the late
fifties and early sixties when his book was being written. In fact, the real
internal product grew at average annual rates of 4.0 percent in the thirties,
6.0 percent in the forties, 6.1 percent in the fifties, 6.1 percent in the first half
of the sixties, and at a slightly higher rate in more recent years.

Thus González Casanova appears to have made the same mistake as many
other writers, domestic and foreign. He underestimated the continued vitality of the Mexican economy, fueled by an increasing proportion of the
annual product that gets invested to produce expansion—a figure that has
recently climbed above 20 percent. Like the others, he believed that the
special circumstances that produced the economic "miracle" were exhaust-
ing their energies and that stagnation was about to begin, but events to date
have indicated continuing expansion.

The lesson may have been learned (perhaps overlearned) since recent
analyses by Mexican economists are more optimistic.[12] Most writers are
concerned about the increasing dependence on foreign borrowing and the
low tax rates inside the country, but they feel that the government, with some
adjustments in policy, can manage the situation. They emphasize the flexibility and diversity of the present economy that have resulted from past
development; indeed, they imply that the country is successfully passing out
of the "underdeveloped" category (per capita income is now over 500
dollars, which is often used as a benchmark). There has been a transition to a
more diversified foreign trade, since the proportion of exports that went to
the United States declined from 85 percent to 64 percent in the years from
1950 to 1967, and the proportion of those exports that consisted of manufactured goods (including, it must be admitted, many agricultural and mineral
products with a low level of industrial elaboration) increased from 7 percent
to 20 percent of the total. Furthermore, the deterioriation in sales expansion
for traditional products such as cotton, coffee, lead, zinc and henequen has
been made up through new products such as fruit, tomatoes, wheat, sulfur
and light manufactures. Merchandise exports increased at an annual rate of 8
percent in the last decade compared to 6.4 percent in earlier years, and

income from tourism increased even faster (Flores, p. 73). Thus, recent trends do not support the charge that the Mexican economy is entering a period of stagnation, internally or externally.

If González Casanova seems to have been too gloomy about economic growth, he correctly predicted that government policies would do little to alleviate maldistribution of income. But has he analyzed all the major causes of marginality and put them into balance? I believe he understates the role of population growth. He occasionally acknowledges it in a brief phrase, but then he dismisses the problem as a distraction coming from those who do not really want to promote development. For example, in *Las Categorías* he mentions birth control as a part of the most reactionary view of society: "Thus, among the extreme conservatives there is a renunciation of a plan for development by those who favor birth control and control of aspirations, who do not believe in development as the way of resolving the fundamental problems of the poor countries" (p. 76).

This perspective leads him not only to reject birth-control programs but also to deny the importance of population growth as a key theoretical variable in the explanation of marginality. In the interview he said, "There are fashions in ways of looking at problems of development. There were some years in which a psychological level was most popular—attitudes, capacity to innovate—but we doubted the utility of that perspective. Then came the faith—and the failure—in such approaches as economic planning or agrarian reform. Now it is family planning. I don't think it will have a great impact on reality, especially if we remember the history of ideas about population. Malthusianism has come and gone in fashion, but the variable of population remains fixed, with relatively stable rates. Of course, methods of contraception have improved, but in terms of population size in the next 20 or 30 years, there's nothing we can do about it. Studies showing fertility by status level show that only the higher strata consciously plan their families—the urban middle class in the more developed countries. Thus, where the neo-Malthusians most want an influence—on the poorer strata— they have the least chance to be effective.

"We can fool people if we adopt the policy of family planning, which appears on the surface to be the easy solution. It might reinforce the status quo and delay awareness of the need to make real social changes. For realists who want action now, neo-Malthusianism is a completely false road; empirical studies demonstrate that."

Of course, no national population policy can change birth rates in the short run; furthermore, all the people who will need jobs in the near future are already alive. But Mexican experience indicates that within its present social structure government policies are unable to produce a major increase in the rate of economic growth. It remains fixed, on the average, between six and seven percent a year, while population growth is more than three percent a year. The economic expansion has been unable to absorb all the growth in the labor force since modern methods on farm and in factory produce a large increase in output with a small increase in the number of workers. Thus, we cannot ignore the question of the relation between the rate of economic growth and the rate of population growth. Although no precise statistics are available, all observers agree that unemployment and underemployment in Mexico are growing at a disturbing pace. This harms not only the unemployed but also puts downward pressure on wage rates and thus reduces the level of living of the lower ranks of the employed workers.

Interestingly enough President Luis Echeverría, who ran as a candidate in 1970 stating that population pressure was not a problem for Mexico, reversed himself after taking office and hearing the reports of his technical advisors. He ordered a plan to make birth-control services available in all government public health agencies for the first time. Because the masses get their medical care through such agencies, the shift in policy may reduce the national birth rate before too long. The timing was particularly appropriate, for the earlier social development of the country probably prepared the population for a shift in desired family size; indeed, some slight reductions in the birth rate were noted before Echeverría switched policy. The president has also ordered a rearrangement in government investment priorities with the aim of increasing employment opportunities in rural areas, and the tone of public policy debates in recent years shows a clear move away from total concentration on output of goods toward an awareness of the need to provide employment.

However, the specific policies adopted so far, be they public birth-control clinics or small shifts in government investment priorities, are inadequate to the task at hand. This brings us back to González Casanova's main point: as long as the present power balance guides policy, major changes are unlikely. He suggests that the masses, if better organized, might be able to exert pressures to improve wages and purchasing power and further invigorate the economy, although the limitations of the external environment (increasing debt to the United States, increasing foreign control over industry linked to the worldwide powers of monopoly corporations) might thwart the reforms. But it is precisely at this point that the formal analysis of González Casanova stops. He is not sufficiently explicit about either the economic policies to be adopted or the political processes necessary to get those policies adopted.[13] He is unwilling to endorse the Cuban route, which ended marginality by emphasizing drastic and immediate redistribution of income, yet his proposals seem more like palliatives than cures.

"We have to find ways of increasing the participation of various groups such as the middle classes, the literates—its's not easy, but it's possible. It's our central task, that of increasing internal democracy in the university, in the labor unions and so on. I'm not the only one concerned with the issue; many people are searching for the methods. One way that has been suggested is to work at the local or municipal level, and another is the classical method of increasing the power of political parties that serve as critics, as opposition to the administration. Yes, I think it may be possible, including the invention of new approaches, new methods. We may not have to reproduce the party system of Europe or the United States. Look at electoral geography: in the urban zones the middle classes show higher proportions voting for minority parties, which shows a trend away from monolithic control. Of course, they might swing either way; they are volatile and might go Left or Right. But at the moment in the United States and Europe the middle classes are not repeating the Fascist tendencies of earlier years. The ideologists and creative thinkers should remember those Fascist years and come up with other alternatives that will be appealing. And of course a big proportion of our working class, for historical reasons, has middle-class characteristics.''

I am tempted to conclude that there is a struggle in his mind between two opposed tendencies: an optimism that springs from a sense of the particularities of Mexican history and a personal commitment to the basic structure of its society and politics, and a pessimism that springs partly from a Marxist-oriented theoretical analysis of exploitation and partly from the very sad events of the decade of the sixties. Indeed, in the years I have known him he was most depressed immediately after the revelations about Project Camelot; suddenly international social science had changed from a hope for future guidance to a military plot aimed at repression of popular movements. The repression in Mexico in 1968 did not make him any more cheerful.

One factor of optimism is patience. How long is one willing to wait until the prosperity of the growth sectors ''filters down'' to the masses? Octavio Paz has written some powerful words on that subject: ''Above all and before all: we must invent models of development that are viable and less inhumane, expensive and insensitive to the present. I said before that this is an urgent task: in truth, *it is the task of our times*. And something more: the supreme value is not the future but the present; the future is a false time that keeps saying 'not yet' and thus it denies us. The future is not the time of love; what man really wants, he wants *now*. He who builds a house of future happiness constructs the jail of the moment'' (*Posdata*, p. 96).

González Casanova's increasing worry about the prospects for Latin America seems linked to his increasing attention to the concept of *exploitation*, both internal and external. It is a concept hard for most North American academics to accept, for our country is the main exploiter. And it is a concept hard for many urban, middle-class Mexicans to accept, for they are the exploiters of their countrymen. Inequality we have long recognized, but the usual tendency is to assume that it is slowly being overcome as the benefits of development spread to the underdeveloped countries and to the underdeveloped regions and strata within countries. When the same facts are interpreted under the concept of exploitation instead of inequality, a basic difference in emphasis occurs: the inequality is no longer viewed as a residue of history that will disappear but rather as something being constantly re-created and revived. Furthermore, the prosperity of the rich men and rich regions is seen as not just the outcome of their own hard work and good fortune, but partly as squeezed out of the labor of the poor and the backward.

The problem with the concept of exploitation is in placing it in an appropriate context of related concepts and then finding adequate measurements that will allow an estimate of its relative significance. González Casanova himself declares that much of the increasing wealth of the advanced countries is due not to exploitation but to improved technology, increasing education and better methods of administration. The question then remains: How much does exploitation add?

We need very careful studies of the flow of capital and profits from country to country and from region to region within a country. Initial investments, reinvestments, transfers within units of multinational corporations, payments of profits and interest—all of these are part of the problem. But new income generated by the investments in the local territory where the factories are built; new jobs created; new sources of foreign exports opened up; new skills in technology and administration transferred to the local population—all of these are also part of the problem. Unfortunately, every study I know has a strong partisan flavor; the writers start the work by praising outside investments or damning them. Then they select part of the data for emphasis and ignore the rest, leaving the reader unable to grasp the total pattern.

Even if we had a good series of empirical studies that measured all of the above aspects of the economic situation, there would still remain a moral issue: What is a "fair" profit? What is "justice"? Is profit to be evaluated by its rate of return on investment? By its ratio to sales? By its relation to "surplus value" (which combines a technical definition with a moral judgment)? Or by its total *effects* on both the local economy and its trading partners? Is it enough if the poor countries get richer or must they actually close the gap with the rich countries?

My own belief is that these questions may not be the crucial ones, fascinating though they are. I suspect that the strategic factor in development is not the degree of exploitation in strictly economic terms (i.e., profit in relation to labor value) but the degree of domination in political terms. Thus the general category of *power* in González Casanova's set of categories may be more useful than that of *exploitation*, as is suggested by the increasing number of Latin American authors who concentrate on the theme of *dependency*.

I doubt that the flow of profit is the core explanation for either the wealth of some nations or the poverty of others. What is central is the trajectory of development over time, and this is determined by power and political decisions. The Russians and the Japanese provide the great examples of development in the twentieth century, and both were led by vigorous governments that maximized their opportunities. Most Latin American nations are developing, but much too slowly. More vigorous government action would speed up the process: higher investments in infrastructure and welfare, land reform, guided diversification of exports, control over foreign firms, etc. Even within the existing structure of international trade and the multinational corporation, it can be done. Or, it can be done within the socialist bloc. But in both cases the crucial decisions are governmental, and the weakness of Latin American governments leaves them unable to act decisively.

According to this view, power is the explanatory key and exploitation may be a distraction stemming from moral outrage. The task for empirical research becomes the careful examination of the linkages between economic and political power, between capital ownership and government decisions; the strengths and weaknesses of Latin American governments must be explained in terms of contemporary capitalism. In discussing the concrete situation of Mexico, this is precisely what González Casanova attempts to do. And in studying the international situation, it is what many of us should be doing. The actions of the American government during the last decade in the Dominican Republic, Cuba and Brazil grew out of linkages with American economic institutions and interests. These in turn had enormous repercussions on the freedom of action of Latin American governments in the immediate past and will continue to have many effects in the immediate future.

However, as González Casanova points out, exploitation is a double-edged concept because it refers both to a division of economic product and to a human relationship between the persons involved. He attempts to design measures of the economic flow and implies that they are "objective," and when the persons concerned become aware of them in "subjective" terms they automatically start to fight over the spoils—thus generating "classes" in the Marxist sense, or colonial-imperial struggles in the Leninist sense.

The relation between objective economic exploitation and subjective protest is much clearer when the situation consists of an owner and his workers than when it consists of a complex network ranging from laborers through commercial intermediaries to international corporations. In the latter circumstances the arousal of the protest feeling will depend upon many factors that connect what *is* with what people think *ought to be*. Actual levels of living, changes through time, norms that determine expectations, comparison with others who are considered appropriate reference groups, ideological leadership, the visibility of differences in income and differences in power—these and other elements will all be operative. Thus, men may *feel* exploited for reasons that are only tenuously linked to the formal definition of exploitation emerging from the theory of surplus value.

The study of the processes that produce consciousness of unfair deprivation is an important political problem, especially when linked to the processes that shape this consciousness into organized group protest. González Casanova attempts to explain why those processes have not gone very far in Mexico, despite poverty and marginality, and he recognizes that the elimination of inequality will only come when political protest is more effective. Similarly, inequities in international relations will continue until more organized and powerful forms of protest and bargaining can be created. In the study of these issues the category of *power* and the category of *exploitation* are likely to merge, and he may oversimplify when he stresses the latter at the expense of the former.

It is easier to discuss these matters and debate with González Casanova because he worked out the formal scheme of categories for the study of development. Those who know the scheme will not slip into misleading models that isolate variables to the point of triviality, whether they be sets of economic variables such as interest rates, capital accumulation or exploitation, psychological variables such as need-achievement or modern values, sociological variables such as class identification or social mobility, or political variables such as mobilization or nation-building. His four "primitive categories" and their elaboration into dynamic concepts are tools to shape research on social change in ways that will lead toward complete rather than partial understanding.

González Casanova's description of the degree to which we choose among the available categories and concepts those which correspond to our own political biases and our needs for personal action is a warning we can all take to heart. I think he clarifies the problem by emphasizing that the moment we seek a social science that is relevant to decisions in the real world (rather than a completely abstract game that has as its sole purpose intellectual pleasure) we are likely to select and emphasize those approaches which are tied to the kinds of immediate actions that we expect to be fruitful, that is, to steps that appear both possible and desirable. Thus our thought inevitably combines rational assessment of reality with ideological assessment of valued goals.

Indeed, there is a pointed example of this process to be found in González Casanova's own work. As he himself said, his most controversial position in Mexican intellectual circles is his faith in the possibilities for democratization of the existing political and economic institutions of the nation. It seems to me that the need for this was demonstrated by his careful descriptive studies showing the degree of marginality that continues to exist (even to be generated) despite the extraordinary growth of the economy in the postwar years. Any observer who fully understands those facts, and who shares values of justice and human dignity, must agree that present trajectories are inadequate and that basic structural reforms are necessary. The argument becomes all the more persuasive when connected with the economists' belief that a more equal distribution of wealth would in fact speed up the growth process and thus benefit all sectors. However, the question of the feasibility of structural change is not so easily decided by empirical evidence and rational theory. It becomes a question of faith as much as logic, since the balance between progressive and regressive political forces cannot be conclusively demonstrated in advance of the specific crisis situation that will bring them into the open and put them to test. Perspicacious men who agree on the description of the current scene and who share the same general values disagree on their predictions of the outcome of that moment of crisis.

The example illustrates the limits of empirical social science, and it helps us understand that those who seek a completely "value-free" approach are likely to arrive at triviality and escapism. On the other hand, it warns those who rush into action, without dispassionate study of all available facts and careful consideration of all alternative theoretical interpretations of those facts, that their action may lead them toward disaster instead of the promised land. We are left then with the continuing challenge: to strive for an approach to development that is meaningful because it is tied to action, that is scientific because it uses explicit and rational theories to explain precisely measured facts and trends and that is humane because its goal is the progressive improvement of the lot of all people.

NOTES

1. "Preámbulo" to *La Industrialización en América Latina*, ed. J.A. Kahl (1965), p. 10.

2. For ethnographic details, see Stavenhagen (1965).

3. For recent information, see Navarrete (1970) and Puente Leyva (1969).

4. See Anderson and Cockroft (1969).

5. In the 1960s average real wages, even of agricultural workers, made some advances because the rate of inflation was reduced at the same time that nominal wage rates improved; however, the inequality of distribution did not change. See Ariel Buira (1968) and Leopoldo Solís (1970), p. 289.

6. One illustration of its effects is the recent sharp reduction by the U.S. government of the flow of *braceros* (agricultural workers) from Mexico to the United States, which has eliminated a very important source of income for poor families. Another is the partial limitation on the importation to the United States of Mexican tomatoes. In both instances Washington yielded to domestic pressure groups but the cost was paid by the Mexicans.

7. The events of the summer of 1968 in Mexico confirm this perspective. A series of very large student demonstrations against certain policies of the government surged to the surface, but unlike the situation in France that same year, the unions in Mexico remained predominantly silent and under government control. The army was called in and completely crushed the protest movement. A parallel might also be drawn with the rightest coup in Brazil in 1964.

8. For Cardoso's reply to this statement, see page 00.

9. The most poignant expression of the mood of Mexican intellectuals in the late sixties is the book by Octavio Paz, *Posdata* (1970); it reflects the disillusionment of a decade that included the U.S. invasions of Cuba and the Dominican Republic, the exposé of Operation Camelot, the military coups in Brazil and Argentina, the long war in Indochina, the invasion of Czechoslovakia, and most acutely, the repression of the student movement in Mexico.

10. The late Toledano, an uncle of González Casanova's wife, was for many years the foremost leader of the radical wing of the labor movement. Lázaro Cárdenas was president from 1934 to 1940 and was a vigorous exponent of land reform to benefit poor peasants, and of state control over the economy; he died in 1970 at the age of 75.

11. The reader familiar with Max Weber will recognize much of this scheme, although González Casanova does not refer to that writer. Weber speaks of class, status, and power, which correspond to González Casanova's categories of wealth, consciousness-values, and power. Weber, being anti-Marxist, excludes exploitation, thus his term "class" does not mean the same thing as class to a Marxist, but merely refers to economic differentiation.

12. See Ibarra (1970); Flores (1970); Solís (1970); Urquidi (1970).

13. Some useful recent discussions of the relationships between economy and polity in Mexico, many by students of González Casanova, can be found in Jorge Basurto, et al. (1972) and Miguel S. Wionczek, et al. (1971).

Bibliography of Pablo González Casanova

Books

1948 *El Misoneísmo y la Modernidad Cristiana*. Mexico, D.F.: El Colegio de México.

1950 *Ideología Francesa sobre América Hispánica*. Paris: University of Paris. Doctoral Thesis.

1953 *Sátira Anónima del Siglo XVIII*. With José Miranda. Mexico, D.F.: Fondo de Cultura Económica. An anthology.

1953 *Una Utopía de América*. Mexico, D.F.: El Colegio de México.

1955 *La Ideología Norteamericana sobre Inversiones Extranjeras*. Mexico,

D.F.: Universidad Nacional Autónoma de México, Instituto de Investigaciones Económicas.

1958   *La Literatura Perseguida en la Crisis de la Colonia.* Mexico, D.F.: El Colegio de México.

1958   *Estudio de la Técnica Social.* Mexico, D.F.: Universidad Nacional Autónoma de México, Colección de Problemas Científicos y Filosóficos.

1965   *La Democracia en México.* Mexico, D.F.: Era.
   1967   Second edition.
   1967   Portuguese: Rio de Janeiro: Civilização Brasileira.
   1969   French: Paris: Anthropos.
   1970   English: New York: Oxford University Press.

1967   *Las Categorías del Desarrollo Económico la Investigación en Ciencias Sociales.* Mexico, D.F.: Universidad Nacional Autónoma de México, Instituto de Investigaciones Sociales.
   1970   Second edition.
   Forthcoming: German: University of Münster.

1969   *Sociología de la Explotación.* Mexico, D.F.: Siglo XXI.
   1970   Second edition.

1970   *Sociología del Desarrollo Latinoamericano: Una Guía para su Estudio.* Editor and collaborator. Mexico, D.F.: Universidad Nacional Autónoma de México, Instituto de Investigaciones Sociales.

Articles

1947   "Un Estudio de Sociología Religiosa." *Revista Mexicana de Sociología* 9, no. 3 (September-December).

1949   "Sociología de un Error: Notas sobre la Mentalidad Primitiva." *Revista Mexicana de Sociología* 11, no. 2 (May-August).

1952   "La Enseñanza y la Investigación de las Ciencias Sociales en México." In *La Enseñanza de las Ciencias Sociales en América Central y el Caribe.* UNESCO.

1952   "Ideología de la Primera Industrialización Mexicana." *Jornadas Industriales* (October).

1952   "El Comercio Francés en las Indias Españolas." *Revista de Comercio Exterior* 2, nos. 1 and 2 (January-March).

1953   "El Problema del Método en la Reforma de la Enseñanza Media." *Boletín de la Asociación de Universidades* 2, no. 2.

1957   "El Don, las Inversiones Extranjeras y la Teoría Social." *Problemas Científicos y Filosóficos* (University of Mexico), second series, no. 2.

1958   "Sobre la Situación Política de México y el Desarrollo Económico." *Cuadernos Americanos* (July-October).

1961   "La Opinión Pública en México." In *Cincuenta Años de Revolución: La Política.* Mexico, D.F.: Fondo de Cultura Económica, vol. 3.

1962   "México: El Ciclo de una Revolución Agraria." *Cuadernos Americanos* (January-February).

         1964   Polish: In *Studies in Developing Countries*. Edited by Oscar Lange. Warsaw.

         1968   English: In *Latin America: Reform or Revolution?* Edited by James Petras and Maurice Zeitlin. Greenwich, Conn.: Fawcett.

1962   "Le Mexique: Société Plurale et Développement." *Tiers Monde* (Presses Universitaires de France) 3, no. 2 (July-September).

         1962   Spanish: *América Latina* (Rio de Janeiro), year 5, no. 4 (October-December).

1963   "Sociedad Plural, Colonialismo Interno y Desarrollo." *América Latina*, year 6, no. 3 (July-September).

         1965   English: "Internal Colonialism and National Development." *Studies in Comparative International Development* 1, no. 4: 27-37.

         1969   Also in *Latin American Radicalism*. Edited by Irving L. Horowitz, et al. New York: Random House.

1963   "México: Desarrollo y Subdesarrollo." *Desarrollo Económico* (University of Buenos Aires) 3, nos. 1 and 2 (April-September).

1964   "C. Wright Mills: An American Conscience." In *The New Sociology*. Edited by Irving L. Horowitz. New York: Oxford University Press.

1965   "Preámbulo." In *La Industrialización en América Latina*. Edited by Joseph A. Kahl. Mexico, D.F.: Fondo de Cultura Económica.

1965   "La Medición de Discontinuidades Intranacionales Mediante Indices Compuestos del Grado y la Tasa de Desarrollo." *Revista Latinoamericana de Sociología* (Buenos Aires) 1.

1965   "Les Classes Sociales au Mexique." *Cahiers Internationaux de Sociologie Contemporaine* (Presses Universitaires de France) 39 (July-December).

         1964   Yugoslav: "Pojava Sistema u Klasa u Mexicu." In *Politks Misso*. Zagreb (Yugoslavia): Fakultet Politiukihnauke.

         1968   English: "Dynamics of the Class Structure." In *Comparative Perspectives on Stratification: Mexico, Great Britain, Japan*. Edited by Joseph A. Kahl. Boston: Little, Brown.

1966   "La Teoría Actual de la Participación Política y la Enajenación." *Revista Mexicana de Sociología* 28 (July-September).

1966   "The Hypothesis of the Underdeveloped World." In *Approaches to Comparative and International Politics*. Edited by R.B. Farrell. Evanston, Ill.: Northwestern University Press.

1967   "Las Ideologías Nacionalistas de los Países Oprimidos." *Cuadernos Americanos*.

1967   "Las Democracias Aparentes en los Países Coloniales y Semi-Coloniales." *Revista de la Universidad de México* (June).

1967   "La Nouvelle Sociologie et la Crise de l'Amérique Latine." *L'Homme et la Société*, no. 6 (October-November-December).

1968 "Rhétorique et Statistique: Analyse des Rapports entre Classes et entre Régions." *Cahiers Internationaux de Sociologie* 45 (July-December).
1968 "Las Ciencias Sociales." In *Las Ciencias Sociales y la Antropología*. Mexico, D.F.: Centro Nacional de Productividad.
1969 "Establissement d'un Plan de Développement en Sciences Sociales." *Inform. Sci. Soc.* 8, no. 1: 149-69.
1969 "L'Avenir de l'Amérique Latine: Une Analyse des Prédictions Actuelles." *L'Homme et la Société* (Paris: Anthropos), no. 12 (April-June): 17-28.
1970 "Aspectos Sociales de la Planeación Universitaria." In *La Planeación Universitaria en México*. Mexico, D.F.: Universidad Nacional Autónoma de México.
1970 "La Violence Latino-Américaine dans les Enquêtes Empiriques Nord-Américaines." *L'Homme et la Société*, no. 15 (January-March): 159-81.
1971 "Las Reformas de Estructura en la América Latina: Su Lógica dentro de la Economía de Mercado." *El Trimestre Económico* 38, no. 2 (June).
1972 "Les Systèmes Historiques." *Cahiers Internationaux de Sociologie*.

Other References

1969 Anderson, Bo, and Cockroft, James D. "Control and Cooptation in Mexican Politics." In *Latin American Radicalism*. Edited by Irving L. Horowitz, et al. New York: Random House.
1972 Basurto, Jorge, et al. *El Perfil de México en 1980*. México, D.F.: Siglo XXI, vol. 3.
1968 Buira, Ariel. "Desarrollo y Estabilidad de Precios en México." *Demografía y Economía* 2, no. 3.
1970 Flores, Edmundo. *Vieja Revolución, Nuevos Problemas*. Mexico, D.F.: Joaquín Mortiz.
1970 Ibarra, David. "Mercados, Desarrollo y Política Económica: Perspectivas de la Economía de México." In *El Perfil de México en 1980*. By David Ibarra, et al. Mexico, D.F.: Siglo XXI, vol. 1.
1967 Lambert, Jacques. *Os Dois Brasíls*. Reissued. São Paulo: Editora Nacional.
1970 Navarrete, Ifigenia M. de. "La Distribución del Ingreso en México." In *El Perfil de México en 1980*. By David Ibarra, et al. México, D.F.: Siglo XXI, vol. 1.
1970 Paz, Octavio. *Posdata*. México, D.F.: Siglo XXI.
1972 English: *The Other México: Critique of the Pyramid* New York: Grove.
1969 Puente Leyva, Jesús. *Distribución del Ingreso en una Area Urbana: El Caso de Monterrey*. México, D.F.: Siglo XXI.
1970 Solís, Leopoldo. *La Realidad Económica Mexicana: Retrovisión y*

Perspectivas. Mexico, D.F.: Siglo XXI.

1965   Stavenhagen, Rodolfo. "Classes, Colonialism, and Acculturation."
         Studies in Comparative International Development 1, no. 6: 53-77. Trans-
         lated from Spanish (*América Latina* 6, no. 4 (1963) by Danielle Salti.

1968   Revised and reprinted in *Comparative Perspectives on Stratifi-
         cation: México, Great Britain, Japan*. Edited by Joseph A.
         Kahl. Boston: Little, Brown.

1970   Urquidi, Víctor L. "Perfil General: Economía y Población." In *El Perfil
         de México en 1980*. By David Ibarra, et al. Mexico, D.F.: Siglo XXI, vol.
         1.

1971   Wionczek, Miguel S., et al.*¿Crecimiento o Desarrollo Económico? Pre-
         sente y Futuro de la Sociedad Mexicana*, vol. 1. *Disyuntivas Sociales:
         Presente y Futuro de la Sociedad Mexicana*, vol. 2. México, D.F.:
         Secretaría de Educación Publica, SepSetentas, nos. 4 and 5.

4
Fernando Henrique Cardoso

The sociological interests of Fernando Henrique Cardoso first focused on the pecularities of Brazil, then broadened to the general situation of Latin America and recently have turned back once again to his own country. He has continually sought theoretical perspectives to illuminate recent historical trends, believing that the concrete reality can only be understood through comparison with other times and places by using abstractions, yet having little interest in the formal elaboration of abstract schemes in and of themselves. He thus follows the procedures of his main models—Karl Marx and Max Weber. Furthermore, the historical events of his own lifetime have been dramatic and have precipitated biographical experiences that clearly influenced the main themes of his sociological writing.

Cardoso was born in Rio de Janeiro in 1931, the oldest of three children; he comes from a line of military men. His paternal grandfather's brother was one of the few high-ranking officers who participated in the abortive revolt of the *tenentes* or lieutenants against the oligarchy in 1922, and he spent some time in jail as a consequence. When Getúlio Vargas led a successful revolution in 1930 and incorporated some of the earlier rebels into his government, General Cardoso became Minister of War. Fernando Henrique's father was both a general and a lawyer, and he carried on a civilian practice when he retired from the army. Toward the end of his career, he was elected a deputy to the Federal Congress. Fernando Henrique calls him "nationalist, liberal, even leftist, but not a Communist," and says that he was skeptical of the ability of the military to run the nation since army politics seemed to be based on intrigue and personal ambition. The son reports that when he was a student he was more in sympathy with than revolt against his father's view of society.

The family moved from the cosmopolitan atmosphere of Rio de Janeiro's Copacabana district to the then more provincial environment of São Paulo about the time Fernando Henrique entered secondary school. He studied in a Catholic school and had a brief period of religious belief, but he drifted away from it before long. Since his father was a "positivist" without religious belief and his mother came from a family that was part Catholic and part Protestant, he reports that an eclectic atmosphere prevailed in the home.

In 1949 Cardoso began to study in the Department of Social Sciences at the University of São Paulo; he might have entered the law school had he not failed the test in Latin that was a prerequisite. It was a period of national history that he characterizes as "the great redemocratization of Brazil, with very intense political movements and many new ideas." Vargas was deposed as dictator in 1945 but was elected as constitutional president five years later, running on a platform of nationalism and industrial development.

At the time that Cardoso was a student, the teaching of the social sciences at the University of São Paulo was being renovated. The student group was small, only about a dozen a year, and their fields ranged widely among all the disciplines. A team of visiting professors from France had a lot of influence, particularly Roger Bastide.

"Bastide was very stimulating. Although he was French, he had a different formation from the French sociologists of the Durkheim school. As a Protestant, he was interested in personal, internal experience, the relations between conscience and the outside world, and he studied religion in order to understand conscience. The more objective style of Durkheim we got through Fernando de Azevedo, the senior Brazilian professor.

"But the main influence on me was Florestan Fernandes, who taught the first-year class in sociology. He was about 28 years old and was assistant to Azevedo. He was very enthusiastic, believed in 'sociology as a way of life', and tried to make disciples out of the good students. However, I had a lot of trouble understanding his class; he was not always clear in his lectures, and he made us read many books that were complicated for beginning students, since they were written in a difficult German style, like Mannheim's *Ideology and Utopia* and various works of Max Weber. We also read a little Marx, but Weber was much more important. Florestan at that time was a functionalist, like Malinowski and Radcliffe Brown.

"But besides those complex European ideas, there was another side to Florestan: he was very empirical in emphasis, and was doing an anthropological study of a small community (Bastide also emphasized ethnography and direct observation). Florestan had been trained by Donald Pierson, the American sociologist teaching at the Escola de Sociologia (a private university in São Paulo), and by Emilio Willems, the anthropologist. Willems taught a seminar for us which was good, very broad, but I never met Pierson. Actually, the American influence on us was weak at that time, and came mainly from anthropology, since we read Robert Redfield on Yucatán, and Ralph Linton's text. We also knew the research methods books of Pauline Young and George Lundberg, and a little about Robert Park, but we had the idea that American sociology meant doing descriptive empirical studies without any imagination. Most of our formation was European. I didn't read Robert Merton and Talcott Parsons seriously until a little later, after I finished my master's degree, and then I became impressed with their functionalism, and particularly with Parson's *The Social System*—I translated some of that for my students.

"It was the Negro question that connected the empirical studies with national issues. UNESCO proposed a project to prove that Brazil was a melting pot society without any problems. Bastide wanted to study Negroes through folk religion, and Florestan wanted to show that UNESCO was wrong, that the Negro was not equal in Brazil. UNESCO gave them some money to help with the research, and while I was a student I worked on the project. In fact, as a student I wrote a paper on some aspects of Negro religion jointly with an anthropology student who later became my wife. We would bring Negroes to the University to talk about their problems, and with Bastide and Florestan we would go and visit in the slums. I learned a lot about the slums of São Paulo in those days, and what I saw of poverty and prejudice had a radicalizing influence on me. Florestan would emphasize the historical perspective, so we read old newspapers and anything we could find that Negroes had written about former times. We made a lot of notes, developed systematic files, and tried to be very empirical in our approach.[1] I suppose that at first we emphasized interpersonal relations more than social structure, but after the earliest publications we all started to move toward a more national and structural orientation.

"Before I even finished my degree I was asked to be an assistant professor in the Faculty of Economics to teach a class on the formation of capitalism in Europe. When I said that I did not know anything about it, the professor gave me a lot of books to read. They were mostly in English which I could not read very easily, but I went to work and I enjoyed it a lot. The experience trained me in the historical approach. But after a while I had some trouble with the professor and lost my job, and I went back to the Department of Social Sciences in the Faculty of Philosophy and became an assistant to Bastide, and later to Fernandes. I taught classes at the same time that I kept doing the

Negro research. With my friends Octavio Ianni and Renato Moreira I went to the south of Brazil to study Negroes in the most advanced part of the country; we kept going back during our vacations for about three years. We gave a big questionnaire to 8,000 high school students, and we conducted about 800 personal interviews. I still have all that material, which we never completely analyzed; the IBM cards from the questionnaires are in the data bank at Berkeley right now. We had no experience with those techniques, and had to teach ourselves how to proceed. We even tried to learn about scaling from *The American Soldier*, but it was impossible, and nobody could help us. The statistics professors were trained in agriculture, and they did not know about scaling.''

Three major influences converged during those years in the mid-1950s. The first was the direct study of the Negro situation in Brazil; the second was a theoretical study of Marxist literature; and the third was participation in radical politics (Cardoso says that during his earlier undergraduate years he was too busy studying to pay attention to political activity). The theoretical study was in the form of a continuing informal seminar that ran for several years with a small group of young faculty members of the university from various disciplines. They went through the Marxist texts with great care, comparing translations in several languages and discussing the basic issues; it took three years to finish *Das Kapital*. Simultaneously, Cardoso was a member of a group centered around a radical magazine, *Fundamentos*, that was connected with the Communist party and attempted to analyze current Brazilian national issues. But in 1956, after the Russian invasion of Hungary, Cardoso split from the Communists. Although he debated his reasons with members of the group, he never denounced them publicly because he did not want to give ammunition to right-wing forces. He says his enemies in the university continued to consider him a Communist long after he took an independent position.

These experiences deepened his interest in the national scene, and he began to shift his perspective on the Negro in Brazil from interpersonal relations to the social-structural framework within which those relations occurred. Increasingly he realized that the current status of the Negro was based on a lower-class position within a capitalist system; the black man had moved from slavery to proletariat. He began to examine the difference between being a rural worker and a factory worker and to study comparatively the situation in Uruguay and Argentina, bordering on southern Brazil, where men did the same work but lacked a slave past. Historically, he analyzed the changing forms of Brazilian capitalism in the nineteenth and twentieth centuries.

The first book on this research was published jointly with Ianni in 1960 as *Côr e Mobilidade Social en Florianápolis (Color and Social Mobility in*

Florianápolis). The second was submitted as his doctoral dissertation and was published in 1962 as *Capitalismo e Escravidão no Brasil Meridional (Capitalism and Slavery in Southern Brazil)*. The difference in titles is an evident indication of the changing perspective: from the description of concrete and observable social relations to the structural analysis of an entire social system.

By then Cardoso's method of work was firmly established: the interpretation of contemporary phenomena through the use of ethnographic field materials based on interview and observation combined with written evidence such as newspapers and historical documents, all sifted and organized in terms of the structure of the total society. He feels that his early work on southern Brazil may be the most carefully documented of any he has done so far, and said that it was quite different from the style of Gilberto Freyre's famous writings on slavery in northeastern Brazil, since he believes that Freyre is biased in favor of the old system and that his methodology is weak and unsystematic.

At this point the focus of Cardoso's research shifted in response to the sociopolitical events then taking place. In the late 1950s Brazil was led by the exuberant President Juscelino Kubitschek and there was hectic industrial expansion; indeed, despite worsening inflation, the boom continued through 1962. There was a widespread feeling that the economy had "taken off" and that the nation was now engaged in self-sustained economic development. Many believed that the business leaders or "national bourgeoisie" were heroes who were moving the country away from centuries of colonial and agricultural backwardness toward a dynamic future based on an independent industrial economy and a modernized democratic polity that would incorporate the masses into active participation.

In order to study this new and exciting phase of Brazilian society, Cardoso and his colleagues at the university organized a Center for Industrial and Labor Sociology. They were aided by a similar center in Paris headed by Georges Friedmann whose protégé, Alain Touraine, spent much time in Chile and Brazil.

"Touraine had an important impact in Brazil. In that period we were influenced by our seminar on Marx; we were theoretically oriented, but somewhat old-fashioned in the sense that we considered Brazilian history to be the repetition of European history. All our interpretations were based on the assumption that the working class was not yet organized enough, mature enough, to accomplish its 'true task'. You will see in the book on the *empresários* or entrepreneurs that I changed my views, even while the research was going on, for I started that book with the same idea, namely that the bourgeoisie was not yet ready for its historical task. But, Touraine wrote an article putting some of our papers in a wider frame of reference, which helped us see that the Brazilian situation was different, not just a repetition of European experience.

"It was hard to start the center. At that time I had been elected by other former students as alumni representative on the council that ran the university, and I fought terribly against the old structure and some of the older professors who were not sympathetic to me. But I had some weight in the council, and we tried to institutionalize research at the university. I got some money from the university, and a friend who was a businessman—Fernando Gasparian[2]—also gave us some money to get the center started. We felt that we had to deal with current national issues, so we got started by studying industrial executives.

"I believed when I started that work that maybe the entrepreneurs as a class could be the new leaders, since that was the mood of the times; Kubitschek, the National Development Alliance and even the Communists believed that. But while doing the research I changed my mind. Some of the more extreme leftists, Trotskyites, thought that I was in favor of national capitalism, but if they read the book they would see that it is not true, because my structural analysis showed me the weaknesses of the position of the entrepreneurs.

"After the interviews were finished, I spent a year in Paris in postgraduate study. I worked with Touraine, a bit with Michel Crozier and studied with Raymond Aron. With Touraine and his group we had a lot of discussions of our Brazilian material. He was interested in social mobility, social process, and that was a good balance for me because I was more oriented toward structural problems."

The interview materials convinced Cardoso that the industrial elite was not able to shape policy by itself and had to make compromises with other sectors such as the agricultural oligarchy and the unionized urban workers, which led to confusions and contradictions and ultimately to inflation, economic stagnation and political chaos—all coming to a head in the troubles of President João Goulart in 1963 and early 1964. The new industries turned out to be unable to stand on their own feet and were forced to seek external help from international enterprises; the state was too weak to make the reforms that were necessary to widen political participation without creating turmoil. Thus Cardoso was not surprised when the elites turned to the Brazilian army and to the financial and political assistance of the United States in order to restore "stability" through a military coup in 1964. The drive toward industrialization and democratization anchored in national autonomy had failed.

"After I had finished the book on the Brazilian industrialists toward the ⸱f 1963 and was back in Brazil from Paris, I had the idea of doing some comparative research on entrepreneurs in Argentina, Mexico and Brazil, and then present that new material in a competition for the professorship which would become vacant when Fernando de Azevedo retired.[3] So I went to Argentina for some preliminary interviews, and I hoped later to develop a more technically oriented research. I also visited Chile; it was my first Latin American experience outside Brazil. Then before we could do much on that comparative research the coup came to Brazil on April 1, 1964, and I had to escape.

"You know, just before the coup, we all felt the tension, we knew a climax was coming. I lived on the same street with Florestan, and we had lots of conversations. We never for a moment thought the leftists would win, that Goulart could successfully lead a leftist transformation. I knew through the industrialists I interviewed that a right-wing coup was being organized, and I had additional information from my father. Actually, because he had recently been a federal deputy, and an uncle had earlier been president of the Bank of Brazil, many of my friends thought that I was somehow active in the government establishment, or wanted to be, but really my interests were more academic. Furthermore, I didn't think the alliance behind Goulart could really make a radical change, though a lot of intellectuals were optimistic about it. Of course, all of the feeling of living through a crisis was reflected in the way I wrote up the material on the industrialists; theory and practice merged.

"But I did not correctly evaluate the coming coup; I thought it would be even worse, and I expected a harsh reaction against me because of my position in the university; I had some conservative enemies. You see, although I was inside the university establishment, I represented the Left, and the Left that was outside the establishment supported me too at some moments. Maybe my behavior was a little ambiguous; I never assumed that I was part of the establishment but I never cut myself off from it—some roads I cannot take. Because of my background I think I have some ability to maneuver within the establishment, to achieve goals, but if I were coopted it could be terrible, so I always put on some defense to keep my independence.

"But in April I was afraid; I was told some people wanted to put me in jail, and in fact, the police came to the university to arrest me and arrested a friend by mistake. I learned that they didn't have my name yet at the airport, so I left on April 18. Florestan was wonderful and refused to appoint anybody to my position, so that when I came back in 1967 I could be nominated for it again. Formally, I was subject to trial by a military court, which might have put me in jail for a month or so, but even when I came back for my father's funeral in 1965 I was not arrested, and actually some of the generals attended the funeral. The reaction in those years was not so strong as I expected."

When he left Brazil after the coup Cardoso went to Santiago, Chile, and spent three years working at the Latin American Institute for Social and Economic Planning (ILPES), which is a part of the United Nations Economic Commission for Latin America. The director of the Social Affairs Division of ILPES was the distinguished Spanish *émigré* sociologist José Medina Echavarría.

"I did not leave Brazil for intellectual reasons, but in those terms it was an advantage; I discovered Latin America. You know, we Brazilians are such nationalists, it is hard to take another perspective. But living in Chile I had contact with people from all over Latin America. In Santiago I met Medina Echavarría, who really is a wonderful man, a European thinker, sophisticated and generous. He let me orient, almost control the division of social affairs in ILPES, to make it more empirical, more sociological. The economists would accept census information, but they didn't understand research like that on the entrepreneurs. Nevertheless we decided to go ahead with that type of study in Argentina and Brazil; we didn't have enough money for Mexico. Earlier when I was interested in Negroes I didn't really think I was a sociologist—more an anthropologist or historian. But in ECLA, with the economists, I became more a sociologist."

Simultaneously with the comparative study on entrepreneurs, Cardoso began to work out a general theory of dependency in collaboration with his young Chilean colleague, Enzo Faletto. He wrote the first paper using that term in 1965, and it represented a step forward in his thinking. The new dimension can be illustrated by comparing the paper with the conclusion of the earlier book on the Brazilian industrialists, which recognized that because they did not have the economic or political power to construct an autonomous industrial system, the entrepreneurs increasingly turned to collaboration with multinational enterprises to solve their problems. As a consequence, they had to turn away from close ties with other sectors in Brazil, particularly the working class. The book suggested that the only alternative to this increasing internationalization of Brazilian enterprise would be socialism.

The new concept of *dependency* is more flexible. It tries to separate analytically the political from the economic forces, and suggests that although the maneuvering limits are indeed set by the external world—by imperialism—the range of possible responses to a given situation depends upon internal political alliances and creativity. Because the history of each country gives it a peculiar mix of possible action, the response cannot be predicted by general theory alone and requires careful study of historical trends and the realities of power in each instance. The key to an understanding of those realities is a focus on the internal response to external dependency.

Furthermore, the perspective Cardoso adopted denies that dependent or nonautonomous industrialization necessarily leads to economic stagnation, which was the view then emphasized by another Brazilian exile temporarily living in Santiago—the influential economist Celso Furtado. Cardoso states that his Marxist training made him sensitive to cycles, and he did not believe that the then-current depression in Brazil was necessarily permanent. After all, Latin America had always been dependent, but there were epochs in which rather vigorous growth did take place and they were likely to return when various countries were able to take advantage of favorable conditions. However, it was true that in the early 1960s most nations of the region were suffering from a downward trend, and it generated pessimism.

The group then in Santiago from many countries shared a common problem: they were seeking new ideas that could explain why the early optimism about development in the postwar years was turning into bitter frustration. The inability of the various national economies to keep moving forward fast enough by becoming increasingly autonomous—as classical economics would predict—and the inability of the political and social institutions to modernize themselves in step with economic change—as functionalist sociology would predict—had to be faced by academic theory. As Cardoso himself expressed it in a recent essay written jointly with his compatriot Francisco Weffort:[4] ''the selection of problems to study in the sociology of development is largely made in terms of practical circumstances and political issues . . . the sensitivity of Latin American social scientists to specific situations and their desire to locate in such situations the 'political nerve center' have been the incentives for legitimate intellectual activity that goes beyond ideological debate.''

The economists in ECLA, under the leadership of Raúl Prebisch, diagnosed the Latin American problem as being one of an inadequate growth rate resulting from deterioration in the terms of external trade; the prices of agricultural and mineral exports were declining relative to industrial imports. But since there was not much that could be done about world prices, the economists suggested two ways out: more industrial production at home to be stimulated by better economic planning, and the development of a Latin American Common Market to expand trade possibilities in the region. However, they did not deal systematically with the internal political forces in each nation that would have to muster the energy and form the consensus required for specific action. Nor did they recognize the degree to which industrialization through import-substitution would lead to the internationalization of enterprises. Cardoso and his colleagues attempted to develop a model that would include those issues, using the key concept of *dependency*. It was a phrase that was then gaining currency in Chile, although used by other men in somewhat different ways.[5] By 1967 Cardoso and Faletto had finished a document that was circulated in mimeographed form and published two years later (after some hesitancy within ECLA about its suitability) as *Dependencia y Desarrollo en América Latina (Dependency and Development in Latin America)*.

The book quickly became very influential, partly because others were working on similar ideas at that time and partly because the critical thrust of dependency theory seemed to be closer to reality than the optimistic tone of earlier theories about self-sustained development. Cardoso reports that Prebisch understood the perspective, although in his own work he used a more narrowly economic style of analysis. The important Chilean economists Aníbal Pinto and Osvaldo Sunkel began to write in terms of dependency. Young sociologists in various countries discovered a congenial new theoretical language; within a short time there were several international seminars devoted to the theme.[6] Cardoso was invited to consult with leaders of the Peruvian military government that was making creative attempts to increase national autonomy and he even found a few specialists in the Inter-American Bank in Washington interested in the subject, although the policies of the bank do not reflect the new insights.

In the winter of 1967-68 Cardoso returned to France, this time to teach at the University of Nanterre in a suburb of Paris, where his friend Touraine was a professor. This happened to be the very time and spot where the French student movement erupted that almost toppled DeGaulle; one of the prominent leaders of that movement was Daniel Cohn-Bendit, a student in Cardoso's class. The experience in France was deeply moving for Cardoso:

"When I first got to France in the fall of 1967 it seemed so sure of itself, so bourgeois, so prosperous. Some people said that DeGaulle was like Louis XIV, only better, because there were no rebellions. Then the students started to protest various rules at the universities; at Nanterre, one of the issues involved sexual freedom in the dormitories—the girls could visit the boys but not vice versa, which seemed to a Brazilian like an issue from outer space. The professors and the administration responded too rigidly to the various protests, finally closing the school. The protests grew, and suddenly various other groups sensed that the government was not as strong as it seemed. Some unions and wildcat groups within unions organized strikes. Before long the fabric began to unravel; the solid society came apart because different groups with different goals converged in opposition, and because communications were tied up since the strikers controlled the radio and television.

"It was necessary to find some way out. DeGaulle and the Communists and the army made a tacit agreement opting for order first and then new elections, and that was enough.

"Such a situation could not happen in Brazil because the separate groups aren't well organized; that's the basic difference. We must not fool ourselves that slogans or clever tactics are enough. I've never been a utopian; ideas don't count unless they express some real force, some power in society."

In 1966 Cardoso had come under the protection of a writ of *habeas corpus* that was obtained for him in Brazil, and the following year he was nominated *in absentia* for the same post with Florestan Fernandes that he had held earlier, although he did not return immediately. At that time there seemed to be some loosening of the authoritarian style of the government and for family reasons he wanted to go home, despite the fact that professionally he was happy in Chile. So he began to make plans to return, and when his teaching was over in France in the summer of 1968 he finally went back to São Paulo. He took with him a manuscript based on one aspect of the comparative study of entrepreneurs that he had conducted from Santiago, namely, the relation between the degree of international dependency of enterprises and the political ideology of their executives. He added some preliminary chapters on the theory of the relationship between social role and personal ideology, written in the form of a critique of North American political science research, and submitted the document in the competition for a chair in political science, which he won.[7]

His timing turned out to be bad. In December of 1968 the government took a sharp swing to the Right, issuing the Fifth Institutional Act that closed the national Congress. It began a new purge of politicians and intellectuals, which included the forced "retirement" of a large number of professors in São Paulo, among them Cardoso and his mentor, Florestan Fernandes. The latter went to Canada for a few years, but Cardoso stayed in Brazil. The vagaries of Brazilian politics permitted him two luxuries, despite the fact that he was considered an enemy of the regime too dangerous to be allowed to teach: he received a "retirement pension" based on his years of service to the university beginning as a young assistant (it came to about half salary), and he was allowed to join a group of colleagues who organized a refuge for those evicted from the university, the Brazilian Center for Analysis and Planning (CEBRAP). They work as a private research and consulting organization, which has received financial support from the Ford Foundation and even gets contracts from local government agencies for certain projects. They are watched closely by the government, but can carry on their work as long as they discreetly avoid delicate topics. The group is a brilliant one, including Cardoso's long-time friends Octavio Ianni, Paul Singer, Francisco Weffort and Juarez Rubens Brandão Lopes—held together by common intellectual interests and by the pressure of political circumstance. Ironically, they are granted the privilege of full-time concentration on their research since most of them are not permitted to teach, yet they chafe under the loss of contact with students who provide so much stimulus, as well as distraction, for true academics.

Thus Cardoso is once again working in his own city along with a team of scholars that includes many who had been his fellow students at the University of São Paulo two decades earlier. He has returned to his first concern: contemporary Brazilian society. But to understand his current focus, it is first necessary to analyze his earlier study of Brazilian entrepreneurs, conducted as a response to the euphoria that dominated the country when the decade of the 1960s began.

Rarely has a work of social science been published with such a prophetic date: Cardoso's *Empresário Industrial e Desenvolvimento Econômico (Industrial Entrepreneur and Economic Development)* carries on its title page the words "April, 1964." On the first day of that very month the constitutional government of President João Goulart was overthrown by a right-wing military coup. The book, of course, was written many months earlier, but reading it with retrospective vision reveals its prescience. The central message of the volume was this: the special conditions of Brazilian development were leading the country toward a crisis that would produce demands for a coup to replace a government that was unable to maintain its authority because the underlying compromises upon which it was based were wearing thin. Economic development had outrun political development, and the system of government no longer expressed basic needs and forces. The existing regime grew out of a merger between three sectors, each unable to rule by itself: the traditional agricultural-commercial elite, tied to the export market (particularly coffee); the new industrial bourgeoisie, which began to emerge in the decade of the 1930s but reached its maximum momentum during the decade of the 1950s; and the new urban masses generated by industrial expansion. The final paragraph of the book reads:

"The possibilities of maintaining the present juggling are not unlimited. Each day the range of possible compromises narrows. The fundamental decisions do not depend only on the industrial bourgeoisie, which it seems has opted for order by abdicating from the attempt to impose its hegemony on society, satisfied instead with the condition of being junior partner to Western capitalism, as well as the advance guard for a national agriculture which very slowly is becoming capitalistic. It remains to be seen what will be the reaction of the urban masses and the popular groups, and who in the country will find the capacity for organization and decision able to carry forward the political modernization needed for economic development. In the final instance the question will become, subcapitalism or socialism?" (p. 187).[8]

Cardoso's book is based on a series of interviews that he and his colleagues at the Center for Industrial and Labor Sociology at the University of São Paulo conducted in 1961 and 1962 with various types of industrialists in different parts of the country. Altogether the owners or managers of 288 firms were interviewed, but the book concentrates on the responses of 82 men who directed very large enterprises (over 500 workers) in the cities of São Paulo, Belo Horizonte, Recife, Salvador and Blumenau. There are occasional quotations from the informants, but the material is mostly used impressionistically, along with historical analysis, in order to explain the trend of events. The book is less a monograph reporting specific research results than it is an essayistic interpretation of the Brazilian crisis in development.

Cardoso begins by noting that the standard literature in sociology and economics gives considerable emphasis to the role of the entrepreneur as the motive force in the development process. Perhaps the classic statement was that of Joseph Schumpeter, who combined the writings of earlier authors such as Adam Smith, Werner Sombart and Max Weber, and produced a theory of economic development based on the role of the entrepreneur as the man who creates "new combinations" by putting together capital and technology in ways that allow substantial jumps in production that lead to the opening of new markets. In so doing he develops new forms of business organization.

In more recent years the predominant style of analysis has shifted to an emphasis on the bureaucratization of the industrial firm. Writers such as Adolf Berle and Clark Kerr have turned their attention to the shift in the role of the entrepreneur as he becomes the administrator of a large enterprise. Instead of being a man of extraordinary personal innovating capacity, he becomes a man able to build change into the day-to-day activities of the firm, making use of systematic research on technology and market opportunities to make long term plans for growth.

Both approaches are becoming out-dated, because under current conditions the intense concentration of capital removes the market more and more from the abstract model of free competition. The role of the government increases dramatically, and the entrepreneur must adjust by learning how to deal with political forces in two ways. He must get government contracts or permits to aid his firm, but he must also generate an ideological position and a set of organizations and pressure groups that will convince the government to act in ways that will help his industry and, indeed, all businesses. Often he must compete in the political arena with pressure groups organized by entrepreneurs in different industries and by other sectors of society, such as wage workers, consumers or farmers.

"Therefore, the managing elites of a contemporary capitalist economy become simultaneously political elites: they go beyond the angle of vision of the isolated firm to a broader view necessary to guarantee ultimate success. But in this activity the dominant classes find themselves challenged by the presence of new groups capable of influencing the system of power, groups created by the very dynamics of modern production" (p. 37).

Obviously, this description of changes in contemporary monopoly capitalism makes us more aware of the fact that "the entrepreneur" is a man located in time and space. No abstract theory of entrepreneurship that fails to place the actor in a specific historical scene can be accepted. It is not enough to say that the industrialist is an innovator who follows rational procedures to seek ever-greater profits. In order to understand his role we must also specify the resources available to him, the market realities he faces, and the political environment in which he operates.

Particularly, when we are interested in dealing with groups of entrepreneurs acting with sufficient strength to change the course of society we must be specific about the historical circumstances. Development cannot be explained by itself; we cannot just say that an increase in the number of entrepreneurs or the rate of investment "causes" development; since that is circular and does not explain how it all got started.

"Furthermore, the notion of underdeveloped society only takes on meaning when there is an explicit reference to a specific relationship between that society and another which is already developed . . . . This means that the notions of 'underdevelopment' or 'process of development' suppose certain types of domination and certain types of social processes that are not purely economic in the traditional sense that the market is the principal regulator of economic life. Full understanding will not come from the study of the ways in which the industrial and developed economies double back on the parts of the world today called underdeveloped. Thus it will be necessary to study colonialism, imperialism, neocapitalism and neocolonialism in order to determine the types of relationship existing between the underdeveloped and developed parts of the world" (*Empresário Industrial e Desenvolvimento Econômico*, pp. 68-69).

Historical analysis should avoid the use of variables that leave out human motivation and human organization. "In the movement from the situation of underdevelopment to development the motivation forward and the resistance to it are not abstract 'factors' but vital 'interests' and 'conflicts'. This means that between stagnation and dynamism there do not intervene 'forces' in the sense that, for example, in a given economic situation potentially favorable to development, the introduction of the final factor will set it off, the way water boils when it reaches the proper temperature. Between one moment and another in the history of society there exists a struggle reflecting the tension between the interests and objectives of different social groups in a double sense: altering the position of that society with respect to other societies, and modifying the internal arrangement of the strata within that society. . . . It is up to the scientific observer to evaluate the connections between the general interests that are being defended, the specific or conscious objectives being sought, and the effectiveness of the actions taken by the various groups involved in the process of development, since social consciousness and the real interests of the groups may not always coincide'' (*Empresário Industrial e Desenvolvimento Econômico*, p. 71).

In sum, Cardoso insists on the importance of a structural analysis of the specific historical situation as a necessary framework for understanding the role of industrial entrepreneurs in any society. Having developed that point, his next task is to carry it out with respect to contemporary Brazil.

Cardoso accepts the influential views of Brazilian development set forth by political scientist Hélio Jaguaribe and economist Celso Furtado but says that they do not go far enough.

Jaguaribe (1962) maintained that the initial growth of the import-substitution industries was carried out by individual entrepreneurs rather blindly, without a clear ideological drive behind their actions and without much support from the state. But he went beyond this analysis *à la* Schumpeter by adding a correction *à la* Keynes: the state had to begin to take action to back up private initiative when the projects became too large for the private sector alone.

This approach is rather close to that adopted by Celso Furtado (1959), who explored the new opportunities of the Brazilian entrepreneurs in the 1930s and 1940s. He said that the new possibilities emerged directly from the difficulties of the export market for coffee during the depression and the disruptions of world trade during World War II. In the first instance, imports could not be paid for; in the second, they were unavailable. The local industrialists who took advantage of these conditions later faced the postwar competition from the revived world market, and the state had to move in to assist them by protective tariffs and distorted exchange rates.

The analyses of Jaguaribe and Furtado, correct as far as they go, leave us with the impression of impersonal and blind economic conditions as the determinant factors and do not deal with the entrepreneurs as human participants. Cardoso feels it is necessary to add a discussion of the formation of new social groups with new ideological goals.

"The economic development of Brazil as a political-economic-social process implies not only the development of a new industry of capital goods and the automatic growth of the economy, but also the formation of new social classes capable of redefining the traditional equilibrium of power and of breaking through economic stagnation internally and externally . . . . The transition from an agrarian exporting society, which is politically dependent on its exterior economic markets, to an industrial society, which is autonomous, requires within Brazil a rearrangement of the system of power and through it a new arrangement of bargaining relations with the world market" (*Empresário Industrial e Desenvolvimento Econômico*, pp. 78-80).

The entrepreneurs who expanded their enterprises to take advantage of the import barriers in the 1930s and 1940s did not begin with a clear vision of the larger process of which they were a part; they were simply maximizing the immediate profits of their firms. As this rather slow and automatic growth gained momentum, it ran into new and unanticipated problems. The infrastructure of roads, schools and public utilities proved to be inadequate, to say nothing of the availability of basic raw materials such as steel and oil. Workers began to flock to the cities looking for jobs in the new industries, straining the supply of housing and water and electricity; the *favelas* or urban squatter settlements mushroomed. The old system of political decision-making—"deals" between different factions based on personal contacts and patronage—was incapable of meeting these new problems.

One response to this emergent situation, which gained resonance from the urban masses, came from intellectuals and government bureaucrats, both civilian and military, who developed a new ideology for Brazil. Instead of a passive nation exporting coffee and importing consumer goods, they foresaw a vigorous new nation learning to stand on its own feet, with an economy that was largely self-sufficient in agriculture, consumer goods and capital goods. They espoused a spirit of pride, nationalism and rapid economic development. One of the earliest examples of this "developmentalist" policy, which was pushed more by the military than by industry itself, was the establishment by Getúlio Vargas's government of state-owned steel mills at Volta Redonda during World War II. Another was the policy a few years later that led to the nationalization of petroleum extraction, which was opposed by many in the traditional upper classes. In both instances there was open and vigorous conflict; one group won over another.

The dream of the nationalists at this stage was an independent capitalism guided and helped by the state but primarily in the hands of Brazilian private owners. What they failed to foresee was the process by which, in a very few years, the local owners would turn toward the international monopolies to gain access to new technology and new capital, with the result that autonomy of decision-making would be lost.

Most of the industrialists themselves had a view that was equally limited. They wanted the state to help them with tariff protection against foreign competition, but they resisted the government activity that was necessary to solve the problems of infrastructure because they were afraid that government intervention might lead to a limitation of their prerogatives.

"The social groups that organized movements for 'economic emancipation' did not suspect that in a few years the national bourgeoisie would ally itself with 'foreign interests' as a way of solving its problems; and the industrial sectors of the national bourgeoisie, who were resisting state intervention in the economy, did not realize that they would be the major beneficiaries of movements favorable to public participation in the economy of the country . . . .

"As a result, the existing policy did not accelerate national emancipation and economic development to the limit that was possible, and it was based on a compromise between the past and the future: the agrarian structure remained archaic, industrialization was not planned and proceeded in terms of deals with international interests, and basic decisions depended upon an agreement between the traditional groups and the new groups that were moving towards power, namely, the urban masses and the national bourgeoisie" (*Empresário Industrial e Desenvolvimento Econômico*, pp. 85-86).

During all this debate the public tended to be manipulated through the mass media and by demogogic leaders rather than by well-organized political parties with clear goals. The government continued to vacillate as it sought temporary compromises between industrialists (some linked to international interests) and agriculturalists; decisions were reached through the old cliques and friendship groups. Thus, the political system never was able to bring the central issues to a clear decision point.

The second part of Cardoso's book moves from these political problems to the specific behavior of entrepreneurs as revealed in the interviews. "The analyses made to this point demonstrate that the actions of entrepreneurs in the process of economic development can only be analyzed and understood as part of a more general process of social change. The idea of absolute autonomy of action by entrepreneurs, even if it is only posited as an analytic tool, would lead to mistakes and would not permit the concrete determination of the meaning of their role. In truth, the structural conditions of society in general limit and characterize the possible forms of innovative behavior in the economic field" (*Empresário Industrial e Desenvolvimento Econômico*, p. 93).

Given the existing system of private property, the first "structural condition" to examine is the way in which a given style of property ownership leads to business decisions. The tradition of the family firm remains strong in Brazil, even though some of the largest companies are beginning to turn to more impersonal forms of administration. The family firm is of course more common in the rural parts of the country, but it continues to have influence in the large cities such as São Paulo and Belo Horizonte. In the sample of firms that was studied, and taking only the larger ones with 500 or more employees, it was discovered that 38 were controlled by the owners directly or by a combination of the owners and the administrators, 29 by public stockholders or a combination of the stockholders and the administrators, 25 by administrators and there were two other cases. Among the smaller firms with between 20 and 500 employees, there was much more direct control by the owners: 176 by the owners and administrators, 51 by public stockholders and administrators, 50 directly by the administrators and four other cases.

In many instances the myth of the founding father remains strong. He is seen as a man of exceptional skills who (with perhaps the aid of some friends) was able to develop a small business into a larger and more successful one and passed it, and often some of his skills as well, directly to his sons. They continue to honor him and they look upon the entire enterprise, including the workers, as a form of extended family. They often reject possibilities of further expansion that would bring a loss of direct control. The continuation of traditional traits can be noted in the fact that among the managers and directors of the largest enterprises less than half had received university education.

Since 1950 there has been a considerable differentiation of management styles as financial groups have merged several firms into giant enterprises, sometimes with foreign participation. Increasingly it is realized that the family may not be the most efficient way to operate a large industrial firm. This is particularly true among the younger managers and those who are employed by firms under government control.

The pressures for modernization come from the growing complexity and size of the larger enterprises, from the competitive pressures of the foreign-owned firms (50 percent of the large firms in the sample were branches of foreign companies and they followed principles of impersonal administration) and, finally, from the competition of large government enterprises.

Yet one should also ask how it is possible in so many instances for the family firms to continue. Despite constant complaint about the lack of personnel both capable and worthy of confidence, which is often given as the reason for not opening branches in regions of economic expansion, such as the Northeast, many family firms are flexible and do adapt to new circumstances.

"One may conclude, therefore, that the persistence of this traditional pattern of control over firms is not just a result of cultural backwardness nor an inadequate entrepreneurial mentality in relation to the new market situation. There are reasons linked to the particular conditions of industrialization in Brazil that permit and at times even promote the maintenance of the family type of control over enterprises. In the first place, the general conditions of the market in Brazilian society are not such as to guarantee that the rationalization of administration will lead to appropriate calculations of the goals of an enterprise, basing them solely on technical, rational grounds. The relatively restricted market is in itself an obstacle for the complete rationalization of economic life. The fluctuations of supply and demand in a market of imperfect competition such as the Brazilian one often require abrupt changes in the planning of firms. Furthermore, the preponderant role that the state exercises in the control over finance and foreign exchange and the relatively small influence that the industrialists as a group exercise over the government mean that firms are often obliged to change their goals and their planning with sudden speed. Changes in the foreign exchange rates can bring a sharp rise in the cruzeiro price of imported machines, making impossible previous plans for expansion; in the same way alterations in the official credit policies require rapid adjustments in the volume of inventories" (*Empresário Industrial e Desenvolvimento Econômico*, p. 105).

Under these conditions firms either must have capital resources of a size that is rarely available to national firms or they must be able to respond quickly to altering conditions, and such response is made more difficult by long-term technical plans. By contrast, the small firm, which is flexible and which deals with a market situation that offers high profits and relatively weak competition, is in a position to take advantage of sudden changes and can thus be more "rational."

But Cardoso indicates that the smaller family firms get into trouble for several reasons.[9] One arises when the heirs of the original founder do not show the same talents that he had. Another stems from the fact that the family's consumption styles often eat up all the profits, leaving no surplus available for investment in expansion; the result often leads families to sell lucrative enterprises to gain cash. At other times these firms get into trouble because they do not have the ability either administratively or financially to grow in the face of their competition and adapt their technology to new market possibilities.

The general conditions of the Brazilian market continue to be confusing with respect to the growth of large, technically managed firms. Such firms obviously have the advantage in industries that require complicated and expensive modern technology. On the other hand, the high rate of inflation, the many possibilities for very large short-run profits and the temptation to use personal connections with the government to get credit or information that permits such profits, supports a certain adventurism among Brazilian entrepreneurs in which the individual or family has some advantages over impersonal bureaucratic administrators.

Cardoso asked his informants to give a history of their firms and discovered three types of founding fathers. He noted that in the traditional situation most innovators were people who through personal experience and personal connection managed to put together enterprises that produced goods for imperfect markets; Cardoso calls them "captains of industry." Those markets were often protected from other producers by distance, which created regional monopolies, or they were aided by government barriers to foreign imports. Under those conditions, there was no advantage in constantly investing more money in expensive technology; instead, the proper goal was to produce in a fixed way by using cheap, unskilled labor and to earn more money by raising prices. Entrepreneurs who used this method of action depended upon personal relationships to get concessions from the government and find purchasers or borrow capital. They followed a paternalistic style in dealing with their workers and considered any organized attempts at collective bargaining to be the result of Communist agitation. "It was the spirit of usury more than that of methodical saving and rational exploitation of the labor force that constituted the primary characteristic of the pioneering industrialist 'who learned to squeeze money from a stone'" (*Empresário Industrial e Desenvolvimento Econômico*, p. 133).

Among the early industrialists were some who followed a different style. They believed in hard personal work and methodical saving and were distrustful of speculative activities. They often refused to borrow money because they did not want to pay high interest rates. They also would do physical and administrative tasks in the enterprise, which in fact were an irrational use of their time, but they found it hard to delegate responsibility. This style of work was more typical of immigrants than of native-born Brazilians. They were the ones who tended to introduce new techniques of production, and when this type of "traditional industrialist" began at a later stage to seek help from engineering and from financial sources outside his own family, he started to transform himself (or his son) into a modern businessman.

Among the larger firms of today one is likely to find managers who represent still another approach. "In contrast to the captains of industry and to the traditional industrialists, modern businessmen are not dominated by an obsession for immediate profit obtained through the manipulation of the market or through official favors, nor do they have an obsessive passion for hard and even irrational work and the accumulation of savings. They are methodical in their work, basing it on a technological understanding of production; they expect profits on a medium-term basis; and they have a sense of competition, rather than monopoly. Furthermore, instead of having a vision limited by the range of their factory, these businessmen are concerned with society as a whole, even though they may lack the conditions for influencing the larger society'' (*Empresário Industrial e Desenvolvimento Econômico*, p. 140).

The new businessmen create continuous organizational and technical change in their enterprises to increase total production and also productivity per man. To a certain point, these attitudes are consequences of the stability of their industries. These men are at the head of large companies with massive financial resources behind them, and they are involved in basic industries undergoing a constant process of substitution of imports which guarantees an expanding market with government protection. But within that market they face competition with other firms, both national and foreign, and find that competition exhilarating. They recognize that their survival in a competitive situation will depend upon more efficient technology and more efficient forms of organization and cost control, and therefore administration cannot be left to trial and error or the entrepreneur's instinct. To some degree these attitudes have been learned from the managers of the foreign firms in their midst. Once national firms began to organize themselves on a scale to compete with the international ones, particularly with the advent of the automobile industry in the late 1950s, then the pressures to modernize spread rapidly.

It should be noted that a full commitment to the building of a specialized industry that will be prepared for the markets of the future involves an act of faith that is not entirely rational. Since the stability of the political regime and the future direction of economic development are somewhat doubtful, it takes an act of faith in order to make large-scale investments that will not pay off in the short run.

Although it may seem that the emergence of these new businessmen brings us closer to the model of the entrepreneur-administrator described in the international literature, it should be recognized that they are not faced with a market based on perfect competition, as is usually assumed in that literature. In order to exist in a contemporary situation, surrounded by branches of big international firms that have special competitive advantages, these men either have to ally themselves in one way or another with the international firms or turn to the state for help. Indeed, the state itself begins to develop enterprises to handle special problems. Therefore, the political aspect of their market situation is always present.

These new businessmen recognize that they have a ''class interest'' and tend to organize pressure groups to influence long-term government policy in ways that will benefit industry as a whole. Instead of just trying to get an advantage for their own factory they try to construct general conditions that will lead to the steady expansion of all modern industry. They not only attempt to apply direct pressure on government but are interested in influencing public opinion over the long run in order to develop an ideology of industrialization that fits their own goals. They believe in the functional integration of political democracy with private property and progress. One industrialist in São Paulo said, "The modern businessman must have a general vision. Today it is not sufficient for him to have specific knowledge about his own industry, for the problem of enterprise is the problem of society" (*Empresário Industrial e Desenvolvimento Econômico*, p. 149).

There is, however, a division among these new industrialists. Those who are part of nationally owned industry tend to maintain closer contact with politicians and use the state as a means of protection against international competition. Those who are linked with international enterprises have a vision of Western capitalism as a whole and are worried about the use of the state apparatus to impose nationalist policies that they feel would be counterproductive because they might lead toward socialism.

It should be admitted that the ideal types developed here of the traditional industrialist, the speculative captain of industry and the new businessman are oversimplified and that most actual business leaders show mixed characteristics. In their daily lives they will be responding not only to certain long-term attitudes they hold but to changing market conditions and the particular economic and social realities they face. As in the past, there are alternative routes to success: hard work and detailed personal control over the enterprise, adventuresome seizing of special opportunities, manipulation of family ties, the use of personal connections and political skill. No single model of the entrepreneur as the agent of change will suffice. Sometimes he creates his opportunities, but often he only responds to situations created by others.

In looking at the Brazilian industrial entrepreneurs as a whole, as a "class," and seeking to explain their political views and actions, Cardoso is constantly struck by their lack of consistency—indeed, their confusion—which he interprets to be a consequence of their recent emergence to prominence. "The Brazilian industrial bourgeoisie has developed as a social stratum very rapidly. It is formed from the merger of different social groups whose industrial tradition is recent: two generations of industrialists constitute the average even among those who are considered as established industrial families. It is common to see even large firms still controlled by their founders. In a fashion that is parallel to the situation of the industrial proletariat, which lacks a clear tradition that orients it to its situation, the recent origins of the Brazilian industrialists make it more difficult for them to orient themselves as entrepreneurs and act as a class. Thus the forms of awareness and definition of political, economic or social objectives that are held by the industrial bourgeoisie often do not match their real class interests" (*Empresário Industrial e Desenvolvimento Econômico*, p. 160).

Furthermore, the heterogeneity of the different groups within the industrial bourgeoisie makes it more difficult for them to discover common denominators to shape their values and their actions. The entrepreneurs stem from immigrants, from old social strata based on land ownership, from new technically trained managers and from people who have made their money through commercial dealings. There are two additional factors: the working class itself, lacking a clear proletarian orientation and enjoying the euphoria of rapid expansion of job opportunities and of real wages in the 1950s, has not pushed the industrialists very hard. And the high rate of return on capital has made it easier for the industrialists to accept the traditional practices that still control the behavior of some of the older men. These social factors intervene and prevent many of the industrialists from reacting rationally and objectively to the market and political situations that face them.

Many industrialists blame the government for inflation and other ills, yet do not feel a sense of responsibility for guiding government decisions in directions that they would consider more appropriate. Indeed, their only contact with the government tends to be in terms of gaining some permit or loan that will be of aid to their own firm. They fail to realize that the inflationary situation of recent years is to the benefit of industrial expansion, and instead they take a typical middle-class attitude and condemn the workers for excessive desires. Furthermore, they are always pushing the government to expand bank credit for business without seeing any connection with the inflation that they complain about. They have excessive swings from pessimism to optimism according to alterations in the business cycle because they lack a long-term theory of industrial growth. They are also ambivalent about government control and investment on the one hand and foreign investment on the other. "Between these two poles the national bourgeoisie constantly waivers, fearing the alienation of the nation's wealth to foreigners, but also fearing the growth of power in the hands of politicians and government bureaucrats" (*Empresário Industrial e Desenvolvimento Econômico*, p. 168).

The lack of clear class-consciousness among the industrialists permits them to identify in a general way with the people and the nation as a whole and to feel that the industrialists' interests are identical with those of the nation. They emphasize that industrial growth in general will be the base of future jobs and prosperity for everybody. Especially those who have recently risen to wealth find it easy to feel an identification with workers, since they see themselves as workers who have become successful.

The result of this lack of solidarity within the industrial group is that *the growth of the industrial sector has not in fact destroyed the old political order that grew out of the preindustrial history of the country*. The personal linkages between men of wealth and politicians continue. Many industrialists belong to landowning families. People seek personal contacts for personal gains and in this there is no clear line of demarcation between industrialists as a class and landowners. The industrialist accommodates himself to traditional forms of political authority: the "patrimonial" state survives.

One fact makes the Brazilian scene strikingly different from earlier patterns of industrialization in Europe and the United States: urbanization and mass society appeared before the economy had developed very far. Mass communications and modern consumption styles put great pressure on inadequate productivity, and the response is to seek state aid and foreign assistance to meet demands. "As we have indicated, the great push for development started outside the industrialist group itself and was based on the combination of foreign capital plus direct state participation in the economy. The private sector of the national economy was thus faced with a difficult choice: to support popular mass movements that were pressing for greater state control of basic sectors of the economy or to associate themselves with the foreign capitalists in order to push for development in the classical mold. The first alternative implied the risk of loss of control of the situation and acceptance of the secondary nature of local private initiative. The second alternative permitted them to identify with the basic values of the Western Christian world but at the same time forced them to accept the massive penetration of the international monopolies. In both cases there was the risk of losing political control" (*Empresário Industrial e Desenvolvimento Econômico*, p. 176).

Since most of the industrialists ended up following their private short-run interests rather than a clear theory of national development, they opted for supporting foreign investment in certain basic fields where national capital was unable to do the job. The costs of this policy are becoming apparent. Inefficiency, lack of national planning and the inflationary spiral force the nation to turn to ever-greater rates of foreign investment. But the flow of that investment depends on conditions that are not under national control, such as the interests of foreign groups and their view of the general political climate of the country. Indeed, the growth of nationalist sentiment in the urban masses did threaten the flow of new foreign capital; the law of the early 1960s regulating the payment of profits abroad, which was pushed by some national industrialists along with most labor unions, intellectuals and elements of the armed forces made it more difficult to attract new investments. The alternative policy of encouraging state investment increasingly frightened the industrialists because of the possibility of a populist take-over of the state.

The growth of production demands the growth of consumption and leads to larger participation by the masses. But, translated into politics, mass participation seems to some to threaten revolution. "Therefore Brazilian policy follows a pendular movement that goes from immobility toward reform and back again, and populist pressures generate counterreactions calling for right-wing military coups. Each time innovating pressures grow they threaten a rupture in the traditional equilibrium, and Bonapartism appears as a solution. But since both poles have some fears of the Bonapartist solution (will it be a coup or a countercoup?) they turn to a new compromise and a new immobility, which in party terms is reflected by the alliance between the PSD and PTB, that is, between the new Brazil which is willing to compromise and the old Brazil which knows that only through compromise can it exist. In these moments of practical politics the national bourgeoisie adopts a policy without grandeur.

"The possibilities of maintenance of this pendular movement in Brazilian politics are not unlimited. The most recent institutional crisis—over the resignation of President Jânio Quadros and the attempts to limit the powers of President João Goulart—expresses fundamentally the incapacity of the traditional classes to maintain control of the state without turning toward the new Brazil, that is, representatives of the urban and industrialized economy. The latter for their part fear the risks of provoking basic changes in the state apparatus and in the traditional structure of the economy . . . . The peculiar situation of the industrial bourgeoisie, placed in the midst of a new economy and a mass society still in the process of formation, makes it fearful and unable to break its ties with the traditional interests, namely the landowners, the traders and the bankers within the nation, as well as the foreign enterprises with which they are allied. Unable to assume political responsibilities, the industrial bourgeoisie thus becomes part of the traditional order of political control. By so doing it may be creating the very possibility that it most fears: losing the historical chance of exercising class leadership for the nation" (*Empresário Industrial e Desenvolvimento Econômico*, pp. 179-80).

Those words were written at a time when the regime of President Goulart was moving toward the Left by endorsing land reform, higher wages for the industrial workers, the vote for the illiterates and state limitations on the remission of foreign profits. Inflation had gotten out of control and reached 80 percent in 1963. The response was a right-wing military coup and a regime that became increasingly repressive at the same time that it succeeded, at least in the short term, in imposing a consistent economic policy. The results of that policy were rapid industrial growth, enormous foreign investment and widening disparities in the distribution of income.

Three years after the book on Brazilian entrepreneurs was published, Cardoso published an essay that took advantage of some new statistics produced by other researchers to reinforce his arguments. It was called

"Hegemonia Burguesa e Independência Econômica: Raízes Estruturais da Crise Política Brasileira" (1967) ("Bourgeois Hegemony and Economic Independence: Structural Roots of the Brazilian Political Crisis"). In this essay he is particulary concerned with trends in the formation of capital and their implications for the control of economic growth. He shows that during the decade of the 1950s the proportion of new investment in fixed capital provided by the state grew dramatically, reaching approximately one-half of the total. In a study of 66 of the largest economic groups (clusters of enterprises with interlocking directorates) in the country in 1960, it was found that 19 were controlled by the state; since the government dominated the larger units, it was able to direct more than half of the total invested capital.

Turning to the privately owned groups, Cardoso reports that more than half of the largest ones were controlled by foreign capital, and that foreigners had minority participation in many others. The larger the enterprises and the more recently they were formed, the greater was the probability of foreign domination. The local firms were mainly in finance, commerce and light industry, and the foreign firms were in heavy industry.

These results point up the fact that the early Brazilian entrepreneurs who started before World War II progressively lost control of the process of industrialization. As firms grew bigger and as technology became more complex—and as the growing market offered more chance for big profits—both the state and foreign firms moved into the action. Therefore, one cannot now base a theory of development in Brazil primarily on the behavior of the independent entrepreneurs of the local industrial bourgeoisie, as was attempted a decade ago. Although they exist and play an important role, the entrepreneurs dominate neither industry nor national political life.

Cardoso also uses the new data to show that over half of private investment came from retained earnings of existing firms, and that industrial wages in the advanced industries barely kept pace with inflation, whereas in small industries and in agriculture wages fell behind prices. He concludes that the process of inflation, low wages and high profits meant that consumers and farmers were being exploited, since their money was being transferred to the hands of entrepreneurs for the expansion of capital. Even the foreigners raised a lot of their funds in local financial markets and through retained earnings, so that actual flows of external capital into the country represented only about 15 percent of new total investment (although much more than that in the crucial growth areas of heavy industry). As a result, the ownership share and the influence of foreigners was greater than the proportion of their own money in the invested capital of their firms.

Cardoso clearly foresaw the trends that culminated in the military takeover of 1964 in Brazil; however, he tended to explain them as peculiarly

Brazilian. In other words, he was writing interpretative contemporary history, not creating abstract models. His primary theoretical emphasis was a polemic against those who, following Schumpeter, constructed a general model of development based on the role of the entrepreneur but failed to specify the concrete circumstances in which that entrepreneur was operating. He felt that the Brazilian circumstances were such as to negate much of the theorizing in the literature.

Later reflection on the Brazilian events seemed to indicate that they shared some characteristics with other countries, as well as showing their own idiosyncracies. After all, Argentina had also gone part way toward industrialization and modernization, but then reached stagnation and military control. Mexico, by contrast, seemed able to avoid the trap and continued to develop. A continent-wide view was required, a way of looking at similarities and differences *within* the region that would go beyond a mere specification of the distinctiveness of the Latin American scene as compared to the earlier paths of Europe and the United States.

Obviously Cardoso's residence in Santiago, Chile, had a lot of influence on this broader view. At ILPES he engaged in a continuous dialogue with social scientists from many countries. He reports that the economists never had any doubt about the importance of the noneconomic aspects of development, but that the sociologists and political scientists had considerable difficulty in specifying those aspects in ways that could be linked to crucial economic variables. Putting aside many social factors (such as immigration, slavery, indigenous cultures), Cardoso concentrated on the political structures that controlled the economic decisions shaping the pattern of development. In the book he wrote with Enzo Faletto, *Dependencia y Desarrollo en América Latina* (1969), he studied the interactions between economics and politics in diverse historical epochs.

At the end of World War II there was general agreement that the more advanced Latin American countries had reached the point where the economic factors were favorable to self-sustained development. "But this optimistic outlook has been weakening since the end of the 1950s. It was difficult to explain why, with so many conditions apparently favorable for passing from the stage of import-substitution to another that would open new fields of autonomous production, oriented toward the internal market, the necessary measures were not taken in order to guarantee the continuity of development; or why, when such steps were taken, they did not reach their objectives. Furthermore, in some cases the rate of economic growth itself has not been sufficient to stimulate the backward sectors of the economy and thereby to make possible the absorption of the manpower created by demographic growth" (p. 6).

In one of the most prosperous countries of the region, Argentina, political conditions were such that economic opportunities were not seized. In Brazil there was a short period of energetic growth and diversification, but the early 1960s brought crisis and stagnation. Only Mexico, with its more diversified export structure and its tourist income, seemed to be able to maintain economic growth—and many suspected that this success was a reflection of the structural changes stemming from the Mexican Revolution some decades earlier. Questions began to be raised suggesting that the key difficulties in Latin America were in the institutional or political realms more than in the economy itself, or even that the very theory of economic development based on growth of the internal market—*hacia adentro*—was in error.

The economic theories that were prevalent in the 1950s and that led to optimism about the possibilities of self-sustained growth presupposed the existence of social groups in the various countries capable of creating sectors sufficiently dynamic not only to move the economy foward but also to transfer basic decision-making from the traditional and conservative elites to modern and progressive leaders. The difficulty with this approach was that it implied a transitional period in which bits and pieces of modernism would grow within the traditional structure, but this process of change was not explained by the model itself. Usually, external factors were advanced as explanations—such as the "demonstration effect" of new styles of consumption coming from the advanced countries or the spreading impact of foreign investments.

Instead of such a model, Cardoso and Faletto prefer one that looks at what is going on inside each developing society and explains change in terms of actions taken by various national groups based on their own interests and not as automatic responses to external stimuli. Alterations in social and political structures only come about when new groups and classes manage through competition and struggle to impose their views on others, taking control of the direction of society; impersonal forces or variables do not explain specific decisions that change the direction of history. "It is evident that the theoretical explanation of the structures of domination in Latin American countries requires that we clarify the connections between internal and external forces, but these connections cannot be understood in abstract terms according to a formal analytic model, and still less in terms of a mechanical or immediate determination of the internal by the external. Precisely, the concept of *dependence* that will be developed in this book seeks to give general significance to a series of facts and situations that appear together in a given moment, and by this means it hopes to establish the relation between internal and external structural components . . . . As the object of this essay is to explain economic processes in terms of social processes, it requires us to find a theoretical point of intersection where economic power is expressed as social domination, that is, in politics. Through the political process, one class or economic group tries to establish a system of social relations that will permit it to impose its view on the whole society, or at least it tries to establish alliances to ensure economic policies compatible with its own interests and objectives. Thus, we will emphasize the following: the economic conditions of the world market, including the international equilibrium of power; the structure of the national productive system and its links with the external market; the forms of distribution and maintenance of national power; and above all the sociopolitical movements and processes pushing toward change, with their various orientations and objectives" (*Dependencia y Desarrollo en América Latina*, pp. 19-20).

"The concept of underdevelopment as it is usually used refers mainly to a type of economic system, with a predominant agricultural sector, a high concentration of income, a limited diversity of output and above all, an external market that prevails over the internal. But this is not sufficient" (p. 23). It is not sufficient because it does not incorporate into the definition the fact that underdevelopment can only be understood in relation to development. That is, the situation of underdevelopment is produced historically when the expansion of early commercial capitalism and later industrial capitalism ties the backward regions into the international market, and these regions become suppliers of essential raw materials for the advanced countries as well as purchasers of their industrial goods. Therefore, internal development in the countries of the periphery is shaped according to the needs of the metropolitan powers that dominate them.

Looking at the situation this way, we recognize that no underdeveloped economy exists as a type or level or stage on its own; thus, we should not expect that any of them will automatically move to the supposed next higher stage. As we redefine and bring into the center of our attention the relation between peripheral societies and metropolitan societies at a given moment of time, we look for the forms of domination that control the underdeveloped society and that must be changed if the economic system is to evolve. Only by studying the conditions that shape decision-making can we explain why some countries are able to take advantage of new economic conditions that emerge in certain historical epochs and others are not.

"In order to undertake this analysis it is necessary to put aside the idea that the action of social classes and the relations among them will move forward in the dependent countries in the same way that they did in the central countries during their phase of original development. All classic studies of the political and economic system at the beginning of development in the advanced countries suppose a free market which acted as the arbitrator among conflicting interests. Within that market economic rationality as measured by profits became the norm of the society, and consumption and investment were shaped by the free play of economic forces. This model further supposes that the possibilities for expansion depended upon the existence of a dynamic group that was able to gain control of decisions about investment, and that was able to influence political activity sufficiently to protect its interests. The rising economic class thus possessed both efficiency and consensus'' (*Dependencia y Desarrollo en América Latina*, p. 30).

But when underdeveloped countries entered world markets later in history under conditions that were predetermined by the advanced countries, they did not face the same market situation that existed in earlier epochs. Their situation always was defined by the relation between the periphery and the center. Although it may be useful to speak of earlier phases in the now-advanced countries that moved them from mercantile capitalism to industrial capitalism to finance capitalism, it does not make sense to see the Latin American countries as passing through the same stages because they may be engaged in mercantile operations at the very moment that the world scene is dominated by finance capitalism.

In sum, the sociological view of economic development emphasizes the values, the interests and the actions of competive groups. Inside a country, the dominant group may have interests parallel to those of powerful international sectors and thus may make decisions that benefit themselves and outsiders at the cost of national growth; they may profit more from the status quo than they would from the transformations that accompany true development. But let us turn to a specific view of the historical epochs through which Latin America has passed in order to try to show how the dependency perspective is more helpful than the abstractions of the classic theory of economic development that leaves out of the picture the real interests of the men who make the crucial decisions.

Cardoso and Faletto start with a look at the situation that existed early in the nineteenth century after the nations of Latin America achieved their political independence from Spain and Portugal. During that period England emerged as the major central power. Her interests involved the maintenance of a steady supply of raw materials, and this was accomplished mainly through commercial ties with local suppliers and not to any great extent by direct investments. The various newly independent countries struggled to organize their political and economic systems in order to take advantage of the new markets made available by the ending of the trade monopolies of Spain and Portugal. Where they had an existing economy that was based on the export of agricultural products, the new problem was to reestablish sufficient internal peace and order so that the supplies would move to the ports and to Europe.

The dynamic elements of the local elite consisted of the commercial people who arranged for the flow of materials, along with the owners of those lands engaged in production for the external market, which can conveniently be called "plantations" since they were efficiently organized for capitalistic profit: they were not stagnant feudal structures, as is often claimed. However, these dynamic elites were not strong enough to control the government by themselves and had to form alliances with the owners of the haciendas concerned with more traditional forms of subsistence production. Through these alliances the labor force was kept under control even when slavery was officially abolished. The local military chiefs who had emerged during the anarchy of the wars of independence had to be subordinated to national power, and to achieve that end the export interests made compromises with regional landlords more interested in the status quo than in economic expansion. The alliance between the two sectors of the elite—the modern commercial-agricultural sector operating plantations and the traditional hacienda-oligarchy sector—was somewhat tenuous and it occasionally broke into struggles between central and regional groups. However, by the middle of the nineteenth century the national forces were winning control throughout the continent.

This style of development left much decision-making in the hands of national elites, since capital was being generated locally by seizing control of unused lands and directing the labor force towards them. Of course the rate of growth did not depend solely on local decisions but also upon fluctuations in international demand for export products such as sugar and cotton (and later, wheat, bananas, beef and coffee). Furthermore, some external investment was channeled toward these countries, most often to improve the efficiency of the exporting system. Money flowed into port facilities and railways, sometimes through direct investment, often by sale of government bonds in London that allowed the local governments to subsidize construction. But the net result of all of this was that although the central powers (mainly England) deeply influenced the general rate of development of the Latin American periphery, they did not substitute themselves for the local economic and political elites. Indeed, the local commercial, military and political leaders increased their powers and in turn generated an expansion of bureaucratic structures that created urban middle classes. The capitals became modern cities, supported by export trade and by government salaries.

"It is easy to understand in these circumstances that the problem of expansion of the export economy was in local terms more a political than an economic problem. In effect, the goal was to assure the appropriation of the land and the domination of the labor force, whether it be by means of slavery, the promotion of immigration, or the creation of obstacles that kept local indigenous groups from gaining control of their own lands. In order to succeed in this task it was necessary to make agreements with landowners who were not directly engaged in the exporting system so that peace and order could be continued even in areas of low productivity'' (pp. 44-45).

There was another type of development in some countries, namely ''the enclave,'' or direct investment by foreign powers in certain areas of production in which the local elites seemed unable to generate either the capital or technology adequate to the task. This was particularly true in mining and the extraction of petroleum but it also occurred in some instances in the export of agricultural crops (bananas). This system developed different social and political effects from the one discussed above. The enclave economy tended to use much capital and little labor; profits were sent to the headquarters of enterprises located abroad, where decisions about new investment and expansion were made. Thus the effects of the enclave in promoting secondary growth throughout the rest of the nation were much weaker.

Having sketched the outlines of ''underdevelopment'' in the nineteenth century, Cardoso and Faletto turn to the period of transition—primarily the first three decades of the present century. ''In fact, the 'period of transition' refers to the historical and structural process by which the expansion of the exporting economy created the bases for the growth of the new social sectors loosely called 'middle''' (*Dependencia y Desarrollo en América Latina*, p. 55).

It has been emphasized in the standard economic histories that the great push towards the development of an internal market came from the world crisis of 1929 and from the interruption of world trade during World War II. Cardoso and Faletto do not minimize those basic economic crises, but their emphasis is upon the varied reactions to them, which they insist must be explained in terms of the relative strength of the political groups in each country that had emerged during their earlier history. Indeed, they feel that the crisis in the political systems of some of the countries began before 1929 as a consequence of the growth of new groups that were not part of the traditional oligarchies. The degree to which these new groups were absorbed into the power system influenced the forms of response to the world economic crisis that came later.

They develop this argument in two parts. The first concerns the transitional periods in those societies that to a considerable extent maintained control over their own productive facilities—the larger countries of Argentina, Brazil and Colombia, as well as Uruguay. The second covers the smaller countries that were enclave economies, such as those in Central America, with key activities owned and controlled from the outside.

Perhaps Argentina offers the clearest example of a country with a dynamic exporting class that was able to establish its hegemony over the whole society. The landowners who turned toward the export production of cereals and meat at the end of the nineteenth and in the early twentieth centuries were able to control the state. Their policies generated a large commercial sector to handle and export the produce, but also began to develop an urban middle and working class sufficient to provide a market for goods beyond mere subsistence. Indeed, the growth in agriculture, processing, transport and commerce was large enough to create a labor shortage, and massive immigration from Europe was actively stimulated. A relatively balanced growth produced modernity and prosperity, and under the leadership of the Radical party the new middle groups were absorbed into the ruling oligarchy. But the crisis of 1929 destroyed the balance and provoked a military coup by the most conservative elements that maintained power until the rise of Perón some 15 years later.

Brazil presents a more complex situation. The traditional local oligarchies were weakened in the nineteenth century by the growth of a legitimate central state under the leadership of the emperor, which brought with it a modest growth of an urban professional and middle class and was able to absorb some renovating liberal ideas from Europe and the United States. These ideas slowly undermined the ideology of the oligarchy and led to the peaceful abolition of slavery and indeed the monarchy itself by the end of the nineteenth century. During this period the large size of Brazil and its regional differentiation led to the development of both a sugar interest in the northeast and a coffee interest in the center, along with the slow growth of production for the internal market. During the 1920s there crystalized an increasing resentment against the landed elites—both plantation and hacienda—which was led by urban professional and military groups. There were several attempts at revolution in that decade, and they finally succeeded in 1930 when the system was faced with the collapse of the external market for coffee. The adroit new regime led by Getúlio Vargas created a compromise between the coffee and sugar intersts and the growing urban groups. The resulting policy gave impetus to industrial production for the internal market in order to maintain employment, as well as granting subsidies to the coffee planters. As the years went by the urban middle and working classes were increasingly brought into the system by a paternalistic populism. The state took a more active role in infrastructure investments and provided some protection to the urban workers through state-sponsored labor unions and social-security systems. While continuing to respect the regional interests of the various agricultural groups, the regime nevertheless gave urban groups a major voice in policy, and industrial production for local consumption boomed.

In Colombia the urban groups were never able to establish themselves with clarity. Various segments within the landed oligarchy fought each other but up until World War II there was no realignment of power sufficient to develop a major push towards internal development.

In all of these instances, a simple economic explanation does not go far enough. One must add a historical description of the actual efficiency of the various groups in coming forward with an appropriate ideology and in organizing their forces in the political realm sufficiently to guide policy in ways that took advantage of economic opportunities. When the major external economic forces changed—such as in 1929—the political response to that change was not automatic but was the outcome of organized struggles, and it varied from country to country. The policies taken as a result of those struggles determined the shape of the following period.

Let us turn to the enclave economies during the period of transition. There was quite a bit of variation from one country to another. In some countries the local producers were all marginal and there was no strong national sector producing for the external market other than the foreign enclave. Indeed, in the Central American countries the foreigners directly owned the land. Consequently, the important local power was essentially political rather than a combination of political and economic as in the case of the larger countries discussed previously. "In the structure of domination of the enclave situation it is possible to have economic exploitation by means of political relations; in this manner the local elites are linked to the foreign firms by acting as their political agents rather than as independent entrepreneurs. The foreign firms themselves establish direct economic relations with the working class and the peasants. The economic weakness of the local elites requires them to maintain good relations with the foreign firms in order to keep themselves in power, and that in turn depends on their ability to keep internal order and place at the disposal of the foreign firms the necessary labor force needed for economic exploitation" (p. 83). In these countries, the "banana republics," the middle class did not have much opportunity to grow. The crisis of 1929 hit these countries very severely and recuperation was slow. In several instances peasants were pushed below subsistence and revolted, but they were repressed by military force.

In other situations where the enclave was based on mining, as in Chile and Peru, a local bourgeoisie could slowly emerge through control of commerce and finance and in the development of more efficient means of exploiting the land. Under these circumstances a more complex internal division of labor developed, and the cities grew. The urban middle and working classes expanded and began to enter politics.

"The political alternatives for these new groups cover a wide spectrum of possibilities. One is the chance of joining some faction within the dominant sector as a means of entering into practical politics, as happened in Chile. Another is the attempt to mobilize peasants and workers in a revolutionary movement, as was tried by the APRA party in Peru. Or, as the limiting case, the landlords may break out of the old hacienda mold and develop a more dynamic capitalist agriculture, without promoting an urban-industrial economy. In this situation the peasants who are not incorporated in either the enclave or in the national-capitalist agriculture are pushed toward the margins of subsistence, and there is not much opportunity for a middle class or an urban working class to grow. This is the case in several Central American countries" (*Dependencia y Desarrollo en América Latina*, pp. 85-86).

In two countries, Mexico and Bolivia, the middle class was able to enter into active politics only by breaking the partnership between the traditional landed oligarchy and the mineral enclave through an alliance with the masses of peasants and workers. Once this process got started in Mexico it moved beyond the original goals of its first leader, Madero, and instead of merely opening politics to elections in which the urban middle class could participate, it led to the destruction of the hacienda class. But until the 1930s and the regime of Cárdenas, who turned to a new alliance with workers and peasants, the power of the enclave economy was not seriously hurt.

In Chile the state was controlled by alliances among local landed oligarchs and members of the commercial bourgeoisie engaged in foreign trade, acting in conjunction with the foreigners who ran the mines. The state was supported through taxes on the mining sector and it began to grow and eventually produced a middle class of bureaucrats and professionals associated with government activity, which gained some participation through the vote. "In the first phase of development, the middle class followed a policy that did not doubt the advantages of the economy of the enclave. Its main purpose was not to challenge the existing system by new forms of economic development that would be autonomous, but rather to invigorate the state and develop its services, which would expand the middle class itself" (p. 92). As the urban popular class began to enter the political game, they pushed for creation of a more autonomous economy that would eliminate the ups and downs in employment stemming from the cyclical export of minerals.

In the enclave countries there were only two situations that permitted partial development of the internal economy. In the first instance, as in Chile, the enclave was established after there already existed in the country a sufficiently strong financial-commercial sector and a sufficiently developed middle class to permit pressures to use the government and other local structures for economic expansion. In the second instance, as in Mexico, the middle class was able to take control of the state by revolutionary means and use it for economic expansion. "In both cases, the energizing of the internal economy began with the pressure of the middle classes allied with the local

industrialists and with sections of the working class and the peasants''
(*Dependencia y Desarrollo en América Latina*, p. 100).

In all the enclave countries, the world crisis of 1929 affected the enclave
more than the rest of the economy, and the decade of the 1930s was
characterized by considerable increase in social tensions and the spread of
strikes and radical political policies. In most of the countries the response of
the local powers to these growing popular demands was repression. Only in a
few were the bases sufficiently strong to permit more progressive groups to
gain control of the state and begin to use it to expand the economy in the
direction of the internal market.

Cardoso and Falleto use the previous analysis to explain the more recent
period since World War II when development moved towards the expansion
of the internal market. The style in which this was done varied from country
to country according to the type of social system that had emerged from the
long period of transition. During that period the division of labor increased in
all the countries and urban middle and working classes emerged. But their
relative strength was not everywhere the same, and the possibilities of
alliances between these new groups and the incipient national industrial
bourgeoisie varied. In some countries the urban masses had grown beyond
the ability of the industrial economy to provide adequate jobs. In some
countries the state was more developed in its administrative efficiency than
in others.

In no country was the industrial bourgeoisie able to take control and
develop the economy on its own. It always had to make alliances with other
groups in order to gain control of the state and use it to channel profits from
the export economy—whether agricultural or mineral, whether controlled
locally or externally—toward investments in new industries and infrastructure.

There were obvious conflicts of interest in all of these situations. If there
was a strong nationally owned export sector, it usually wished to keep
control of profits rather than have them redirected into new industries. The
masses often demanded immediate distribution through higher wages rather
than investments for future payoff. The middle class was often more interested in expanding government jobs than in creating industrial jobs for
workers.

In each instance various local groups had to be combined for political
action, and usually this was done under the ideology of a populist developmentalism with a strongly nationalist tone, for only through such a
mobilization could enough consensus be reached for an effective state
policy. There were three typical approaches: (1) liberal industrialization,

mainly directed by private entrepreneurs and requiring a strong preexisting local agricultural exporting group linked with the internal market through commerce and finance; (2) a national-populist form in which the industrial bourgeoisie was supported by the political power of sectors of the middle and working classes; (3) industrialization directed mainly by the state, which occurred when the local export sector was weak.

The case of Argentina is perhaps the clearest one of the development of a rather strong national bourgeoisie during the period of the export economy. Both the agricultural exporters and the commercial groups connected with them had developed early in the present century. Alongside of them began to grow an industrial sector. The cities expanded, and a portion of the middle class and the upper parts of the urban working class were incorporated into the electoral process. When the conditions following the world economic crisis of 1929, and later World War II, made it advantageous to expand industrial production for the internal market, these groups were able to take advantage of the new conditions. The growth of industry was for a time sufficient to absorb much of the new manpower that was moving toward the cities from the farms.

Eventually, however, the system began to be strained. The early and easy phase of import-substitution ran its course. The urban masses increased their pressure for higher wages and more political participation. For a brief period under Perón immediately following the war there was enough foreign exchange available for the system to meet most demands, and it was possible to have a populist policy that was not too threatening to the bourgeoisie. But this alliance was fragile; and when inflation and mass pressures ran up against inability to expand either the export market for agricultural goods or the internal market for industrial goods, the crisis became acute. Since the state had been functioning as an arbitrator between groups and as the agent of control over foreign exchange and imports, but not as a major direct participant in the economy itself, it was unable to move decisively to take over the role of the dynamic leader for further growth. The combination of free enterprise and populism proved short-lived.

The Brazilian situation was different. When the external market for coffee collapsed there did not exist in Brazil a large and strong industrial sector. Therefore it was up to the state to develop the first push towards the internal industrial market. This was done under Vargas in the 1930s, and at first it appeared to mean the exclusion, by the revolution that put him in power, of the coffee elite. But he compromised with them and supported coffee prices by government purchases. His policies used foreign-exchange controls to create a protected internal market that fostered local industries, and he greatly increased government investments. At first even the landlords were satisfied, since the rural masses were not included in the dominant political alliance and their interests were subordinated. Indeed, they paid the costs of the new development.

As time went on the easy phase of import-substitution was exhausted and the various groups in the alliance began to make new demands. The industrial bourgeoisie recognized the need for advanced technology and greater efficiency in production, and it turned more toward ties with foreign enterprises; as a result it became more hostile to state enterprises. The urban masses demanded higher wages, and the contradiction between consumption and investment became sharper. When Goulart attempted in the early 1960s to strengthen his power base by turning to the poorer sectors of the urban and rural masses, the alliance broke and he was removed by military force.

In Chile, we have the case of the enclave economy that faced a sharp crisis in 1929 when the export of saltpeter collapsed. The government began a more active policy through the control of foreign exchange to channel any export earnings that could be obtained into the growth of internal industry in order to provide jobs. This policy reached its peak in the late 1930s when an alliance between the middle class (mainly government employees) and the organized urban working class assumed power in "popular front." During World War II, and with the improvement in the export price of copper, the policy had a certain vigor. But in later years it was unable to expand either production or jobs at a sufficient pace to appease the urban masses, and runaway inflation was the result. The national bourgeoisie attempted to gain control under Alessandri but was unable to maintain an effective alliance with the masses through populist slogans. During all the postwar years various groups—national bourgeoisie, state employees, urban workers—increased their political organization, and open class conflict dominated the scene.

"If during the early period of the development of the internal market the impulse towards a policy of industrialization was sustained by a relatively stable balance between nationalism and populism, the period of diversification of the capitalist economy—based on the formation of a capital goods sector and the strengthening of the entrepreneurial groups—is symbolized by the crisis of populism" (*Dependencia y Desarrollo en América Latina*, p. 130).

When the terms of trade deteriorated in the late 1950s the fragility of the political alliances became clearer. The agricultural exporting groups were pinched by the fall in prices and were less willing to support any transfer of profits from their sector to that of industry. The demands for further capital investments using high-level technology in industry were so great that they produced rampant inflation and repeated foreign exchange crises. Simultaneously the urban masses were increasing their demands and getting more efficient in their methods of protest so that clashes between organized labor and industry became more acute. Both Argentina and Brazil went through similar crises and found themselves unable to maintain the pre-existing alliance that included so many sectors; they turned to military solutions. Only Mexico, with its strong postrevolutionary state, was able to continue developing; yet even that country came increasingly to depend upon foreign investments and loans to keep the system going, and internal tensions mounted as a result of inequity in the distribution of the new production. Mexico's growth was the most vigorous of all in the region, but not sufficient to absorb the marginal populations.

Cardoso and Faletto suggest that the present form of capitalism in Latin America, in terms of the current structure of political and economic forces in relation to the realities of the world market, faces a dead end. There appears to be no solution adequate to maintain the alliance between the modernizing industrial sector that demands increasing investments, the still powerful agricultural export sector that faces declining profits and the urban middle and popular sectors that demand increasing consumption—to say nothing of the vast mass of rural workers (many drifting toward the cities) who have so far been completely left out. The Latin American countries are unable to control the prices of their exports in the world market and they are unable to channel the various internal conflicts of power in ways that maintain reasonable stability under democratic institutions. So they increasingly turn to external capital for short-run solutions to their economic problems, and turn to the military for short-run solutions to their political problems.

This is not to say that there is an economic determinism that allows us to predict the course of history. But Cardoso and Faletto do maintain that a careful analysis of the structural conditions that emerged from the political residue of past history, plus the realities of the existing world economic markets and the world political situation, set clear limits on the possibilities of action. Under these present limits the maneuverability of any Latin American political system is narrow and the result is a permanent state of crisis.

The early development of industrialization was based primarily on local capital, both private and public, aided by protectionist tariff policies. Once the markets began to grow, outside capital found it profitable to invest, either to take part in the expansion of the markets or to compete with existing firms within them. In the early 1950s there was a flow of industrial capital towards Latin America. But this style of growth—presided over by Frondizi in Argentina, by Kubitschek in Brazil and by Alemán in Mexico—faces inherent limitations. The market it serves is a relatively small one, depending on the urban middle and upper working classes. Once this market is served through the easier import-substitution industries, the rate of growth tends to slow down. To keep it going requires moving toward capital-goods production, which in turn demands larger investments and more complex and imported machinery. Local firms join with international enterprises, and they use a technology that produces more goods with fewer men. In response the urban popular forces begin to pressure the government to take a more active role to create jobs and maintain wage levels. The previous alliances that made possible a combination of development and populism under nationalist slogans come apart. There are even conflicts of interest with the working class between those attached to the most modern and productive industries and those attached to the more traditional and less productive industries, just as there are conflicts of interest between the entrepreneurs in each of these sectors.

The relationship between the peripheral economies and the metropolitan centers changes drastically when one moves from an agro-exporting situation to an industrial situation designed to produce for internal markets. The new flow of international capital is in the hands of a small number of very large firms, and the external government debt of the peripheral nations grows rapidly, so the crucial decisions about economic growth tend to be concentrated more and more in the hands of foreigners. Under these particular conditions, the development of modern industry and the increasing complexity of the economy do not lead toward the autonomy that pure economic theory often predicts. These countries are not able to develop the internal social discipline, the restraint on consumption necessary to promote saving and investment, and the redefinition of national goals that are required to shift productive forces toward the new industries with some sense of national purpose and balance. Instead, the decisions about which industries may expand are made by the foreign firms, and the links between economic power and political power that ordinarily should unify a nation tend in this instance to weaken it.

"When it is not carried out under the control of the national society, this type of industrial revolution creates a new type of dependency. In the situations of underdevelopment described earlier the national state was able to control within its own frontiers a series of political instruments that could respond to the pressures of the external market (for example, a monetary policy or a defense of the level of employment), and thus to protect a part of national autonomy in basic decisions about investment and levels of consumption. But under the new type of development the control mechanisms of the national economy partially escape the internal political system" (*Dependencia y Desarrollo en América Latina*, pp. 149-50).

If this occurs in the context of the cold war, in which there are constant maneuvers in expectation of a World War III, then the local authoritarian groups become identified with the security interests of the Western bloc headed by the United States. The Brazilian regime of Castelo Branco is the clear example. When such an authoritarian solution appears, it is not so much the industrialists that trigger it but rather the members of the civil and military bureaucracies. The government is not just the expression of the class interests of the industrialists, since they are in fact unable to impose their view, given internal divisions and external linkages. "Currently the armed forces as a technical, bureaucratic corporate group take over the state in order to serve interests which they believe to be those of the total nation (*Dependencia y Desarrollo en América Latina*, p. 156).

"In consequence, the dominant themes of the present historical moment relative to development become: the formation of a supranational market that can resolve the problems of economy of scale and of the lack of market demand within societies in which participation in modern consumption is restricted; the authoritarian corporative reorganization of the political regime in search of stability within the context of mass societies but without offering full political participation to the popular masses; and the accumulation and increasing concentration of capital within a structure of unequal distribution of income" (*Dependencia y Desarrollo en América Latina*, p. 160).

Cardoso and Faletto offer the following concluding statement: "From a methodological point of view, the principal task of this book was to reconsider the problems of 'economic development' from a perspective that emphasized the political nature of the processes of economic transformation. At the same time it tried to demonstrate that reference to 'historical situations' in which economic transformations take place is essential for the understanding of such transformations as well as for the analysis of their structural limits and the conditions that make them possible . . . .

"The current conditon we call 'internationalization of the internal market'. It is no longer a question of the export interests subordinating those dealing with the internal market, nor of rural interests opposed to urban ones. On the contrary, the current situation of dependency is that in which the 'external interests' are placed more and more within the sector of production for the internal market (without abolishing, of course, the earlier forms of export production), and consequently they ally themselves with political interests based on the local urban populations. The formation of an industrial economy in the periphery of the international capitalist system currently minimizes the effects of exploitation of the colonialist type; it is now necessary to seek a consensus between foreign interests and a combination of national social groups linked to modern capitalist production: salaried work-ers, technicians, entrepreneurs, bureaucrats, etc. Thus, the great political themes of the preceding period of the early formation of the internal market—populism and nationalism—are losing impetus as a result of the new type of dependency.

"We know that the actual course of history, although marked by given conditions, depends in great part on the daring of those who propose to act in terms of historically viable goals. Therefore, we do not engage in the vain pretension of attempting to define theoretically the probable course of future events. The future will grow out of collective actions shaped by a political will that will bring into being a new reality which is today glimpsed only as a possibility" (*Dependencia y Desarrollo en América Latina*, pp. 161-66).

Cardoso and Faletto thus end their book with an activist plea for imagina-tive new political combinations that might break out of current contradic-tions. At the same time they warn both academic and revolutionary theorists against tight "models" that claim to explain the past and predict the future; those models too easily lead toward either fatalistic resignation that "noth-ing can be done," or naive optimism that history is preordained and radical triumph inevitable.

Cardoso has published a large number of articles in scholarly journals, but most are "occasional papers" prepared for international conferences and are reworked versions of his main books; thus, they need not be discussed here.[10] However, one of them is different because it shifts emphasis from the entrepreneurs to the workers; it was written jointly with Mexican sociologist José Luis Reyna and was published in English in 1968 as "Industrialization, Occupational Structure and Social Stratification in Latin America."

The paper uses comparative statistics to show the effects on the labor force of late industrialization under current dependency conditions, and then makes some deductions about the consequences for the system of social stratification.[11]

The first measure of the extent of change in recent decades in Latin America is the proportion of the population living in urban areas, defined as those in towns with more than 2,000 inhabitants: it increased for all of Latin America from 30 percent in 1925 to 46 percent in 1960. The biggest part of this new urban population has been employed in the "tertiary" or service sector, and not in the manufacturing sector as was the case in the countries that industrialized in the last century; modern technology produces more goods with fewer men. The basic facts are shown in Table 3, which demonstrates that although farming employment has decreased from 61 percent to 47 percent of the labor force, manufacturing employment has not

TABLE 3
Employment in Latin America, 1925 and 1960

	1925	1960
Farming	61.3	47.3
Mining	1.0	1.0
Manufacturing:		
Industrial	3.5	7.5
Artisan	10.2	6.8
Construction	1.6	4.9
Basic services	3.2	5.2
Trade and Finance	6.7	9.2
Government	2.2	3.7
Miscellaneous services	7.9	12.1
Unspecified activities	2.4	2.3
Total	100.0	100.0

Source: Cardoso and Reyna, 1968, p. 24.

changed at all, remaining at 14 percent. It should be noted, however, that within the manufacturing sector, artisan jobs have been steadily replaced by jobs in modern factories. Construction jobs have increased, but the bulk of the new urbanites has been absorbed in commerce and services. (Although government employment has grown, it has not expanded as much as some theorists imply when they talk of the bureaucracy as the sole base of the middle class.)

The countries of the region can be grouped into three categories: (1) those which industrialized first, namely Argentina, Chile and Uruguay—they have grown slowly in per capita manufacturing output in more recent years, approximately *doubling* the per capita product from 1930-60; (2) those countries which began to industrialize during the Great Depression, especially Brazil, Colombia and Mexico—they increased per capita industrial product from *three to four times* in the same three decades; (3) those smaller countries where industrialization has not even begun. It is not heartening to note that after the initial spurt occurred the rate of increase in manufacturing output has tended to slow down.

It is also disturbing to note that the later the industrialization begins, the less impact it has on the labor force. Argentina had absorbed 20 percent of its manpower in manufacturing by 1925; that figure grew by only one percentage point in the succeeding 35 years. Brazil increased its per capita manufacturing output by more than four times in the same period, but the proportion of the labor force working to produce that output increased only from 12 percent to 13 percent. Indeed, of all the major countries considered, only Mexico absorbed manpower in industry during this period, the proportion increasing from 11 percent to 17 percent.

It is interesting to compare this situation with that in the countries of early development. If we go back in time to the point where one-half the labor force was in agriculture (approximately the figure for Latin America today), we find that France (in 1886) had 29 percent employed in the secondary or manufacturing sector, and the United States (1880) had 25 percent—figures to be compared with Brazil's 13 percent or Mexico's 17 percent. In the nations of early development, the big growth of the tertiary sector came *after* a large proportion of the labor force had been absorbed into industry. In Latin America, it comes *before* the massive growth of industrial jobs—indeed, the latter never occurs at all.

As a proportion of *nonfarm* jobs, the industrial sector is losing ground in Latin America because of the shift from artisan to more efficient factory methods of production. From 1925 to 1960, it declined from 30 percent to 26 percent in Argentina, from 36 percent to 28 percent in Brazil, from 33 percent to 23 percent in Chile and even in Mexico it dropped from 36 percent to 30 percent. For all of the region it declined from 35 percent to 27 percent. Of course, the absolute number of men and women working in industry has gone up at the same time that the proportion has declined. By 1960, the majority of those working in industry in the larger countries were employed in big factories employing more than 100 workers. And within the industrial sector, between one-fourth and one-third of the workers were in fact white-collar employees. For the total labor force, the white-collar segment ranged from almost 40 percent in Argentina to 15 percent in Brazil.

Unemployment and underemployment is known to be widespread in Latin America, but has not been precisely defined or measured. It is particularly acute among the half of the population still engaged in agriculture, and among the 15 percent of the labor force classified as "miscellaneous services and unspecified activities," where some sample surveys place unemployment at 25 percent. These are the categories which include the bulk of the "marginal" population—those not benefiting from modernization of the economies.

How can these data be combined with other material to produce a portrait of the stratification system? One clear conclusion is that many authors use misleading stereotypes that do not take into account the complexity of the real situation. Cardoso and Reyna offer a more realistic assessment in these terms:

"The flexibility of the traditional leading classes operates in a framework of economic dynamism, as revealed by the data presented in this paper. This dynamism, which is not sufficient to incorporate the whole population into the expanding economic system, does, however, permit upward social mobility sufficient to force the traditional dominating classes to 'share command' with the new politically or economically powerful sectors (capitalist entrepreneurs of immigrant origin, technical or professional sectors—mainly the military—of the old or new middle classes, etc.); this dynamism seems capable of creating expectations, fulfilled up to a certain point, of upward social mobility among the popular classes'' (p. 48).

Studies of social mobility show that "structural mobility"—that produced by expansion of the upper segments of the job structure—is high in the big cities, but "replacement mobility"—caused by circulation of individuals within a theoretically fixed structure—is quite low. In other words, some people rise as a result of the new types of jobs; but those who were on top in the old structure stay on top in the new one.

"The information presented limits the validity of pessimistic interpretations, like those denying the evidence of the existing dynamism in the industrializing Latin American societies, as well as the validity of naive interpretations establishing an immediate link between the limited achievements of industrialization and economic development and the attainment of social development patterns characteristic of the 'mass industrial societies' . . . . Actually, it is within what is usually called the urban-modern sector that marginal groups have become established, unincorporated by the dynamics of economic expansion. On the other hand . . . the new social groups do not completely displace the traditional sectors, and these latter apparently are much more flexible than assumed in commonly held theories on oligarchies'' ("Industrialization," pp. 49-50).

The economically dynamic sectors produce a "policlassist" center capable of absorbing new groups and producing considerable mobility. But at the same time, those who move from declining rural zones to the expanding cities are split; while some enter modern jobs with high productivity and relatively good pay, others are pushed into the kinds of service jobs that have low productivity and exist mainly because unemployment exists.

The older theories of "dual society," which posited a traditional sector in agriculture and a modern sector in the cities with very weak links between them, will not serve. It is clear that the modern and dynamic policlassist center is producing several groups at once: a small, integrated industrial proletariat, a growing middle class, a new bourgeoisie—but at the same time, urban marginals and rural unemployed. The old and new elites blend rather than stand in sharp conflict, and the urban masses divide between those who wish to protect good jobs and those who seek them. This division inhibits the formation of a class-conscious and effective political force among either the workers or the middle class.

At the same time that he was working out the dependency theory with Faletto in the mid-1960s, Cardoso was supervising a field survey in Brazil and Argentina designed as a continuation of his earlier study of the Brazilian industrial bourgeoisie. But this time the focus was more concentrated: he wanted to discover how the dependency situation of a man's business affected his ideological perspective. The sample that is the core of the study consisted entirely of executives of firms that were locally controlled, although they had varying degrees of relationship with international enterprises in the form of credits, technological assistance contracts and so forth. There were 71 Argentinians and 100 Brazilians among the respondents, the latter group divided into two equal-sized segments of men from very large firms and men from medium-sized units. A standard questionnaire was used, but unfortunately some items were not repeated in both countries. The material was published in 1971 as *Ideologías de la Burguesía Industrial en Sociedades Dependientes (Argentina y Brasil)* [*Ideologies of the Industrial Bourgeoisie in Dependent Societies (Argentina and Brazil)*].

The book does not make a major new contribution to dependency theory but does add some specification regarding the political views of the executives of large enterprises. Particularly, the data trends cast doubt on the commonly held hypothesis that those executives are likely to provide important leadership that will help their nations break loose from the difficulties inherent in the current style of dependent industrialization. To do so, they would need a vision of national goals that would transform their own interests into a coalition of forces able to unite their countrymen to the point that effective policies for breaking bottlenecks would be adopted. They would have to support programs to enlarge local markets for industrial goods, which would require land reform and other means of redistribution of income, and they would have to generate projects for creating jobs for the marginally employed instead of just destroying jobs through ever-more efficient imported technology. Such measures would require vigorous use of the state to transform society and could only occur through open political conflict to impose new policies against the will of traditional interests.

But the responses of the industrialists in both Brazil and Argentina indicate a blurred view that vaguely assumes that what is good for industry is good for the nation; sharp conflicts of interests are not perceived. A little over half of the respondents, for example, deny that there is any basic split between industrial and agricultural goals; an even greater proportion (especially among the Brazilians who run the larger firms) deny that land reform would be an effective means of enlarging local markets. In fact, there seems to be no clear policy at all for accomplishing the latter goal. The managers appear more concerned with increasing the productivity of their factories than with selling their products.

Interestingly enough, the industrialists do not themselves feel as powerful as they often appear to be to their opponents. Only 10 percent of the Brazilian respondents say that the great industrialists are the most powerful single group in the country as of the mid-1960s, since most believe that the power lies in the hands of the military. Even in retrospect only 26 percent of the respondents put the industrialists in first place during the years of the Kubitschek regime, with half of them saying that the politicians were the ones who held the real power in those years.

Two-thirds of the Brazilians indicate that the long-run interests of industry will best be served by "the cohesion of the productive classes, including the landowners"—and they mean here the capitalists of the country. (A fifth of them believe that "strengthening the block of Western countries" is of greater importance.) The Argentinians are slightly less interested in alliances with the landowners and slightly more concerned about help from various other groups in society, including the organized workers. Indeed, they seem to have a view of society that is more sharply differentiated into various interest groups, and the more power they see in the hands of groups other than themselves the more willing they are to enter alliances to protect their position.

In order to make the analysis more precise, Cardoso developed an index for classifying the respondents with respect to their dependency situation, based on the amount of foreign connections their firms had. It should be remembered that *all* of these firms were 80 percent or more nationally owned, so the measure involves the less overt aspects of dependency such as use of foreign credits, licenses for technological processes and ownership of a minority of the stock shares by foreign interests. About half the firms did have international ties of one sort or another. The bigger the firm, the more likely the ties.

Noting that most of the industrialists preferred to avoid alliances with other sectors of society (particularly the workers), Cardoso sought to find the special characteristics of the minority who favored such alliances. He discovered that they tended to come from those enterprises that had the least connection with international firms. These more "independent" entrepreneurs were the ones most likely to be involved in "old-fashioned" production for the local mass market, namely food and clothing, and also most likely to hold "populist" views. By contrast, the leaders of the more dynamic and complex industries, which hold the key to the future, were precisely the ones least interested in internal political action to incorporate the urban workers and rural peasants into modern markets by sharing power with them. Instead, these entrepreneurs preferred to tie themselves ever more closely to international markets; they were the ones who took measures to increase exports and they were the ones who attempted to rationalize production through complex imported technology and efficient personnel methods, which means fewer workers per unit of output.

Cardoso admits that each group is responding to real, if short-run, interests, thus he is not saying that the industrialists have a view of politics that contradicts their own requirements. The older food and textile industries are precisely the ones that least need outside help and most need a local mass market. But the conclusion is a sad one for those who had hoped to see their society completely transformed through industrialization.

"Therefore, to the degree that the economic system becomes internationalized, it will produce a separation between political aspirations defined locally and economic actions defined in terms of the exterior. Furthermore, it will bring a growing sense of participation in the world economy, and a lessening sense of the significance of internal political participation in the form of conflicts and compromises between various social-class groups for the purpose of promoting political reform" ("Industrialization," p. 222).

I have been using the phrase *dependency theory* to describe Cardoso's work, but it is an imprecise expression. Actually, *dependency* is a perspective, a frame of reference, not a theory in the scientific sense of the term. It directs the attention of the analyst to certain aspects of an historical situation—the relation between the internal economic and political forces and the external powers that dominate the world economy—but it does not tell the analyst just what those relations will be. In other words, it tells him *how* to study history, but does not tell him specifically *what* he will find as he does so.

Cardoso believes that this general perspective is more useful for Latin America than the structural-functionalism that has been the predominating sociological approach until recent years. The latter assumes a natural equilibrating of forces; it suggests that when a new economic group, such as the local industrialists, begins to operate and expand it will automatically gain sufficient political power to protect its interests. It assumes that political mobilization will move apace with the emergence of the new urban masses, and that the polity will provide adequate mechanisms to absorb them into decision-making. In general, it assumes that economic changes are gradual and steady and that they, in turn, produce gradual and steady modernization of the social and political institutions. It assumes that small "dysfunctions" created by change will produce tensions leading to adjustments and new equilibria. Most of all, it assumes that the key "variables" interact in standard ways regardless of the historical context. These asumptions are reflected by methodological techniques that intercorrelate many indices of aspects of modernization to discover the ''normal'' patterns of congruence, placing countries of diverse background into the same matrix.

But the structural-functional approach has not been matched by real events. Old economic sectors retain political power long after their days of productive glory. New political groups emerge and occasionally, as in Cuba, seize power in order to drastically restructure the economy. The ''deviant'' instances are often better clues to real situations than the presumably ''normal'' or standard patterns that emerge from the computer.

An alternative to structural-functionalism that has gained strength in Latin America is a form of Marxism that uses ''imperialism'' as the central explanation of the trend of events. Cardoso emphasized in the interview that he elaborated the concept of dependency in part to combat oversimplified use of the concept of imperialism. ''When I wrote about dependency it was not supposed to be a substitute for imperialism, but an addition to it, since imperialism is used too much in the sense of external determinism. It is important to remember that there are historical options, alternative political possibilities inside a nation. Both concepts are more questions than theories; it is a misunderstanding in my view to think that you solve problems in terms of dependency. Each situation needs analysis. There are no contradictions between a class-oriented and a dependency-oriented analysis; we can use them both as flexible tools. We have to study the relations between the classes inside the country and between the classes in a world sense.''

Unfortunately, just as there are ''vulgar Marxists'' who degrade the original work of Marx by reducing it to mechanical slogans, there are beginning to be ''vulgar *dependentistas*'' who use the new ideas in unimaginative ways. There is particularly strong motivation to do so among those who use abstract theory to guide them toward ideological construction, that is, to generate ideas that can be transformed into slogans for political use. Indeed, for Latin Americans whose frustrations grow in precise ratio to the gap in development that separates them from the most advanced countries, there is a great temptation to focus blame on powerful outside forces and to attack those among their fellow countrymen who ally themselves with the outsiders in order to promote personal interests at the cost of national goals.

Cardoso is concerned about misuses of his scholarly writings. ''Of course, you cannot immediately derive political objectives from my work. Between a theoretical work and practical action one must fill in with ideology; I am not an ideologist and don't want to be one. When some people tell me, well, your idea influenced that political movement, I'm worried about it, because they may put any idea inside the *dependencia* framework; it is possible to use the word *dependence* as pure rhetoric. But the word doesn't explain anything at all, it only opens a way of getting at knowledge about the concrete facts . . . . I am not interested in a new pseudotheory or mythology, a new scholasticism. It only makes sense if you can combine theory, research, the historical moment, and practice—but it is hard to play that game, to move among the levels, and it takes flexibility, both intellectual and emotional.

"Maybe there are some contradictions in my work; it seems at some places that I'm pleading for national autonomy, but I'm also saying that the nation is losing importance. I'm trying to demonstrate that the trend in the structural situation of the world economy means that the least important frame of reference may be the nation. Yet how far can we go with the idea of dependency without the nation? What would that mean? It's an open question. But I don't want to pose false solutions."

I showed Cardoso the comment of Pablo González Casanova: "Many South American writers are now emphasizing the concept of dependency, which is interesting, but somewhat different from our line of thought. What you have to do is to seek ways of reaching independence, to look for processes of decolonization, techniques of augmenting national power and negotiating capacity. That is a less ascetic way of looking at it."

Cardoso replied, "There are two problems there. First, Pablo is discussing the vulgar notion of dependency, which is not mine. Second, he still believes in the national state, he is thinking of problems through the optic of the state. You know, all of us Latin American sociologists, intellectuals, we are elitist men, we belong to the elite. It's very difficult for us to think without using the state. Pablo is stressing the peculiarity of the Mexican way, in terms of its state. I'm trying to find some general patterns that transcend a particular country or its style of government; I am European in that sense. I believe in science as a general statement, as a general theory; I would like to explain the particular situations as linked to a more general pattern. In that sense, the Marxist influence is strong. I'm not thinking that the general patterns are the result of abstract models, no, but rather the result of concrete social movements. You can see in the social movements some general structures. To build science is to grasp those structures. But most of the Latin American sociologists are national thinkers, thus they are ideologists."

Cardoso went on to admit that his books do not contain a practical a guide for maximizing autonomy. He said that sometimes it was possible to use the state to overcome aspects of dependency and offered as an example the current programs of the governments associated together in the Grupo Andino, the Andean countries trying to form a common market with very strict rules governing the activities of foreign enterprises. But he suggested that in the long run the state is losing potency vis-à-vis the multinational corporations and that theories that see the state as the center of action may miss much of the basic trend. When I asked if this did not also imply that imperialism was changing, that Washington might well be losing its control over the multinational firms, he readily agreed and re-emphasized that the dependent countries must always analyze their own situations by studying what goes on at the center, in the metropolitan countries. He added:

"I'm more interested in the political problem than the economic one, although I recognize the connections between them. It is not just a question of reducing economic dependency; you can do that and still have different kinds of regimes, more or less democratic. One does not automatically lead to the other. I'm trying to think about ways of increasing participation by the masses, not just always thinking of different styles of elitist or statist solutions. Not just the participation of the industrial working class, because by itself that makes no sense in Latin America, but all the popular classes.

"The intellectuals in Latin America are important because they are the voices of those who cannot speak for themselves. The bureaucrats and politicians can speak for the state; we should try to take a wider view. Unfortunately, dependency theory is too often used as a guide for the state. It is not always used to think about making devleopment more equal, more free, in terms of the popular classes. That's just what has been missing in my work. I must consider the other side of the question, not the state, not the nation, but people. That's the reason we at CEBRAP are now studying poor people in Salvador, in cooperation with the University of Bahia, and also in São Paulo. We are studying their work, their community lives, how they are connected with one another. How do they get a job? What net of relations protects them against hunger? What are their spontaneous organizations? We want to understand spontaneous social movements at the bottom of the social structure. Maybe those views are influenced by the earlier Negro research. Then I learned that the church, the carnival, sports—those things are very important, much more than we imagine. Those are the ways people participate and socialize. Of course, we know that intellectually, but it's really difficult for people like us to understand all that. I don't want to write a book on the confrontation of the masses and the elites; no, something more objective. What are the real possibilities for change, seen from the point of view of the people without power? Organized strikes, wildcat strikes (Weffort is studying that); religion; football; riots—expressions by the people. You know, we liberals easily sign petitions, protest torture and so on, but we must learn to influence the regime from the bottom, not from the top."

The current research in Salvador is based on a combination of direct observation of spontaneous forms of social organization, especially among the poor, and a questionnaire interview with a random sample of over 1,000 people representing the total population of the city. Participating are sociologist Juarez Rubens Brandão Lopes, who has considerable experience studying the informal patterns of social life among industrial workers, economist Paul Singer and some younger sociologists at CEBRAP who have recently completed advanced training in the United States and are adept with the newer techniques of the social survey.

Cardoso recognizes that he is not skillful at multivariate statistical analysis based on carefully constructed measures of social dimensions, but tried it anyway in the comparative study of entrepreneurs in order to move closer to proof instead of just relying on historical insight. And he is hoping that the new field work will further advance the ability of the team to choose significant theoretical problems and then study them with the best available empirical tools.

Cardoso views the present state of sociology in Latin America (and political science, since he sees little distinction between them) in a "moderately optimistic" mood. Two forces came into contact in the past two decades and created the new sociology: a critique of structural-functionalism that is leading to a better theoretical perspective and the absorption of more precise techniques of empirical investigation. He said that the coming together of these forces has produced a particular shock at the international graduate school in sociology at FLACSO in Santiago, with the result that there is a lot of debate and considerable zigzag in styles.[12]

"In all of Latin American sociology the preoccupation with political problems is central, and of course the capacity to choose the key problems is the fundamental aspect of good sociology—not just its general quality or its technical capacity, but its ability to ask the right questions. And I think we are learning to do that. The experience of living in a society which is changing like ours pushes us to do that . . . .

"What I try to do is to illuminate with certain intellectual categories a particular historical situation. And I try to keep up with the newest techniques—I've done some game theory with the computer—but the available techniques are still weak. They are based on empirical generalizations, attempting to capture the constancies, the regularities of a situation, emphasizing the most stable aspects. One can in a given investigation develop instruments for detecting the current tensions and conflicts, the values of the actors. But there is no methodology for understanding the forces that are emerging, and yet change is always my main preoccupation, what in Hegelian-Marxist dialectic would be called the negation of the situation. For example, concerning dependency: what really interest me are the new forms of dependency—the emerging forces, the dialetic of what is developing against the current situation, hidden within it, like those forces that erupted when I was in France. If we understood them we might learn how to transform society without starting from the state; change from above has failed in Latin America, in the sense of absorbing the masses. All we can do is to participate, to get a lot of information, to develop some perception, some insight, but the insight by itself guarantees nothing. Lots of journalists have good intuitions, but cannot predict anything, or give a real explanation. To explain means to put the particular fact inside a larger pattern, to make comparisons.

"Now it seems to me that there is increasing awareness of this in Latin American sociology. We are no longer content with merely verbal explanations. We are trying to ask key questions and to collect precise facts. There has been a lot of data collection recently, some of it by agencies with responsibility for government planning, so we know much more about social conditions in different countries. There is more interest in the study of concrete situations. And at the theoretical level, there is more flexibility. In Brazil, for instance, it is clear that we are moving toward more theoretical freedom, whether it be structural-functionalist or Marxist; there is less dogmatism, more desire for information."

Cardoso's desire to move the focus of research away from a total concentration on the state and toward a study of social participation (which he called Maoist and I called Tocquevillian) appears to be influenced by a feeling that the military regime in Brazil is likely to be around for a long time, so that ways must be found to influence it rather than cling to a vain hope that it can be overthrown. This view parallels that of González Casanova who speaks of the need to democratize the regime in Mexico by working inside its own structures.

However, Cardoso does not agree with those who give encouragement to military regimes as the only ones in the Third World countries that are capable of furthering development. Indeed, he protests the official view of many governments (especially the one in Washington) that puts "development" ahead of "democracy" to the point of strengthening military regimes in order to provide the stability that is supposed to promote development. Unfortunately, one of the rationalizations for that policy is taken, perhaps vulgarly, from the structural-functionalist wing of sociology that predicts that industrialization, mobilization and participation will grow together, so development should enhance democracy. The Brazilian experience clearly contradicts that prediction. Some theorists take a further step and evolve complex models of different types of military and authoritarian regimes, implying that some are better than others, grading them according to the degree of national autonomy a regime seeks and its efficiency in promoting development.

In a recent paper called "Alternativas Políticas na América Latina" ("Political Alternatives in Latin America")[13] Cardoso denies that the new military regimes are essentially nationalist. "It seems to me that the predominant tendency in the key countries of the region—Argentina, Brazil and Mexico—is above all internationalist, although developmentalist." He says that despite nationalist slogans that are used for demogogic purposes, "the form adopted for economic development is, basically, that of closer association among three sectors: that directly controlled by the state (which is increasing its capability to intervene); the local capitalists; and the multinational corporations." In contrast to some observers who see these sectors as engaged in conflict, each seeking domination, Cardoso sees them as increasingly engaged in cooperation. The state acts neither as a neutral forum where competing interests seek influence nor as the agent of a single sector or class within the society; rather, it is a bureaucratic structure with a developmentalist ideology of its own (sometimes mixed with cold-war ideals of saving Western Christian civilization) that attempts to direct the whole process.

The unifying perspective shared by all three sectors is an elitist determination to control events. In contrast to the earlier national-populist regimes like that of Perón in Argentina or Vargas in Brazil, these new governments do not have leaders who seek to mobilize support from the urban masses. Even in Mexico, the most "revolutionary" of the examples, the president is chosen by the bureaucracy and is not supposed to develop a strong mass following of a personal type; the government strictly limits, by force if necessary, presssures from below for a more rapid distribution of the fruits of development among the workers, farmers and marginal poor. All of these regimes stress elitist control of mass appetites in order to encourage rapid capital accumulation, which is seen as the central requirement for development. The results bring high profits, expansion of firms through reinvestment of earnings and steady growth in the size and power of the efficient enterprises, whether they be owned by the state, by local capitalists or by the multinational corporations—or indeed, often by a combination of all three in the form of mixed firms.

Who benefits from this type of development? Under favorable circumstances, rapid growth as measured by the gross national product can be achieved by these bureaucratic regimes; Mexico has maintained it over a long period and Brazil is enjoying a boom at the moment. But income distribution gets more unequal through time and the benefits of development flow increasingly into the hands of the enterprises; their savings are protected, and as a result their power grows. Local firms and international ones both gain at the expense of the consumption of the masses. From this perspective, the slogans of the regimes are not very meaningful; the degree of nationalism that is stressed gives little clue to the shape of practical policies. Nor does the degree of "participation" in the electoral process; lots of people vote in Mexico, but they have little real choice of candidates or programs. What counts are the actual policies put into practice and their beneficiaries. Only in the Chile of Allende and the Cuba of Castro have redistributive policies been central to the development effort.

Thus many of the current issues debated in academic halls seem irrelevant. It does not appear to matter much whether the governing elite is "militaristic" or "civil-bureaucratic" or based on the "national bourgeoisie"; it does not appear to matter much whether politics are organized in a one-party or multiparty system; it does not appear to matter much whether the slogans stress a liberal free-enterprise or a statist public-enterprise economy; it does not seem to matter much whether populist or even revolutionary rhetoric is used during election campaigns. The central question concerns the participation of the masses, not just in the forms of politics but in the actual distribution of income, and that is determined by those who control big enterprises and therefore dominate the accumulation of capital.

Cardoso insists that we must move away from simplistic theories that imply an automatic equilibrium between politics and economics, without attention to the substantive realities. It is not true, as some on the Left assert, that capitalism automatically leads to exploitation and repression of the masses; but neither is it true, as some on the Right assert, that socialism automatically brings totalitarianism. There have been capitalist regimes ranging from one political extreme to the other, and socialism as well shows wide divergences in the amount of liberty and participation granted citizens. "It seems to me that the crucial question for the decade of the seventies is this: how to link the economic objectives of development with practical policies that are neither authoritarian nor totalitarian . . . . The decisive issue may be the attitude of the United States in terms of its ability to co-exist with both capitalist and noncapitalist patterns in Latin America without defining everything within the narrow framework of the cold war or the 'security of the hemisphere'. But it is also important for the Latin American politicians to re-elaborate democratic forms of accomodation for the anticapitalist protests that will arise from the masses during development, and not treat them all as problems of 'national security'." And finally, it is important for the Left to learn how to protest in ways that will bring a productive response from the regimes, rather than generate more repression, as violence tends to produce more violence.

In the abstract Cardoso would prefer socialism, since he believes that under current dependency conditions capitalism thrives on vast inequalities in the distribution of income, and indeed, may even require them to promote capital accumulation. But he is a realist, and sees few indications that in a country like Brazil there is much current chance to create socialism; in the interview he said:

"Of course we live in a society where there are aspirations for change, for modernism. The people are on the move. But they want to reach their objectives with a minimum of risk. When the state offers them protection under some form of populism, they accept it. They are not going to accept an adventurist line of the *guerrilla* type because they are going to die and they know it. But yes, they can accept more limited and practical objectives that have less risk . . . . To learn how to build real participation from the bottom in modern, bureaucratic society is a work that will take patience, maybe generations. You can't make a real transformation, Socialist or otherwise, just from above.

"What seems to me most important at this moment, in order to give the people a chance to participate in what is going on, is to guarantee that the flow of information be kept open. If not, our societies will become static; and in places just that is occurring, for there is less information and more coercion, and of course there's a relation between the two. I doubt that liberal democracy can function well in Brazil because the social classes do not have organizations to represent their interests, therefore a formal liberal democracy would not be a genuine opening to the people. That's why I have so much interest in studying just how the people actually live, how they relate to each other—whether in the church, the community, the factory, during strikes, during spontaneous movements for occupying land, even in the rural areas where things are changing very fast. I want to find out how to increase the opening for the people—*la apertura para el pueblo.*"

In evaluating the work of Fernando Henrique Cardoso, I would like to begin by offering an explanation for its widespread impact in Latin America. It seems to me there is a double reason, one strictly intellectual and the other connected with the political mood of the times.

The intellectual reason is that Cardoso offered an alternative just when abstract and formal theories were losing their luster because they did not seem to offer adequate explanations for Latin American conditions. After World War II, various long-range theories of development came to the forefront of social science. (Let it be remembered that for the previous decades cyclical theory was the central problem, as a response to the years of the Great Depression.) In economics, sociology and political science there was a rush to offer theoretical guidance to the Third World countries, stimulated by a combination of scientific interest and policy needs. Experts from Europe and the United States spread around the globe; the U.S. government began tentatively with technical assistance under Point Four and expanded into general programs of developmental aid culminating in the Alliance for Progress; the United Nations established special agencies for similar purposes. The practitioners needed theoretical guidelines; the professors needed to feel that they had something important to say.

Naturally, the initial phase involved the adaptation of the social science theory then in vogue in the advanced countries to the dilemmas of the backward countries. Each discipline used its own jargon and the international conferences on the theme heard learned papers on "the role of the entrepreneur," "international division of labor and comparative advantage," "industrialization and import-substitution," "urbanization and modernization" and so on. Many authors thought they were writing about general principles, universally applicable, but of course they were just making abstractions out of the concrete experience of the early-developed nations. Within sociology, the two dominant frameworks were structural-functionalism, epitomized in the work of Talcott Parsons and applied to the Third World by such men as Marion J. Levy, Bert F. Hoselitz and Wilbert E. Moore,[14] and a contrasting approach originating from Marxism and relying more on European than U.S. sources for inspiration. Both approaches forced the Latin American facts to fit into the standard theories, regardless of the distortions involved.

Latin American scholars responded at first either by becoming enthusiasts of one of the imported models or by nationalistically rejecting all ideas based on the experience of other countries in other epochs and instead seeking idiosyncratic concepts based on local reality. The next step was to seek a new synthesis that would take what seemed useful from older theories but make major adaptations to fit local experience. And the most significant fact about local experience that came increasingly to the forefront of discussion was the timing and the speed of Latin American industrialization: many countries of the region were attempting to accomplish in a very short time what had been a process spread out over decades or centuries in the countries that first industrialized, and they were doing it at a historical moment in which the existence of the advanced countries was the central condition that governed their choices. World markets for industrialized goods were already functioning and had barriers that made it difficult for newcomers to enter; the technology for industrial production already existed and was based on intensive capital investment to save manpower; the legal structure of enterprises was well established and gave them control over technology and capital flows. Yet the orthodox theories did not give much weight to these circumstances and seemed to suggest that Argentina, Brazil and Mexico could follow the same route to industrialization as did England, France and the United States. However, the Latin American scholars understood that their countries were facing situations that were new and possibly unique.

Germani dealt with this problem by emphasizing the speed and phasing of social change, pointing out the tensions and problems that arose when various aspects of modernization came together very quickly in unexpected sequences. He concentrated on the internal processes of change within a country, and although he recognized that the stimuli for various alterations in society were external in origin he was mainly interested in what happened when they were absorbed into the local scene.

In his most influential book González Casanova emphasized the peculiarities of the Mexican situation (his later work on exploitation, which has some striking parallels to the dependency perspective, has not yet had time to circulate much in Latin America). He dealt with its revolution, its progress toward a unique type of state-private capitalism, its proximity to the United States. His concept of internal colonialism was adopted by some as useful to other countries, but mainly those with large Indian populations.

Cardoso offered a reaction to the same basic problem of Latin America's situation that seemed more universal in form and more directly applicable to policy issues, and yet at the same time remained deeply rooted in local reality. The book on dependency (the one that earned him his international reputation) put the current behavior of industrialists and governments into a frame of reference that allowed comparisons with past epochs of the economic history of the region, and it allowed the observer to contrast the situation in one country with that in another. By spelling out the structural conditions, it seemed to make possible the use of some of the abstract theories about the development process in general that stemmed from the experience of the countries that had undergone the transformation in previous years. Most particularly, it clarified the crucial points of contact between the local scene and the international context. Thus, dependency theory looked like a way out of the intellectual dilemma—a theory that was rooted in the Latin American reality, yet one that used abstract concepts of wide applicability.

When these intellectual advantages were joined by a political one, its popularity was assured. The political point grew from the apparent economic stagnation of the early 1960s, which in Brazil and Argentina brought military regimes to power and in Mexico generated new questions about the viability of the system. The resulting pessimism created a political need to find a scapegoat, and the outside forces of imperialism were readily at hand. As the optimism of the early postwar years faded, so did theories of "take-off" that predicted continuing and automatic economic growth and social transformation once the initial difficulties were surmounted. Furthermore, ideas connected with liberal policies of international free trade and foreign investment came under growing suspicion; they sounded too much like propaganda for the ever-expanding multinational firms. Demands for local autonomy increased, but when it was noted that the new national industrialists themselves were turning towards international integration and that the governments maneuvered ever closer to Washington, the hope for autonomy was replaced by despair. Dependency theory was grasped as the weak man's answer to imperialism; it was imperialism as seen from the bottom looking up and suggested that if the process could be better understood it might be mastered. Therein lies the difficulty: when an intellectual theory satisfies political and emotional needs it is only too easy to substitute belief and conviction for analysis and inquiry. This is a problem not only for Latin Americans seeking more autonomy; it is shared by those of us in the United States who are opposed to the imperialist style of many of our government's policies and are seeking justifications for basic changes.

Cardoso tries to avoid the temptation of building elaborate theoretical schemes because he prefers to emphasize historical specificity. He uses abstract concepts, but mainly as tools to illuminate concrete reality by making a few careful comparisons. Then comes a problem. Cardoso occasionally finds himself pushed toward turning the perspective of dependency into a formal theory of dependency and then testing it with more precise empirical tools. He too is tempted by current modes of science-making. He started to "test" his theory in the volume that compares industrialists in Brazil with those in Argentina, and the result is not convincing. The book does inform us about the ideological positions of such men, but the opinion measurements are poor and the statistical manipulations are weak; indeed, there are very few differences among subgroups of respondents that are even statistically significant (Cardoso makes no such tests himself, but the reader's eye can make estimates), let alone of such magnitude as to lead toward "proof." The author argues theoretically about the supposed importance of patterns of small variations, but he does so with an apologetic tone. Yet the theory of dependency is especially appropriate to the study of elites, for they are the ones who must openly choose between various currents of political life and cast their lots with those that lead either to more dependency or more autonomy. Thus, if the theory can be used in logico-deductive fashion elites should make the easiest test, and the difficulties with that test are disturbing.

It is even more doubtful that the perspective of dependency can be turned into a general theory useful for studying all aspects of social life in the Third World, particularly at the level of concrete studies of the social organization of the masses, which now concerns Cardoso. True, the general framework of the lives of the masses is influenced by the dependency situation, both in the sense that the economies and polities of their nations respond to it and in the sense that some of the stimuli individual men receive from the mass media are reflections of it. But when one wishes to study something like the informal social organization of the people, then the dependency situation is only a distant part of the framework, and many other concepts of sociology are still relevant such as local patterns of stratification, interpersonal interaction networks, extended family structures, effects of migration from rural to urban zones, opportunities for upward social mobility, changing values and aspirations, emerging forms of class consciousness.

If the dependency perspective is to lead us further into research on the contemporary scene, I believe its direction should be toward case studies of specific political decisions, such as those which determine the levels of tariffs or exchange rates, the rules for foreign investments or the deals that bring outside military aid. We need analysis of the recent historical record to the point that reveals just which groups pressured in each direction, with what degree of success. But when it comes to studying "the opening for the people" in terms of the total fabric of mass social life, we should not rely too much on a perspective that comes from another set of problems.

I may here be arguing with some of his followers more than with Cardoso himself, for he retains a cautious flexibility of mind. Unfortunately, "dependency" is becoming a magic word in Latin America. Some beginners in social science who have not lived through the disillusionment of discovering the weaknesses in all social theory believe they have found the key to complete understanding. Those who generate social theory are burdened with a responsibility: one of the major criteria for the utility of theory is the ability to guide fruitfully the work of many others besides the originator of the theory. We are engaged in a collaborative enterprise. Cardoso himself is aware of the problems that stem from excess theoretical enthusiasm. "At certain times I may have tried to force empirical tests of general theory in the book on the Argentine and Brazilian entrepreneurs, but it is not my basic desire to formalize the theory. Indeed, in subsequent writings I have issued a polemic against formalization. I know that some younger scholars are attempting to turn the theory of dependency into a logico-deductive model in order to generate specific hypotheses for test. But that is not the procedure that I refer to when I insist on the necessity of linking theories with facts, because behind my thought stands the shadow of Marx. Or better, the force of Marx: the link between them is through practice."[15]

By practice, Cardoso does not necessarily mean the transformation of theory into ideology to shape direct political action. He recognizes the legitimacy of that function but feels that it should be carried out more by politicians than by academics. His own goal is to use theory to guide research and thought for the purpose of increasing our understanding of major social trends. Contemplation is part of the active life if it centers on crucial issues and succeeds in illuminating the fate of men.

NOTES

1. Florestan Fernandes's book on race relations in São Paulo was published as *A Integração do Negro na Sociedade de Classes* (1964), and appeared in English as *The Negro in Brazilian Society* (1969).

2. Currently publisher of the critical journal *Opinião*, for which Cardoso writes articles on current issues.

3. The Brazilian university system at that time followed the old French pattern. There were a limited number of "chairs" for full professors, which were obtained through open competitions. The candidate presented, besides his past record, a new work and was examined by a committee of experts. The chair gave lifetime tenure, and its occupant controlled the work of several younger assistants who did much of the teaching. There were two chairs in sociology at São Paulo.

4. "Introducción" to *América Latina* (1970); also in *Mudanças Sociais na América Latina* (1969).

5. Two books in English give alternative approaches to that of Cardoso but within the broad dependency framework; both authors were in Santiago in the middle 1960s: André Gunder Frank (1969) and Keith Griffin (1969). A general review of the literature on dependency is Susanne Bodenheimer (1970).

6. In fact, many of the basic ideas in the book were disseminated before its publication, because Cardoso was then teaching classes at the University of Chile and at the international graduate school in sociology that is part of FLACSO, the Facultad Latinoamericano de Ciencias Sociales, located in Santiago.

7. The material was published in 1971 in three languages; the Spanish title is *Ideologías de la Burguesía Industrial en Sociedades Dependientes (Ideologies of the Industrial Bourgeoisie in Dependent Societies)*.

8. The reader who is unfamiliar with the Brazilian scene in recent decades can find much help from two books of contemporary history: Skidmore (1967), which tells the story up to 1964, and Schneider (1971), which details the aftermath.

9. For a comparative study in Mexico, see Davis (1968).

10. Some of them are collected in Spanish in *Cuestiones de Sociología del Desarrollo de América Latina* (1968) and a larger number in Portuguese in *Mudanças Sociais na América Latina* (1969).

11. Another Brazilian sociologist has been writing on the same theme with important impact; see Gláucio A. Dillon Soares (1968).

12. The school has been a major training ground for younger sociologists from many Latin American countries. Its first director was the Swiss Peter Heintz; he was succeeded in the mid-1960s by the Brazilian Gláucio Ary Dillon Soares, who stressed the new empirical techniques; he in turn was succeeded by the Spanish-Paraguayan Luis Ramallo. The school was closed after the military coup in 1973. Cardoso taught at the school when he lived in Chile and returned to it from time to time after he returned to Brazil.

13. Published in *O Modelo Político Brasileiro* (1973). See also his "Associated-Dependent Development" (1973).

14. When I first began to study development, I attempted a summary of the current literature; in retrospect, it seems to capture the mood of that period: "Some Social Concomitants of Industrialization and Urbanization" (1959). Many examples of field studies in Latin America were collected in my reader, *La Industrialización en América Latina* (1965).

15. Cardoso: personal communication (1973).

Bibliography of Fernando Henrique Cardoso

Books

1960   *Côr e Mobilidade Social en Florianápolis*. With Octavio Ianni. São Paulo: Editôra Nacional.

1961   *Homen e Sociedade*. With Octavio Ianni. São Paulo: Editôra Nacional. A reader for students.

1962   *Capitalismo e Escravidão no Brasil Meridional*. São Paulo: Difusão Européia do Livro.

1964   *Empresário Industrial e Desenvolvimento Econômico no Brasil*. São Paulo: Difusão Européia do Livro.

1968   *Cuestiones de Sociología del Desarrollo de América Latina*. Santiago de Chile: Editorial Universitaria. A collection of his essays. Includes articles 21, 32, 33, 36, plus parts of *Empresário Industrial*, 1964.

    1969   French: *Sociologie du Développement en Amérique Latine*. Paris: Anthropos.

1969   *Mudanças Sociais na América Latina*. São Paulo: Difusão Européia do Livro. A collection of his essays. Includes articles 13, 18, 19, 21, 32, 33, 35, 36, 38, plus introduction (with Weffort) to *América Latina*, 1970.

1969   *Dependencia y Desarrollo en América Latina*. With Enzo Faletto. Mexico, D.F.: Siglo XXI. First circulated as a mimeographed document of ILPES, Santiago de Chile, 1967.

    1970   Portuguese: *Dependencia e Desenvolvimento na América Latina*. Rio de Janeiro: Zahar.

    1971   Italian: *Dipendenza e Sviloppo in America Latina*. Milan: Feltrinelli.

1970   *América Latina: Ensayos de Interpretación Sociológica-Política*. Edited with Francisco C. Weffort. Santiago de Chile: Editorial Universitaria. A reader.

1971   *Política e Desenvolvimento em Sociedades Dependentes*. Rio de Janeiro: Zahar.
1971   Spanish: *Ideología de la Burguesía Industrial en Sociedades Dependientes (Argentina y Brasil)*. Mexico, D.F.: Siglo XXI.
1971   French: *Politique et Développement dans les Sociétés Dépendantes*. Paris: Anthropos.
1973   *O Modelo Político Brasileiro*. São Paulo: Difusão Européia do Livro. A collection of his essays. Includes articles 40, 44, 45, 46, 48.
1973   *Estado y Sociedad en América Latina*. Buenos Aires: Nueva Visión.

Articles

1.   "O Estudo Sociológico das Relações entre Negros e Brancos no Brasil Meridional." With Renato Moreira and Octavio Ianni. *Anais da II Reunião Brasileira de Antropologia*. Bahia, 1957, pp. 88-98.
2.   "Desenvolvimento Econômico e Nacionalismo." *Revista Brasiliense* (São Paulo), no. 12 (July-August 1957), pp. 88-89.
3.   "O Café e a Industrialização." *Jornal do Comércio* (Rio de Janeiro), 19 January 1958, p. 5.
1960   *Revista de História* (São Paulo), (commemorative supplement on coffee).
4.   "Educação e Desenvolvimento Econômico." *Revista Brasiliense* 17 (May-June 1958): 70-81.
5.   "A Estrutura da Indústria de São Paulo." *Diário de São Paulo*, 30 April 1959.
6.   "Estabilidade no Emprêgo." *Arquivos do Instituto de Direito Social* 13, no. 3 (December 1959): 23-28.
7.   "Polarização dos Interêsses de Patrões e Operários numa Indústria Paulistana." *Ciência e Cultura* (São Paulo) 10, no. 4 (December 1958): 213-14.
8.   "O Negro e a Expansão Portuguêsa no Brasil Meridional." *Anhembi* (São Paulo) 32 (year 8), no. 94 (September 1958): 16-21.
9.   "As Exigências Educacionais do Processo de Industrialização." With Octavio Ianni. *Revista Brasiliense*, no. 26 (November- December 1959).
10.   "Condiciones y Efectos de la Industrialización en São Paulo." With Octavio Ianni. *Ciencias Políticas y Sociales* (Mexico, D.F.) 5, no. 18 (October-December 1959): 577-84.
11.   "Proletariado e Mudança Social." *Sociologia* 22, no. 1 (March 1960): 3-12.
12.   "Educação para o Desenvolvimento." *Anhembi* 39 (year 10), no. 115 (June 1960): 35-43.
13.   "As Condições Sociais da Industrialização de São Paulo." *Revista Brasiliense*, no. 28 (March-April 1960), pp. 31-46.
14.   "Atitudes e Expectativas Desfavoráveis à Mudança Social." *Boletim do Centro Latinoamericano de Pesquisas em Ciências Sociais*, 3, no. 3 (August 1960): 15-22.

15.   "Os Brancos e a Ascensão Social dos Negros em Pôrto Alegre." *Anhembi* 39 (year 10), no. 117 (August 1960): 583-96.

16.   "Roteiro para a Defesa da Escola Pública." In *Diretrizes e Bases da Educação*. Edited by Roque Spencer Maciel de Barros. 1960, pp. 446-55.

17.   "Condições e Fatôres Sociais da Industrialização de São Paulo." *Revista Brasileira de Estudos Políticos* (Belo Horizonte), no. 11 (June 1961), pp. 148-63.

18.   "Le Prolétariat Brésilien: Situation et Comportement Social." *Sociologie du Travail* (Paris) 3, no. 4 (1961): 50-65.

19.   "As Tensões Sociais no Campo e a Reforma Agrária." *Revista Brasileira de Estudos Políticos*, no. 12 (October 1961), pp. 7-26.

20.   "O Método Dialético na Análise Sociológica." *Revista Brasileira de Ciências Sociais* 2, no. 1 (March 1962): 85-106.

21.   "Industrialização e Sociedade de Massas." *Sociologia* 26, no. 2 (1964).

22.   "Educação e Mudança Social." *Pesquisa e Planejamento* (São Paulo), no. 5 (June 1962), pp. 55-65.

23.   "Criação da Universidade de Brasília." *Universidade de Brasília* (1962), pp. 63-66.

24.   "Le Brésil Contemporain: Analyse Socio-Politique." Louvain (Belgium): Université de Louvain, Institut d'Etude des Pays en Développement, February 1963. Mimeographed.

25.   "El Empresario Industrial en América Latina." Santiago de Chile: CEPAL, 1963.

26.   "Le Préjugé de Couleur dans le Brésil." *Présence Africaine* (Paris), no. 53 (1965).

27.   "Unidades e Dispersão: Santa Catarina e Rio Grande do Sul." In *História do Brasil*. Edited by Sérgio Buarque de Holanda.

28.   "Das Hautfarbevorurteil in Brasilien." *Staden-Jahrbuch* (São Paulo) 11-12 (1963-64).

29.   "The Structure and Evolution of Industry in São Paulo: 1930-1960." *Studies in Comparative International Development* 1, no. 5 (1965): 43-47.

30.   "El Proceso de Desarrollo en América Latina: Hipótesis para una Interpretación Sociológica." Santiago de Chile: ILPES, November 1965.

31.   "Children and Youth in National Development in Latin America." Santiago de Chile: UNICEF, December 1965.

32.   "The Entrepreneurial Elites of Latin America." *Studies in Comparative International Development* 2, no. 10 (1966): 147-59.

33.   "Industrialization, Occupational Structure and Social Stratification in Latin America." With José Luis Reyna. In *Constructive Change in Latin America*. Edited by Cole Blasier. Pittsburgh, Pa.: Pittsburgh University Press, 1968.

        1967   DADOS (Rio de Janeiro).

34.   "Directrices para un Programa de Trabajo entre Economistas y Sociólogos." *Economía y Administración* (Concepción, Chile) 2 (year 2), no. 5 (1966).

35. "The Industrial Elite." In *Elites in Latin America*. Edited by S.M. Lipset and A. Solari. New York: Oxford University Press, 1967, pp. 94-114. 1967 Buenos Aires: Paidós.

36. "Los Angentes Sociales de Cambio y Conservación en América Latina." Santiago de Chile: ILPES, August 1967.
   1969   *L'Amérique Latine par Elle-Même*, Christianisme Social (Paris), 1969, pp. 25-54.

37. "Des Elites: Les Entrepreneurs d'Amérique Latine." *Sociologie du Travail* (Paris), no. 3 (July-September 1967).
   1968   *Pensamiento Crítico* (Havana).

38. "Hégémonie Bourgeoise et Indépendance Economique." *Les Temps Modernes* (Paris), no. 257 (October 1967).
   1968   *Brasil Hoy*. Mexico, D.F.: Siglo XXI.
   1968   *Desarrollo Económico* (Buenos Aires) 8, no. 29 (April-June).
   1968   *Brasil nos Tempos Modernos*. Rio de Janeiro: Paz em Terra.

39. "Structural and Institutional Impediments to Development." Stockholm: United Nations Expert Group Meeting on Social Policy and Planning, September 1969. Mimeographed.

40. "Aspectos Políticos do Planejamento." In *O Planejamento no Brasil*. Edited by Betty Mindlin. São Paulo: Perspectiva, 1970.

41. "Participación Social y Desarrollo: La Clase Obrera y los Grupos Marginales." *Boletín ELAS* (Santiago de Chile) 4, no. 6 (December 1970).

42. "Les Obstacles Structurels et Institutionnels au Développement." *Sociologie et Sociétés* (Montreal) 2, no. 2 (November 1970).

43. "Dependência, Desenvolvimento e Ideologia." *Revista de Administração de Emprêsas* (Rio de Janeiro) 10, no. 4 (December 1970).

44. "Industrialización, Dependencia y Poder en América Latina." *Revista Paraguaya de Sociología* 7, no. 19 (September-December 1970).

45. "Teoria da Dependência ou Análises Concretas de Situações de Dependência?" In *Estudos I*. São Paulo: CEBRAP, 1971.

46. "Comentário sôbre os Conceitos de Superpopulação Relativa e Marginalidade." In *Estudos I*. São Paulo: CEBRAP, 1971.

47. "Considerações sôbre o Desenvolvimento de São Paulo: Cultura e Participação." With Candido Procópio Ferreira de Camargo and Lucio Kowarick. In *Recursos Humanos da Grande São Paulo*. São Paulo: GEGRAN, 1971.

48. "Imperialismo y Dependencia." *Sociedad y Desarrollo* (Santiago) 1, no 2 (1972).

49. "Notas sobre el Estado Actual de los Estudios sobre Dependencia." *Revista Latinoamericana de Ciencias Sociales* (Santiago de Chile) 4 (1972).

50. "Associated-Dependent Development: Theoretical and Practical Implications." In *Authoritarian Brazil*. Edited by Alfred Stepan. New Haven, Conn.: Yale University Press, 1973, pp. 142-78.

Other References

1970   Bodenheimer, Suzanne J. "Dependency and Imperialism." *NACLA Newsletter* 4 (May-June).
        1971   Reprinted in *Readings in U.S. Imperialism*. Edited by K.T. Fann and Donald Hodges. Boston: Porter Sargent.
        Edited by K.T. Fann and Donald Hodges. Boston: Porter Sargent, 1971.

1968   Davis, Stanley M. "Entrepreneurial Succession." *Administrative Science Quarterly* 13 (December): 402-416.

1964   Fernandes, Florestan. *A Integração de Negro na Sociedade de Classes*. São Paulo: Faculdade de Filosofia, Ciências e Letras.
        1969   Reprinted as *The Negro in Brazilian Society*. New York: Columbia University Press.

1969   Frank, André Gunder. *Capitalism and Underdevelopment in Latin America*. Revised edition. New York: Monthly Review Press.

1959   Furtado, Celso. *Formação Econômica do Brasil*. Rio de Janeiro: Fundo de Cultura.
        1963   Reprinted as *The Economic Growth of Brazil*. Berkeley, Calif.: University of California Press.

1969   Griffin, Keith. *Underdevelopment in Spanish America*. London: Allen and Unwin.

1962   Jaguaribe, Hélio. *Desenvolvimento Econômico e Desenvolvimento Político*. Rio de Janeiro: Fundo de Cultura.
        1968   Revised as *Economic and Political Development: A Theoretical Approach and a Brazilian Case Study*. Cambridge, Mass.: Harvard University Press.

1959   Kahl, Joseph A. "Some Social Concomitants of Industrialization and Urbanization." *Human Organization* 18 (Summer): 53-74.

1965   ——. *La Industrialización en América Latina*. México, D.F.: Fondo de Cultura Económica.

1971   Schneider, Ronald M. *The Political System of Brasil: Emergence of a Modernizing Authoritarian Regime, 1964-1970*. New York: Columbia University Press.

1967   Skidmore, Thomas E. *Politics in Brazil, 1930-64*. New York: Oxford University Press.

1968   Soares, Gláucio A. Dillon. "The New Industrialization and the Brazilian Political System." In *Latin America: Reform or Revolution?* Edited by James Petras and Maurice Zeitlin. Greenwich, Conn.: Fawcett.

5

Conclusion

When reading or listening to the words of Gino Germani, Pablo González Casanova or Fernando Henrique Cardoso, I am constantly reminded of one simple fact that sets them apart from most North American social scientists: the Latin Americans start from their particular national or regional situation and then borrow or develop theoretical tools to help them understand that situation, whereas most North Americans reverse the procedure and start with theoretical models and then look for examples to illustrate or test them. Therefore, when the North American scholars began to be interested in the Third World, they established as the highest academic goal the creation of a general theory of development, and most participants have become identified with one or another approach to such a theory. For example, economists are divided between "monetarists" and "structuralists," and sociologists between those who stress the role of individual creativity and entrepreneurship (via the Protestant ethic or perhaps need achievement), and those who seek explanations in terms of more general processes such as technological advance, urbanization, social differentiation, cultural diffusion and the demonstration effect. The commitment to the theoretical model tends to come first, and the search for "appropriate" field sites to test it or modify it comes later. Indeed, the highest academic prestige goes not to the person who applies theoretical perspectives to historical description in order to produce the most convincing portrait of the growth of a single society, but rather to the person whose theoretical and methodological sophistication allows him to make wide-ranging generalizations that cover many societies. The first is put down as "an area specialist," while the second is raised up as a "true scientist."

At the moment, many members of the avant garde in the United States who study development meticulously define a half-dozen or more separate numerical indicators connected with their favorite abstract model, and then collect information from dozens of countries on each one. The style demands that each indicator be "culture free," that is, abstracted from local idiosyncracies so that it will presumably measure the same "thing" in all countries. Only then can the indicators be combined and manipulated in the computer to produce mathematically stated "laws" of development. The more complex the computer operation, the more valued is the result. Once published, the "law" becomes a challenge to the next investigator to show that certain deficiencies in measurement or in statistical treatment weaken its power, and so a new research is proposed to overcome the problems. This endless process produces many generalizations, sometimes with increased refinement, but they are so limited in application that they offer little understanding of what is going on in any given Third World country and even less guidance for the making of practical decisions. As a secular form of theological disputation for professors in rich countries, the exercise causes no great harm and fills the lives of its practitioners with intellectual satisfaction; as a guide to the perplexed in the Third World it becomes increasingly "academic" in the pejorative sense of being irrelevant.

The contrasting approach of the scholars considered in this book is to attempt to define crucial problems for study in terms of the most important practical issues their societies face. For them, development is not just a question of intellectual disputation, but also a matter of national survival. They recognize that practical problems cannot be understood and solved solely by looking at their surface manifestations, and that policy debates in the newspapers or the corridors of government palaces are concerned with momentary aspects of the situation rather than underlying trends. So they take the issues that are currently being debated and seek intellectual frameworks for their study and comprehension that will dig beneath the surface and reveal basic trends.

However, the very selection of topics for study has an ideological and theoretical bias. Although these scholars are more concerned with an exploration of national reality than they are in testing academic theories of development, they nevertheless cannot escape certain theoretical choices that guide their research. Indeed, the synthesis that dominates their conclusions is to some degreee implicit or inherent in the way they formulate the issues for study in the first place, and that is true of all social scientists. For example, the economists who shaped the study of development in the decades of the fifties and sixties at ECLA in Santiago tended to look at it as a continuous process, even though one that might for convenience be divided into recognizable stages. It was taken for granted that a steady accumulation of capital, the improvement of technology, the expansion of industry, the increase in autonomy of national economies, the growth of cities, the bureaucratization of many aspects of social organization, the spread of the electoral franchise and an increase in national integration were all parts of the same on-going process. Academics at the time wrote of the correlations between economic development, social development and political development as measured by indicators of the trends listed in the previous sentence. Some form of traditionalism based on landowning oligarchies was the beginning of the transformation, and some form of participatory democracy and welfare capitalism was the conclusion of the transformation. The only other path toward economic development that was recognized was a Socialist trajectory, which might bring advance in gross national product but was presumed to bring totalitarian rule along with it and thus was not viable in the Americas. Germani accepted most of this dominant perspective, and studied details of the social transformation within the given larger pattern.

González Casanova and Cardoso had serious doubts not just about the details but about the pattern itself, doubts that emerged both from observations of their own countries and from the influences of Marxist theory. They noted that development could proceed for a while along the path just outlined and then run into "contradictions" that blocked it. The local political power of the landed oligarchs might not decline at the same rate as the economic strength of the new industrialists increased. The new industries in turn might be dominated by foreigners and thus not provide an adequate base for national integration. The spread of the rewards of the new economy might be limited by old social structures, national and international, and thus inhibit both the prosperity and the social and political participation of major sectors of the population. As a result of these problems, crises might arise that could not be handled by "normal" political channels and would lead to military solutions. In the place of an inexorable march toward modernity, there might occur conflicts that would destroy the neat correlations among aspects of development. Instead of thinking of those conflicts as aberrations or deviations from the model resulting from inadequate and irrational policies that could be improved under the guidance of an enlightened social science, they saw the conflicts as inherent in the special kind of development that was occurring in Latin America.

This split in perspective is too basic to be resolved by any of the techniques of contemporary social science; it goes far beyond the question of testing academic theories through the application of appropriate measurements. People who read the same books of contemporary history respond to them in opposite ways, depending upon their foci of attention, and those who predict the next phase of history expect different outcomes. Consequently the particular research problems chosen for study reflect overall perspectives that are imposed upon, not natural to, the social situation that is the object of investigation. Once the perspective has been chosen, detailed research that is disciplined, "objective," "scientific," even relatively "value free," can be executed, but that does not negate the necessity of making an original choice of viewpoint.

The great power of the sociological tradition resides less in its ability to resolve technical problems of research (although that ability is steadily improving), than in its ability to enlighten men about the overall perspectives they are using in half-conscious ways. That enlightenment comes from contrast, from the recognition of alternative modes of organizing society or alternative modes of explaining society. Thus the contrasts among our three authors are as revealing as their similarities. Many particular themes they study and many techniques they use to collect and analyze data are indeed similar, and many sources of their thought are also the same. But their outlooks on the trajectory of history are contrasting.

The selection of specific problems for study, guided by a theoretical framework that focuses attention on crucial historical trends, leads toward a synthesis of each nation's reality. Its purpose, according to these scholars, is to produce an approximation to total understanding that will be sufficiently powerful to enlighten the citizen about the key features of his social situation and lead him toward more intelligent actions for improvement. That purpose is often expressed in the phrase "the test of theory is praxis," as contrasted to the approach that builds "science" for its own sake. If the researcher is a democrat at heart, the ultimate consumers for his work are not other academics who read technical journals or bureaucrats who seek to maximize the "cost-effectiveness" of a specific government program, but rather groups of citizens who wish to participate more effectively in the exercise of political power. Thus the final report on the research is most likely to be a book addressed to a wide audience using theories and measurements to explain social life for the purpose of guiding action to improve it.

This emphasis on action should not distract attention from the fact that all three men considered here think of themselves as social scientists and not as ideologists or politicians. They follow a style that all the earlier masters of social science took for granted, from Smith and Malthus, through Tocqueville and Marx, to Weber and Durkheim. All of those authors were concerned with the great issues of the times in which they lived such as social integration, change, power and justice, and they addressed themselves to general audiences. Only more recently have the social sciences in the United States become more technical, more narrowly academic, more intent on imitating the natural sciences and consequently more isolated from the general public.[1] Although they address a wide public, these Latin Americans distinguish their work from ideology on several grounds: they do not attempt to enhance the program of any organized party or faction; they do not use a style of rhetoric that deliberately aims to convince rather than enlighten; once the problems for study are chosen, they attempt to follow methods of observation and analysis that are as "objective" as possible; their final product is a synthesis of various aspects of the situation that is more general and long range in view than the discussion of a particular political issue being publicly debated at a given moment.

Within these broad frameworks of both similarity and difference, all three authors have had to face certain technical issues in social science: (1) the role of general theory versus historical specificity; (2) the proper uses of empirical, especially statistical, data; (3) the contrast between the specialization of the disciplines and the integration of the real social world. These are hoary issues and I do not wish to attempt here a thorough discussion of them, but only desire to present a brief evaluation of the positions of the three authors under consideration.

All three men seek a theoretical base that is abstract and general enough to place the specific situations they study in a wider framework for purposes of comparisons. Thus Germani writes of the modernization process, González Casanova stresses structures of internal colonialism and exploitation and Cardoso is concerned with situations of dependency. Yet all three are students of history and do not wish to lose sight of the specific context within which those more general processes or situations occur. They continually struggle with the problem of the relationships between general concepts and concrete situations. At times they swing in one direction and work out some of the logical implications of concepts that indicate similarities of structure or process in divergent situations, and at times they swing in the other direction and emphasize the particularities of time and place, the sequential and limited facts of real history that create uniqueness.

Among the three, Germani is most likely to emphasize the generalities, González Casanova and Cardoso the specifics, yet all three attempt some combination of both perspectives. Germani handles the problem by specifying stages of history (within one region of the world) that offer sufficient internal homogeneity to permit useful comparisons. He then applies to countries within those stages certain concepts about the change processes that originated in other historical situations, but emphasizes that the outcomes will be somewhat different precisely because the situations are different. For example, mobilization and participation are general processes, but they work themselves out differently in the countries coming late to modernization as compared to those that arrived early, partly because the former can imitate the latter. He tends to use historical fact to limit and modify the workings of general processes of change. He does not seek new concepts that are rooted in historical differences, but rather tries to explain those differences as specific modifications of more general trends. The effect of his approach is to emphasize the general over the particular.

González Casanova and Cardoso are more likely to stress concepts that define the historical situation as having key features that make it different from others. For them the central dynamic of history may well stem from that difference, rather than from other aspects of the situation that show similarities. They too write of historical stages, but the stages are described in ways that highlight divergences rather than parallels. For example, a country in Latin America that was established with an enclave economy controlled by foreigners based on the export of a single mineral product will not enter the modern stage of industrialization in the same way as a country that began with a diversified agricultural export trade controlled by local elites. Of course, there will be some similarities as per capita income goes up and standardized technology is imported, but the social structures absorbing these new developments will be different. The theme of their writing is to describe a limited number of alternative types of adaptation to industrialization (late versus early entrants, peripheral versus central powers, mineral versus agricultural exporters, etc.) and then highlight the features of each type that separate it from the others. Thus, they emphasize the similarities within types that make meaningful comparisons possible and the divergences among types that make universal laws impossible.

These alternatives in emphasis on how history should be combined with theory are related to differences in the uses of statistics. Germani seeks the pattern of correlation among indicators of modernization that applies all over Latin America, indicating that the differences occurring among nations are confined to the level of the indicators and not to the pattern of relationship. He describes the level that currently defines the most advanced stage and implies that other nations will approach it in time. The general pattern is shown by large correlations among the key indicators: the percentages of the population living in big cities, graduating from secondary schools, holding white-collar jobs and voting in elections. He ranks the countries according to their degree of modernization and finds that a given stage of modernization produces similar ranks on all of the indicators. This correlational approach to statistics is closely linked to a *functionalist* theoretical model, since it measures the "goodness of fit" of the data to such a model in terms of steady historical evolution.

Germani follows a parallel path when doing internal studies in Argentina.

He seeks to depict degrees of integration into the urban scene and suggests that there is a continuous process of adaptation that makes migrants come to resemble old-timers, leading them all toward a new style of integration of work, family, group participation and general values that produces modern men, differentiated in some ways by social strata but all sharing full citizenship. Many aspects of this process can be quantified in indicators of demographic behavior, voting choices and subjective attitudes and opinions. The data from the census and from sample surveys provide the numerical details.

González Casanova speaks of his "obsession" to use the newer statistical methods in conjunction with forms of dialectic theory. In *Democracy in Mexico* the tables of data were used in descriptive ways to indicate the degree of concentration of wealth in the country, the continuing existence of marginality and the extent of foreign penetration. But each indicator was treated separately and there was little attempt to measure correlations. The data served as illustrations, as support for the theoretical argument, not as "tests" of specific propositions stemming from that argument. In his more recent work there are three other uses of statistics: the sample survey of stratification in Mexico City, the search for factor-analytic patterns to measure regional differentiation and exploitation within Mexico and the creation of statistical time series for Latin American comparative history. The first two are close to publication, the third is just beginning. None are available for comment here.

Cardoso has mainly used historical and ethnographic methods with a minimum of statistical data. He made one attempt to use a questionnaire for the study of Brazilian and Argentine entrepreneurs, aimed at a test of theoretical propositions about the degree of relationship between a firm's dependence on foreign financial interests and the political attitudes of its executives, but the results were meager. He is currently engaged in research in the state of Bahia that includes rather extensive use of opinion surveys. In principle he seeks to integrate numerical data with theoretical ideas, but has not yet offered many examples that can serve as models.

When they use numbers, these authors have been closer to descriptive statistics than to experimental statistics. That is, they collect data that help portray a given situation by improving our level of detailed knowledge of the distribution of certain indicators among a specified population. This is an extremely useful exercise, and I do not use the word "descriptive" in a pejorative sense (the way many professors do in doctoral examinations when they refer to a student's dissertation as "mere description" or "just journalism"). I believe that careful description is one of the most powerful tools of modern sociology, for it dispels the "common-sense" myths about reality that so often distort understanding and decision. It can be ethnographic depiction of the inside view of the life of some subcommunity of people—be they Indians in the jungle or residents of urban slums—who appear exotic to outsiders who fail to grasp their full humanity. It can be statistical description of the unequal distribution of wealth and income, which shows how narrowly the benefits of industrialization are shared. There are varieties of form, but good description is a weapon against ignorance, ethnocentric distortion and inhumanity of view.

The uses of statistics to describe reality, however, are not identical with the uses of statistics to test theory. Descriptive statistics can give some support to theory in the same way that historical examples can illustrate general trends and help convince the reader that the author's view of the direction of those trends is a reasonable one. But the full test of theory should approach the experimental model. That requires a formalized logico-deductive theory, leading to an experimental situation in which crucial variables are combined in a pure form that excludes or controls for disturbing variables and allows one to confirm or deny precise predictions that are made in advance by deduction from the theory. That is the central model for the most powerful natural sciences of our epoch, and thus it serves as the model for those who wish to make the social sciences more "scientific."

Yet Germani, the man among the three who most desires to follow that model, admits that when he deals with the larger issues of the theory of modernization he is inclined to use the method of broad historical comparisons with mainly qualitative materials. His more detailed statistical studies of Argentine society may have theoretical relevance, but cannot confirm or disconfirm the general theory he uses. Indeed, most of his empirical studies in Argentina were initiated more for descriptive than for theory-testing purposes and had the goal of making precise measurements of social trends in the country. I suspect that when we have available further examples of the uses of statistics from the new research of González Casanova and Cardoso, they too will be closer to the descriptive than the experimental model.

This discussion leads to a crucial question that remains unanswered: Can statistics be used in the experimental manner to test broad theories of social change? Certain small-scale theories of interpersonal interaction have been subjected to experimental test in the laboratories of North American social scientists, and perhaps with enough ingenuity we might make the procedures applicable to larger theories of social structure and social change. Indeed, some scholars who are devotees of numerical measurement believe it is already being done in recent massive U.S. studies, such as in the work of James Coleman, Otis Dudley Duncan or Christopher Jencks.

At this point, I remain skeptical. Actually, I believe that the large studies currently in vogue in the United States are much closer to description than experimentation; although they relate certain variables to one another in complex patterns, those patterns are essentially systematic descriptions of momentary relationships. They do not test theoretical models of higher orders of generality that purport to explain the present and predict the future. Once again, I do not denigrate their utility, but believe that the utility comes precisely from their quality as better descriptions than we previously had of aspects of current social reality in the United States that are themes of political controversy. However, they are far from contributing to a formal theory of society that would be applicable to all times and places; thus, they are not building blocks for an abstract science of society that follows the model of the abstract sciences of nature.

Given certain trends of thought in the worldwide social science community, there are pressures on Latin American sociologists to formalize their theories and test them by an approximation to the experimental procedure. However, if they did so they would lose the particular historical character that makes their contributions especially interesting. The quantification of history to make description and comparison more precise will aid them; the formalization of history in the direction of universal laws will lead them away from the reality that is the object of their study. I believe that their ties to specific Latin American issues will save the three men discussed here from the temptations of excess formalization. In addition, González Casanova and Cardoso have the protection that comes from their appreciation of good Marxist theory, which uses abstractions to help the observer rise above his particular situation but always leads him back toward historical specificity, since it says that in the last analysis the purpose of theory is not controlled experiment in which "all other things are held equal," but rather effective action in the real world where all things hang together.

Obviously, much of the debate as to whether or not sociology is a "science" is a discussion about semantics: the participants use different definitions of science and each claims his is the correct one. For Marxists, true social science is that analysis of capitalism which stems from the work of the master. For statisticians, it is the use of good quantitative indicators. For experimentalists, it is a set of logico-deductive propositions—based on a general and abstract theory—that are tested in crucial empirical situations, usually by the technique of disproving null hypotheses. For some men of the current generation of Latin American sociologists it is the attitude expressed by Germani when he wrote about his polemic against the *pensadores* and ideologists who failed to offer evidence to support their conclusions: "I do not accuse those who happen not to accept the views I like of being unscientific or irrational; what I am defending is an attitude toward the highest objectivity historically and personally possible. If one does not make any distinction between what he likes and a scientific statement, when one says that all social science is ideology, then efforts toward a higher (not an absolute) objectivity and toward instrumental rationality are lost. My emphasis is on the attitude, on the effort toward an objectivity that goes beyond the personal, psychological, historical and social conditions under which the individual mind is working. It is an effort which will always be defeated in the final instance, but at least we should try as much as possible to stretch the limits.''[2]

Perhaps the very word *science* causes us as much pain as pleasure, since it invokes the sacred connotations of a new form of contemporary religion. If we attempt to imitate the physical sciences we promise too much, inevitably fall short and suffer from a continuous inferiority complex. But if our goal is merely an attempt to discipline our personal biases through the use of a comparative method that rises somewhat above them, along with efforts to collect rigorous and quantified evidence, we can do so without engaging in semantic arguments about labels. Social scientists waste too much effort talking about what they are proposing to do—instead of just going ahead and doing it.

These three men, along with their fellow sociologists and political scientists in Latin America, have usually concentrated on questions of development that were on the fringes of formal economics, the branch of social science that has greatest maturity in both theory and method. González Casanova and Cardoso have been more explicit about that focus than Germani, and indeed they have often begun their analyses by criticizing the economists for overemphasizing growth in physical output of goods and for underemphasizing such issues as the distribution of income, the increase in unemployment, the regional inequalities in growth or the political processes that shape crucial decisions about economic policy. Whey then do treat such issues, the economists often do so in common-sense ways that appear amateurish. But these sociologists may commit the obverse sin: they often write like amateur economists. They offer prescriptions for avoiding recession and invigorating output, and discuss the basic social and political requirements of economic development without presenting a clear model of the economic system itself. Since they insist upon a synthetic approach that is broad enough to have policy implications they are willing to foresake narrow disciplinary boundaries.

The difficult challenge is to combine breadth with rigor. Nobody can be a professional master of all branches of modern social science, since the technical requirements of each branch have grown so demanding that it takes years of study to master them. Nevertheless, we must find some way to reach synthesis of the disciplines or else policy decisions of government and trends in public opinion will be shaped by studies in economics that do not include adequate consideration of social and political factors. How can we reach synthesis without sacrificing technical quality? I do not believe that sociologists can provide it by developing a new version of Comte's "Queen of the Sciences" that encompasses all important viewpoints within itself. I do believe that we should first narrow and sharpen the sociological focus and then formally link it with the economic focus. Unfortunately, even after decades of effort, serious and effective conversations between sociologists and economists are rare, and each group tends to act like an amateur in the other's field whenever its own disciplinary focus proves too thin to cover the issue at hand.

There are two themes in the works of our authors that offer particularly good possibilities for detailed research in sociology and political science in the near future. They have broad application to policy issues in development and are more complementary than competitive with the work of most economists, namely, the study of imperialism/dependency, and the analysis of mass participation in social decisions.

González Casanova and Cardoso are both deeply concerned about the issues of imperialism and dependency, although they use slightly different language in their analyses. The perspective of the Third World is one of weakness facing strength. It watches the backward countries trying to catch up with the advanced countries by imitating their technology and many aspects of their social organization, but it finds that those who control the means of modern production have the power to set the rules by which they will share its secrets. The problem would be simpler to handle if reality consisted of undeveloped societies making arrangements with developed societies to borrow money and machines; the bargaining process for setting the terms would then be the focus for a study of the decisions that shape the future. But reality is more complicated than that because the outsiders are also inside; they have their own branch factories in the underdeveloped countries and they have partnership arrangements with various local entrepreneurial groups that limit their activities so as not to upset the world markets of the parent firm. When one views political power as the reflection of economic strength, then one must recognize that elements in the political structures of the underdeveloped nations actually represent interests that stem from the developed nations, and a simple bargaining process between "insiders" and "outsiders" is impossible to find since there is no sharp line of division between them.

There is ample room for a specialized field of sociology and political science that concentrates on the roots of power in various aspects of social structure, national and supranational, and the impact of that power on the decisions that shape economic development. As I suggested before in my comments on the work of González Casanova and Cardoso, it appears to me that the next step in the research is to move from the historical and structural outlines of the process that they have given us to a more detailed study of entrepreneurial and governmental decisions in the Latin American nations in ways that might indicate degrees of power and thus lead us toward greater precision of analysis. (Incidentally, this would be an ideal project for cooperation with North American scholars since the home offices of the multinational corporations in New York and their influences on government policy in Washington are crucial parts of the total problem to be studied.) We need case studies of actual events that could pinpoint the relative strength of various interest groups and could show the channels through which they operate.

More precision in these studies would be particularly useful as an offset to the tendency to exaggerate that exists in such an emotional area of research. It is a great temptation for nationalist ideologues to blame all local troubles on imperialist forces and for internationalist ideologues to claim that imperialism is a myth that exists only in the minds of Communists. Unfortunately, the concepts of dependency and exploitation that were first introduced in academic discourse are now used in extreme form in public debate in ways that may be counterproductive to the goals of the academicians. For example, if one overemphasizes the power of outside interests in shaping national policy he may be pushed either toward a romantic dream of revolution or else its opposite, an apathetic despondency in the face of the difficulty of reform. Neither mood leads toward responsible action.

Obviously, if one is sure that imperialism is to blame for everything bad, then the only way out is a revolutionary upheaval that would break all ties with imperialist interests—in other words, the path of Cuba. But most serious observers are convinced that under present conditions successful revolution in major Latin American countries is close to impossible because the right-wing forces are too strong (especially with United States support) and would reproduce the counterrevolutionary triumph that Brazil experienced in 1964. Ironically, the success of Fidel Castro in Cuba alerted conservatives throughout the continent and made it much more difficult for revolutionaries in other countries.

On the other hand, acceptance of the realities of power need not mean that all changes in the direction of human betterment are impossible. In the face of regimes that are moving from old styles of oligarchical rule to new styles of corporate and bureaucratic domination, often with military underpinnings, the sociologists considered here all urge an increase in genuine mass participation, both at the formal level of national politics and at the local level of community and factory involvement. But we seem to face a basic contradiction: according to certain aspects of their own analyses, particularly those of González Casanova and Cardoso, the dynamic groups in the Latin American countries that keep growing in power are elitist and tied to international capitalism, and opposed to genuine mass participation. Those groups stress a style of development that calls for expansion of a form of industrialism that produces goods mainly for middle-class consumers, and that generates high profits for reinvestment by using a labor-saving technology which leaves the masses of men in city and countryside marginal to the fruits of development. The men in charge are satisfied and simply want more of the same. The earlier national populism calling for immediate redistribution of income has weakened as a political force, and technocratic rule with military support seems to be growing as the alternative. Such has been the obvious trend in the last decade in Brazil, with Mexico and Argentina following paths that were not very different.

However, from time to time there are reversals; the discussion of conflict in the writings of these sociologists is matched by real struggles in national reality, with outcomes not completely predetermined. For example, the military rulers of Argentina finally recognized that they could not solve the nation's economic and social problems and instead of further tightening the repression decided to reopen the door to electoral politics. The Peronists won by reiterating some of the old populist slogans and by invoking the still-powerful prestige of the aged leader. But it is not clear at this writing in 1973 whether their victory represents a true return to earlier policies, or merely the most obvious channel for registering disgust with the military dictators.

In Chile the Popular Unity coalition of President Salvador Allende represented a major step forward from earlier leftist forces. It was an ideological rather than a personal movement with an explicit policy of transformation to democratic socialism. However, it faced the very pressures from local and international capitalism that dependency theory would predict, and its early political success was not translated into economic progress sufficient for survival.

González Casanova clings to a belief that the Mexican system still has enough of its revolutionary inheritance to permit a revival of the reformist spirit and a redirection of trends away from the recent course of increasing monopoly of political and economic power. He hopes that the system can be reformed from within by democratizing the organs of the official party apparatus, as well as by strengthening groups on the outside that could be more effective in the role of "loyal opposition" such as independent labor unions, student and professional groups and new types of political parties. The current attempts of President Luis Echeverría to institute reforms are still in their early stages, and certainly demonstrate that there are elements within the official system that are aware of deep problems and can generate new proposals. But unfolding events also demonstrate the great vigor of the conservative elements who oppose change and have so far been able to limit the reforms to minor readjustments of policy.

In Brazil the military and the technocrats have indeed provided rapid growth in economic output, but much of the dynamic underlying that expansion comes from a flood of new investment from the United States that cannot long continue, and the whole process is held together by overt repression of mass protests that grow along with increasing maldistribution of income and increasing unemployment. Cardoso's hope is for a strengthening of social organization outside of the state system in ways which might, under more propitious circumstances, lead toward a form of socialism that would provide an open and equalitarian society and enhance individual liberty. He recognizes that such a solution could only come about if the new structures were built from the bottom up by the masses themselves, rather than imposed from the top down by a new elite, even one claiming to speak for the masses.

In the introduction to this book I wrote that much of the impetus for the work of sociologists and political scientists in Latin America came from a reaction to the growing influence of economists, particularly the approach of *desarrollismo* or developmentalism that was being publicized by the technicians at ECLA, the United National Economic Commission for Latin America, led by Raúl Prebisch. In the mid-sixties Prebisch left Latin America and did noble work representing all the countries of the Third World at UNCTAD, the United Nations Conference on Trade and Development. At the end of the decade he returned to ILPES and ECLA in Santiago and prepared a general report on the state of Latin America for the Inter-American Development Bank entitled *Change and Development: Latin America's Great Task*. It is a document that presents a synthesis of up-to-date technical economic analysis, infused with a deep awareness of human needs. It shows that considerable economic progress was achieved in recent years; indeed, the goal that was set by many agencies of 2.5 percent annual growth in per capita product was almost reached during the period from 1950 to 1970. But the maldistribution of income around that average figure was more distorted at the end of the period than it had been at the beginning, and the various gaps between regions and sectors have grown worse. To begin to remove these distortions, especially the shocking amount of underemployment, he offers calculations of necessary paths for the future: the total growth in physical output would have to increase from the current annual rate of a little over 5 percent up to a sustained rate of at least 8 percent; birth rates would have to decline; middle-class consumption would have to be restrained so as to permit more investment (up from 18 to over 26 percent of domestic product); foreign economic assistance would have to grow and under new and more favorable terms; drastic land reforms would be necessary; new forms of labor-intensive technology would have to spread—and these improvements would have to continue at a steady pace for several decades before surplus labor could be absorbed.

Prebisch recognizes that all of these changes require fundamental reorientations of government policy in many nations, both in Latin America and elsewhere, but he fails to suggest how those reorientations can be brought about. His only recommendation is more effective "persuasion" of the rulers by the experts. Thus we face exactly the same impasse today that existed in 1950: genuine economic development that includes social progress is impossible without firm political direction, and such political direction is impossible without mass support from a citizenry willing to make the necessary sacrifices because they are steps toward a more just society. Very few governments in Latin America can generate such support.

Latin American sociologists and political scientists have entered the great debate and have clarified many aspects of the total development process that previously were not given proper weight in the discussion. But the new voices have not provided neat solutions to thorny problems. Those who expect them to do so might ponder the words of Peter Berger and his colleagues in *The Homeless Mind*:

"If the passion with which one engages oneself in the struggles of one's time can consist of both ice and fire, then surely sociological analysis belongs to the icy part. Sociology is essentially a debunking discipline. It dissects, uncovers, only rarely inspires. Its genius is very deeply negative, like that of Goethe's Mephistopheles who describes himself as a 'spirit that ever says no.' To try to change this character is to destroy whatever usefulness sociology may have—especially its moral and political usefulness, which comes from sociology being held in balance, simultaneously and within the mind of the same person, with the affirmations of moral passion and human engagement" (p. 234).

NOTES

1. Thomas S. Kuhn (1970) asserts that the transition from general treatises understandable by laymen to technical journals for specialists is a mark of maturity in science. But Kuhn does not deal with a special characteristic of the social, as compared to the natural, sciences: their central purpose is the improvement of public policy. In democratic societies, policy making includes the enlightened participation of citizens who themselves can combine judgments about political values or ends

with judgments about the effectiveness of means to reach those ends. Social science is particularly useful for weighing alternative means, but it would be naïve to hand over all the decisions to experts, for they might well become dictators.

2. Gino Germani (1972) personal communication.

Authors

1973   Berger, Peter, Brigitte Berger and Hansfried Kellner, *The Homeless Mind: Modernization and Consciousness*, New York: Random House.

1970   Kuhn, Thomas S., *The Structure of Scientific Revolutions*, Chicago: University of Chicago Press.

1970   Prebisch, Raúl, *Change and Development: Latin America's Great Task*, Washington, D.C.: Inter-American Development Bank. Republished in 1971 by Praeger, New York.

Indexes

Subject Index

Alliance for Progress, 3, 5, 6, 185

Argentina, 10-12, 160-62, 167, 171, 182; compared to Brazil, 155-56, 165-66; electoral politics in, 207; political ideology and social problems in, 35-36; social integration in, 200-201; twentieth-century modernization of, 55-61. *See also* Perón, Peronism

Authoritarianism, 53, 54, 67; and national development, 64; of the working class, 56-57, 69 n14. *See also* Fascism

Boletín (of the Institute of Sociology, Buenos Aires), 28

Brazil, 14-17, 171-73, 182, 201; economic development and ideology in, 143-45; economic firms in, 145-49; industrialists in, 140-43; Negroes in, 131-33; political participation in, 206-207; politics in, 161, 165-66, 181

Brazilian Center for Analysis and Planning (CEBRAP), 139-40; 181-82

Cardenism, 93

CEBRAP, *see* Brazilian Center for Analysis and Planning

Center for Industrial and Labor Sociology, São Palulo, 15, 133-35, 141. *See also* Industrialists

Center for Research in the Social Sciences, Rio de Janeiro, 14, 34, 77

Center-periphery relations, 94-97, 157-59, 168

CEPAL, *see* United Nations Economic Commission for Latin America

Chile, 162-64, 166, 171, 183, 207

Colegio Libre de Estudios Superiores, 30, 32, 34

Colombia, 160, 161-62, 171

Colonialism, 94-95. *See also* Exploitation, Internal colonialism

Columbia University, 34, 35

Communist party, 25-27, 31, 132. *See also* Marx, Marxism, Political ideology

Dependency, 16-17, 92, 136, 137, 156-70, 205-206; assessed, 186-88; compared to imperialism, 177; compared to structural-functionalism, 176-77; ideology, 174-76; internal, 139; internal politics, 174-78; Marxism, 180-81; multinational corporations, 178-79; stratification, 170-73

Desarrollismo, see Developmentalism

Deteriorating terms of trade, theory of, 4-5

Development, stages of, 48-50

Developmentalism, 3, 7, 91-92, 208-209

Disequilibria, 48-52, 67; and mobilization-integration, 46-48, 69 n13

Di Tella Institute, 36, 64

Dualism, *see* Exploitation, Internal colonialism

ECLA, *see* United Nations Economic Commission for Latin America

Economic development: birthrate, 6; comparative statistics on, for Latin American countries, 50-51; early impediments to, 5-6; empiricism, 90-91, 110-111; foreign investment, 152-55; history, 154-55, 157-62; ideology, 144-45, 149-52, 165-66, 181-84; labor force, 171-72; noneconomic concomitants of, 6-8, 41-51; politics, 19-20, 81-83, 86-89, 155-58, 205-206; primitive concomitants, 107-109; secularization, 42-51. *See also* Industrialists, Modernization

Economic elite, *see* Industrialists
Economic planning, 4-5
Empiricism, 79-80; and the analysis of economic development, 90-91, 110-111; and political ideology, 97-101, 104-109. *See also* Latin American social science
Enclaves, 162-70
Entrepreneurs, *see* Industrialists
Exploitation, 13-14, 99-103, 117-21, 186-87. *See also* Enclaves, Internal colonialism

Fascism, 23, 24-26, 40-41, 53, 56, 90-91, 109; compared to Peronism, 31; and socialization, 64. *See also* Authoritarianism, Political ideology
FLACSO, *see* Latin American Faculty of Social Sciences
Ford Foundation, 34, 35, 68 n5
Fundamentos, 132

Harvard University, 20, 24, 36, 63

Ideal types, 39, 42
ILPES, *see* Latin American Institute for Social and Economic Planning
Imperialism, 52-53, 179, 187, 205-206. *See also* Dependency, Enclaves, Internal colonialism
Industrialists, 133-35, 139-43, 201; class interests of, 149-52, 174-76; comparative study of, 135-36, 165-67; family control of business, 145-47; government encouragement of development, 6-7; market structure, 147-50; politics, 12-14; styles of leadership, 147-51
Institute of Social Research, Mexico, 76-77, 78
Internal colonialism, 84-93; compared to class structure, 95-96. *See also* Enclaves
Internal markets, *see* Enclaves
Irrationalism, 21, 36-41, 56-57

Latin America: history of economic development in, 41-51, 155, 157-69; labor force characteristics of, 170-73; regional common market, 137, 178, 179. *See also* individual country entry
Latin American Faculty of Social Sciences, 9, 21, 34, 77, 180, 189
Latin American Institute for Social and Economic Planning, 15, 136, 155, 208
Latin American social science: compared to North American, 196-97, 201, 203; evaluated, 180-81; ideology, 18-20, 36-37, 75, 111, 121, 177-78; irrationalism, 36-41; secularization, 38; social problems, 17-18; World War II, 1-2. *See also* Marxism, North American social science, Political ideology

Marginality, 85, 116. *See also* Internal colonialism
Marxism, 8-9, 25-26, 43, 132-34, 137, 177, 197, 203; as an analytic tool, 89-90, 91-94; compared to empiricism, 97-101, 106-109; compared to structural-functionalism, 53-54, 185-88; Latin American social science, 36-37. *See also* Political ideology
Mexico, 12-14, 161, 163, 167, 171-72, 182-183, 201; compared to Brazil and Argentina, 155; economic development in (economic planning, 87-89, 114-116; measures of modernization, 84-85; spirit of reform, 18-19); multinational corporations in, 13-14, 82-83; *Partido Revolucionario Institucional* (PRI), 82, 85; politics in (political participation, 206-207; political reformation, 207-208; political structure, 81-84, 111-114); population growth and government policy in, 115-16
Modernization, 10-12, 41-43, 200-201; effect of history on, 47-48; ideology, 53-54, 66-67; social class, 55. *See also* Disequilibria, Economic development, Secularization
Multinational corporations, 7, 16, 51-52, 82-83, 178-79

National Autonomous University of

Mexico, 12-13, 74, 76-77
Negroes, 131-33, 179
North American social science, 8-9, 21, 27-28, 37, 38-39, 75, 195-97. *See also* Empiricism, Latin American social science, Marxism, Structural-functionalism

Operation Panamericana, 6
Organization of American States, 3-4

Peronism, 10, 30-31; Argentine modernization, 55-57; Germani's thought, 65-66
Political ideology: economic development, 53-54, 89-93, 181-84; explanations of social change, 97-101, 104-110; Latin American social science, 75, 111, 121; secularization, 44-47; social class, 55-57. *See also* Fascism, Marxism, Peronism
Project Camelot, 110, 117, 122 n9

Rationalization, *see* Secularization
Rockefeller Foundation, 34, 35, 68 n5

Secularization, 29, 68, n10; disequilibria, 46-47; economic development, 42-51; effect on the family, 45; Latin American social science, 38; political ideology, 44-47; Roman Catholic Church, 40-41
Social class, 66, 83-86, 172-73, 179-80; internal colonialism, 93-97; political ideology, 53-54, 55-57; social mobility, 59-61, 62-63
Social participation, 181-84
Sorbonne, 76
Standard Oil Company, 16
Statistical analysis, 201-203
Structural-functionalism, 9, 41, 43, 51, 67; compared to dependency, 176-77; compared to Marxism, 185-88. *See also* North American social science

UNCTAD, *see* United Nations Conference on Trade and Development
Underdevelopment, 157
UNESCO, 8, 9, 14, 34, 77, 131
United Fruit Company, 16

United Nations, 3, 185; Conference on Trade and Development, 208; Economic Commission for Latin America, 3, 7, 48-50, 136, 137-38, 197-98, 208
United States, 13, 184-85
University of Bahia, 179
University of Buenos Aires, 10, 23, 53, 64
University of California, Berkeley, 35
University of Chicago, 35
University of Chile, 4
University of Mexico, *see* National Autonomous University of Mexico
University of Nanterre, 138
University of Rome, 25
University of São Paulo, 131
Uruguay, 160, 171

World Bank, 5
World War I, 53, 54, 59-60
World War II, 12, 36, 59, 60, 164, 165, 166

Name Index

Note: No reference is made to information on Cardoso, Germani, or González Casanova; please see the chapter devoted to that sociologist.

Allende, Salvador, 183, 207
Anderson, Bo, 128
Aron, Raymond, 30, 134
Azevedo, Fernando de, 130, 135

Baer, Werner, 22
Baran, Paul, 36
Bastide, Roger, 131-33
Basurto, Jorge, 128
Becker, Howard, 29
Berger, Peter, 209, 210
Berle, Adolf, 141
Bodenheimer, Susanne 22, 189 n5, 194
Booth, Charles, 28
Branco, Castelo, 169
Braudel, Fernand, 76
Buira, Ariel, 128
Butelman, Enrique, 30

Cárdenas, Lázaro, 18, 76, 89, 122 n10, 163
Castro, Fidel, 183

Cicourel, Aaron, 33
Cockcroft, James D., 193
Cohn-Bendit, Daniel, 138
Coleman, James, 104, 202
Contreras, Enrique, 77
Cosío Villegas, Daniel, 76
Crozier, Michel, 136

Dahrendorf, Ralf, 41, 90
Davis, Kingsley, 41
Davis, Stanley M., 194
De Gaulle, Charles, 138
Deutsch, Karl, 41, 69 n13
Díaz, Porfirio, 83
Di Tella, Torcuato S., 33, 68 n4, 73
Duncan, Otis Dudley, 202
Durand, Victor Manuel, 77
Durkheim, Emile, 8, 26, 29, 39, 130, 198

Echevarría, José Medina, 30, 68 n1, 72,
    136
Echevarría, Luis, 78, 116, 207-208

Faletto, Enzo, 16, 136, 138, 155-70
Fernandes, Florestan, 130-31, 135, 139,
    189 n1, 194
Flores, Edmundo, 128
Frank, André Gunder, 194
Freud, Sigmund, 8
Freyre, Gilberto, 133
Friedmann, Georges, 76, 133
Fromm, Erich, 29, 30
Frondizi, Arturo, 33, 35, 167
Frondizi, Risieri, 33
Furtado, Celso, 141, 194

Gasparian, Fernando, 134
Goldsen, Rose K., 33
Goulart, João, 134-35, 140, 153, 166
Graciarena, Jorge, 32-33
Griffin, Keith, 194
Gurvitch, Georges, 76

Hirschman, Albert O., 22
Horowitz, Irving Louis, 33
Hoselitz, Bert F., 185

Ianni, Octavio, 132, 133, 139
Ibarra, David, 128
Imaz, José Luis de, 73

Jaguaribe, Hélio, 143, 194
Jencks, Christopher, 20

Kahl, Joseph A., 194, 195
Kenworthy, Eldon, 73
Kerr, Clark, 141
Kubitschek, Juscelino, 6, 133, 167
Kuhn, Thomas S., 20

Lambert, Jacques, 96, 128
Lasky, Harold, 30
Lazarsfeld, Paul K., 34, 104
Lenin, V. I., 100
Levene, Ricardo, 27, 30
Levy, Marion J., 185
Lewin, Kurt, 30
Linton, Ralph, 131
Lipset, Seymour Martin, 90
Lopes, Juarez Rubens Brandão, 139, 180
Lundberg, George, 131

Malinowski, Bronislaw, 30
Malthus, Thomas, 199
Mannheim, Karl, 29, 30, 130
Marx, Karl, 8, 30, 42-43, 52, 90, 93,
    129, 130, 188, 199
Mead, George Herbert, 30, 41
Mead, Margaret, 30
Médici, Garrastazu, 7
Meister, Albert, 33
Mendieta y Núñez, Lucio, 68 n1, 76
Merton, Robert K., 34, 131
Mills, C. Wright, 21, 96
Moore, Wilbert E., 185
Moreira, Renato, 132
Moreno, J. L., 30
Mussolini, Benito, 25, 31, 36
Myrdal, Gunnar, 52

Nasatir, David, 33
Navarrete, Ifigenia M. de, 128

Organski, Kenneth, 64

Pareto, Vilfredo, 8, 26, 40
Park, Robert, 131
Parsons, Talcott, 27, 29, 30, 34, 39, 41,
    51, 69 n25, 131, 185
Paz, Octavio, 117, 122 n9, 128
Perón, Juan, 11, 30, 32, 33, 55-57, 62,
    163, 182
Pierson, Donald, 131
Pinto, Aníbal, 138
Pinto, Luis A. Costa, 14, 32, 33
Pozas, Ricardo, 77

Prebisch, Raúl, 3, 22, 137, 138, 208-209,
     210
Puente Leyva, Jesús, 128

Quadros, Jânio, 153

Radcliffe-Brown, A. R., 130
Redfield, Robert, 131
Reyna, José Luis, 170-73
Riesman, David, 30

Schneider, Ronald M., 195
Schumpeter, Joseph, 141, 155
Scobie, James, 73
Silvert, Frieda, 33
Silvert, Kalman H., 33, 48
Singer, Paul, 139
Skidmore, Thomas E., 195
Smith, Adam, 141, 199
Smith, Peter, 73
Soares, Gláucio A. Dillon, 195
Solís, Leopoldo, 128
Sombart, Werner, 141

Sorokin, Pitirim, 41
Stavenhagen, Rodolfo, 22, 128
Sunkel, Osvaldo, 138

Thomas, W. I., 29
Tocqueville, Alexis de, 193
Toledano, Lombardo, 93, 122 n10
Tönnies, Ferdinand, 29
Touraine, Alain, 133-35

Urquidi, Victor L., 128

Vargas, Getúlio, 129, 130, 144, 161,
     165, 182

Weber, Max, 8, 29, 39, 42-43, 122 n11,
     129, 130, 141, 199
Weffort, Francisco, 139, 179
Willems, Emilio, 131
Wionczek, Miguel S., 128

Young, Pauline, 131

Znanieki, F., 29

Transaction Books
$5.95

Modernization, Exploitation and Dependency in Latin America

Joseph A. Kahl

Scholarly discussion of the fate of the Third World has long been dominated by North American and European authors. Yet in recent years the writings of Third World social scientists have often been creative, and are worthy of more attention in the United States. This book makes the work of three outstanding Latin American sociologists readily available to the English-reading public: Gino Germani of Argentina (who has moved to Harvard University); Pablo González Casanova of Mexico; and Fernando Henrique Cardoso of Brazil. Their major writings are summarized, and then interpreted in the context of material from extensive interviews with the authors. In these interviews, the authors explain the events—personal, professional, and political—that have had major influence on their thought.

Their views range from Germani's synthesis of orthodox European and American sociology, as adapted to his detailed empirical studies of the modernization of Argentina and other countries in this hemisphere, through González Casanova's interpretation of the forces of exploitation, internal as well as external, that dominate the Mexican political system, to Cardoso's influential revisions of Marxist theory to deal with the basic situation of dependency that shapes the range of options open to the Latin American countries, especially Brazil. These "inside" views of the development process often sharply diverge from the dominant opinions among "outsiders." By understanding the differences, readers in the United States can gain direct insight into Latin American social reality, and can find ways of improving North American social science by bringing to the surface some unstated assumptions.

One theme common to all three authors is their concern with issues that arise from policy debates: they focus on questions of practical import, rather than abstruse theoretical models. Yet they use sophisticated tools of social science that go beyond ideological rhetoric, and thus discipline political argument with scholarly rigor.

Dr. Kahl is professor of sociology at Cornell University. He is the author of numerous articles and several books, which have been published in both English and Spanish, on Latin American culture and development.

Library of Congress: 75-43190
Printed in the U.S.A.

ISBN: 0-87855-584-6
Cover design: Barbara J. Ciletti